Building Natures

Under the Sign of Nature: Explorations in Ecocriticism

Editors
Michael P. Branch, SueEllen Campbell, John Tallmadge

Series Consultants
Lawrence Buell, John Elder, Scott Slovic

Series Advisory Board
Michael P. Cohen, Richard Kerridge, Gretchen Legler,
Ian Marshall, Dan Peck, Jennifer Price, Kent Ryden,
Rebecca Solnit, Anne Whiston Spirn, Hertha D. Sweet Wong

Building Natures

MODERN AMERICAN POETRY, LANDSCAPE ARCHITECTURE, AND CITY PLANNING

Julia E. Daniel

UNIVERSITY OF VIRGINIA PRESS

CHARLOTTESVILLE AND LONDON

University of Virginia Press
© 2017 by the Rector and Visitors of the University of Virginia
All rights reserved
Printed in the United States of America on acid-free paper

First published 2017

9 8 7 6 5 4 3 2 1

Library of Congress Cataloging-in-Publication Data
Names: Daniel, Julia E., author.
Title: Building natures : modern American poetry, landscape architecture, and city
    planning / Julia E. Daniel.
Description: Charlottesville : University of Virginia Press, 2017. | Series: Under the sign of
    nature: explorations in ecocriticism | Includes bibliographical references and index.
Identifiers: LCCN 2017027098 | ISBN 9780813940830 (cloth : alk. paper) |
    ISBN 9780813940847 (pbk. : alk. paper) | ISBN 9780813940854 (e-book)
Subjects: LCSH: American poetry—20th century—History and criticism. | Cities and
    towns in literature. | Parks in literature. | Landscapes in literature. | Landscape
    architecture. | Ecocriticism. | City planning. | Urban parks.
Classification: LCC PS310.C58 D36 2017 | DDC 811/.509321732—dc23
LC record available at https://lccn.loc.gov/2017027098

Cover art: Detail from a map showing Calvert Vaux and Frederick Law Olmsted's design for
Prospect Park. (From William Bishop, *Manual of the Common Council of the City of Brooklyn,*
1871/Wikimedia Commons)

Contents

Acknowledgments

This book had its small beginning when David Chinitz introduced me to Wallace Stevens's lovely bijoux of a poem, "Tea." First thanks therefore to David for the countless times you helped me set my course and right my little ship. In you, I found a wise and generous scholar and friend. Thanks also to my mentors Suzanne Bost and Jack Kerkering for their bottomless reservoirs of intellectual energy and kindness. Pamela Caughie, Joyce Wexler, Suzanne Gossett, and Melissa Bradshaw also did much to help me discover my critical voice, and for their effort and example, I am deeply grateful. My thanks as well to Loyola University for the support afforded me by the Crown Fellowship.

I could not have completed the research for this book without support from Baylor University, particularly a summer sabbatical and a University Research Committee grant that made the required archival work possible. Carey Newman of Baylor University Press lent me his expertise and enthusiasm when both were sorely needed. I am especially grateful for the assistance of my keen-eyed graduate students Allyson DeMaagd and Kayla McKinney of West Virginia University, and Seth Muller at Baylor. To my phenomenal writing group, the Pittman Gang, without whom the introduction would remain in shambles, I thank you all: Tara Foley, Sarah Ford, Hope Johnston, and Coretta Pittman.

My profound thanks to the talented archivists at the Newberry Library, the Hartford History Center, the Brooklyn Historical Society, and the New York Botanical Garden. To Edward Smkye of the Passaic County Historical Society, as well as to the dedicated staff of Elizabeth Park and the rangers at Mount Rainier, I owe you all a great debt for your dedication and erudition. Every day, I also give thanks for the countless citizen volunteers who sink their love into the dirt of these parks. To Carl Smith, I owe a debt of thanks for his excellent work on the *Plan of Chicago* and for assistance with ferreting out the identity of Sandburg's mysterious violet-eyed architect. I also owe much to the perceptive feedback I received from audiences at various conferences of the Modernist Studies Association, the Modern Language Association, the William Carlos Williams Society, the Association for the Study of Literature and the Environment, and the Chicago Institute for Nature and Culture.

To the dear friends and colleagues who have helped me become a better scholar in ways large and small, may all your kindness return to you. I was uniquely lucky to have begun my career with a talented cohort of supportive, sparkling graduate students, particularly Alison Lukowski, Natalie Kalich, Erin Holliday-Karre, Allison Fagan, Lacey Conley, Cynthia Wallace, and Faith Bennet. A number of my colleagues at West Virginia University and Baylor University have been especially supportive during the process of making this book a reality, including Timothy Sweet, Lowell Duckert, Richard Russell, Lisa Shaver, Kevin Gardner, Maura Jortner, Alex Engebretson, Bill McDonald, and Ginger Hanchey. I am also grateful to my editor, Boyd Zenner, for the countless ways she has championed this project. My thanks also to the anonymous reviewers of the manuscript, whose insights have helped me immeasurably, as well as to the attentive labors of my exceptional copy editor, Susan Murray.

My parents taught me the sound of each letter and the name of every flower. It is a literacy and an inheritance that brings me great joy and, I hope, happiness to those I teach. To them, Kathy and John Barrett, and to my stellar, gifted brother, Dominic, I give my love and overflowing thanks. I offer here special gratitude to my mother, who served as a talented photographer and as a guide through Prospect Park and Elizabeth Park (when my hugely pregnant self could hardly take another step), as well as a needed pair of extra eyes in the dim light of many a reading room. She also raised me with a healthy suspicion of all the "natural" prairie landscaping in our neighborhood, a suspicion that forms the hidden root of this book. Thanks also to my in-laws, Marcia and Jack Daniel, and my brother-in-law, Max, for always cheering me on with enthusiasm and love.

Finally, to my husband, Spencer Daniel, for the innumerable ways he has loved this book into being and carried our whole family in his arms along the way (indeed, all the way from the Monongahela River to the banks of the Brazos). You are good and wise and patient beyond words. I love you and hope you find this book a worthy read. And to my children, John and Joy, who kicked in my womb as I walked in the parks of Chicago, Hartford, and New York: I love you dearly and I promise to take both of you to Central Park if you promise to hold my hand.

Building Natures

Introduction

On 21 September 2014, New York's High Line Park reached completion. The elevated railroad track that once carted goods around the city was re-purposed as a green path running above the streets, sending grass and pedestrians in curves through the geometry of onlooking skyscrapers. Thanks to the artistry of Piet Oudolf, the planting designer, and the work of the landscape firms James Corner Field Operations and Diller Scofidio + Renfro, the blight of a languishing industrial apparatus transformed into a lush road that now offers New Yorkers new vistas on their city. But, as with similar projects in other urban centers, what now seems like an obvious architectural, social, and ecological improvement was hotly contested during different moments of its design and construction. How would the park affect property values? What about gentrification? How could the ecological impact of the park be measured? What design would balance sustainability and the cultural past of the space? And who would pay for it all? And who would use it? And manage it? When the project was finished, Michael Kimmelman of the *New York Times* raised the ghost of these concerns: "[The park] is a Rorschach test, signifying different things—about urban renewal, industry, gentrification, the environment—to different people. Occupying an in-between sort of space between buildings, neighborhoods, street and sky, the park makes a convenient receptacle for meaning."

For all of its contemporary innovation, the receptacle of High Line Park brims with the same contradictory meanings that the American public has wrestled with since the establishment of landscape architecture, city planning, and parks management in the late 1800s. Kimmelman's comments here could just have easily been made about Central Park during the early days of its creation. When Central Park opened to the public in 1857, the fringe of trees edging gently rolling lawns performed the double task of obscuring and reframing the skyline beyond its margins, as it does today.

And, as with High Line Park, Central Park occasioned lively debates about class, race, urban renewal, public health, and, ultimately, the relationship of nature, the common good, and design. Given how contentious that debate was, it is something of a miracle that Central Park was ever completed. Some promoted its health benefits, while others argued that its dampness in the autumn would foster disease. And with trains providing easier access to the country, why should the city commit a fortune to a park that would simply prove a breeding ground of vagabondage? Nonetheless, park advocates won the day. The black community of Seneca Village was forcibly evicted to make room for Frederick Law Olmsted's architecture. Ironically, that same architecture was designed to foster neighborly mingling among the diverse inhabitants of New York. As late as 2011, archaeologists were still unearthing Seneca artifacts from the earth in the park: an iron tea kettle, a bone toothbrush, the remnant of a child's shoe.

Like High Line Park, where railroad ties and trestles from the 1930s mingle with compost and honeysuckle, Central Park is a literal container of its own material past and present. And as metaphoric containers for community meaning and memory, our parks are often overburdened and overdetermined. If Kimmelman presents parks as convenient receptacles for meaning, some of those meanings are often inconveniently contradictory. Parks express a longing for a democratic, green utopia where citizens might attain health, civility, and refreshing contact with nature during a Sunday stroll. At the same time, parks embody long and fraught histories of displacement and disenfranchisement, the imperfect attempts to regulate behavior that deviates from middle-class mores, as well as the cognitive dissonance involved in consuming heavily designed, managed, and regulated spaces as either innocent pastoral rambles, sublime wilderness, or wholesome frontier.

And as goes the park, so goes the city. From the first generation of American city planners to the present, parkscapes have served as fundamental components of holistic city design, as well as the imagined stage on which political life could be most amiably performed. It was at the turn of the twentieth century, just as the frontier receded from view, that the profession of city planning began theorizing and constructing unified urban spaces rather than patching over bits of urban decay as needed. These theories presented the city in terms of teeming, organic metaphors—a human body, a plant, a walled garden, a new frontier—while materializing this rhetoric in connected park systems, utility and traffic infrastructures, and the chaos of construction they required. At the same time, the National Park Service (NPS), and park management as an emerging profession, sought to protect a national frontier myth from urban encroachment while also catering to city dwellers with an appetite for wilderness sports. Caught between preservation and recreation, the NPS designed and maintained wilderness museums that simulated a frontier experience while accommodating the millions of visitors that flooded these spaces in the early 1900s. In many, often overlooked ways, national parks were (and are) the city park writ large, in that they were designed specifically to provide a green space for the weary urbanite. And while not hemmed in by skyscrapers, these frontier memorials react against the expanding city centers around their protected margins. Like the city park, they exist as emerald islands in an urban sea. The result of these new architectures and disciplines is a distinctively modern American experience in which nature, whether within or beyond city limits, exists primarily as a built reality. More precisely, these architectural zones materialize different kinds of nature, from the rugged frontier of the NPS to the meditative pastoral lawns of public parks. What emerges is an American topography of built natures, where different designs and social uses realize different and, at times, competing visions of what nature can and should mean for a modern community.

Among the countless park goers who moved through these works of green architecture were American poets who brought with them a heightened sensitivity to the park's character as art object, nature fantasy, and social playground. Modern poets turn to the park as an ideal stage for exploring the American inheritance of pastoral and frontier myths, as well as the possibilities and failures of an art form addressed to an economically and ethnically diverse public. This book traces the influence of landscape architecture, city planning, and parks management on American poetry in order to demonstrate the many ways modernists actively engaged with these new professions and aesthetics, as well as their complex social afterlives. As Adam Sweeting has shown, literary production and attempts to build nature into urban environments have a long-standing relationship in the American cultural landscape, including the work of writers like William Cullen Bryant and Washington Irving to sell the public on Central Park (93–94). This project picks up the timeline where Sweeting's ends to demonstrate how modernist poetry, particularly the works of Carl Sandburg, Wallace Stevens, William Carlos Williams, and Marianne Moore, responds to the legacy of these spaces. A study of their poetry requires that we understand the park locations in their verse as dynamic art objects informed by new aesthetic principles articulated by these emerging professions.

The pronounced linguistic artifice of poetry in particular provides rich ground for beginning an exploration of nature as artifice. In the 1990s, many early ecocritics turned our attention back to a kind of prose invested in the mimetic representation of the nonhuman world, such as the nature essays of Thoreau or Rachel Carson. And as happens in the tidal pools of any critical school, subsequent waves of ecocriticism expanded the texts under consideration. Nature poetry, and the very meaning of such a loaded term, became a locus of new interest, often for the ways it evaded the mimetic passions of prose in favor of ecopoetic moments of aural or visual enactment. As Scott Knickerbocker has argued, the poetic emphasis on language's conventionality can serve as a vital tool for exploring relationships between the human and the nonhuman world, a realm that exceeds the words we use to negotiate it. The sonic and visual textures of poetry, what John Elder has called "the most distilled form of literature" (313), foreground language in ways that prose typically does not. Presenting language as an act of building, rather than a smooth mirror, can disrupt the apparent mastery of our human utterances about the superabundant material cosmos around us. In this regard, the poetry draws our attention to the minute word choices that evoke, efface, mirror, and muddy our shared preconceptions about what nature is, what it does, and how it is constructed. The ecopoetic conception of poetry as an act of linguistic making is particularly well suited to this project. The writing I study here is invested in an exploration of nature as a built phenomenon, and so the self-aware act of poetic crafting brings attention to the similarly crafted greenspaces of parks. And just as an ecopoetics can revel in moments when the scaffolding of our language fails us, so too do the poets under consideration enact cracks in the emerald facade of parkscapes in their playfully crafted slips of language and artfully broken lines.

More broadly, the pastoral functions as a dominant style in American city parks, and many of the poets who engage with these spaces also take up the poetic heritage of the pastoral in order to complicate a verse tradition and a landscaping aesthetic with shared cultural roots. In his study of appropriations of the pastoral in the modern novel, Jeffrey Mathes McCarthy has demonstrated how the naiveté associated with the charm, purity, and escapism of the pastoral receives tragic or ironic treatment in a modernist context. In poetry, as opposed to the novel, modernists can make the question of pastoral landscapes their central concern. Without the burden of

eidos: type, species, form, essence

eidos

plot, the poets treat our idyllic visions as discrete εἶδος: small pictures of idealized natures that offer refreshment for the human body and mind, as did the Greeks and Romans. And, as Anabel Patterson argues, the Virgilian pastoral always refers "to something other than itself . . . specifically to the historical circumstances in which it was produced" (3), a moment marked by war, class unrest, and expanding urbanism. The ancient Roman and the modern New Yorker alike sought relief from these similar historical pressures under the shade of the beech tree. But while Tityrus reclines in a country dreamscape beyond the city, Wallace Stevens can hoof it to the shady lawns of Central Park and never leave Manhattan. The poets considered here explore how landscape architects and city planners reconstruct pastoral fantasies, as well as how these idealistic architectures tend to collapse. In doing so, the poets close the loop of a strange ouroboros; an ancient poetic tradition influences later schools of landscape painting that fire the imagination of park designers whose spaces are then celebrated and critiqued in a modern incarnation of pastoral verse.

Parks serve as recurring backdrops and occasional foregrounds in a wide variety of modernist poetry. Some poets treat the park primarily as a site of class identity and conflict, to the point that natural elements barely receive mention. In these pieces, parks at times represent the height of middle-class decency and a corresponding yawning ennui, such as when the stifled gentleman speaker of T. S. Eliot's "Portrait of Lady" can be found "any morning in the park / Reading the comics and the sporting page" (10). Many poets also use the park to explore tensions between high and low culture, as well as the rift between the haves and the have-nots. Ezra Pound's bourgeois lady in the park of "The Garden" observes the "filthy, sturdy, unkillable infants of the very poor" with a horror that stems from her own anemic upper-class perspective (26). From the opposite vantage point, Langston Hughes's impoverished speaker in "Park Bench" terrifies the wealthy Central Park visitor with the suggestion that, one day, he might move from his park bench over to Park Avenue. Another major middle-class concern about parks was the mingling of the sexes. Parks could provide a wholesome site of public courtship or, alternatively, a location for unseemly liaisons. E. E. Cummings mocks these fears by framing the park as a fertile world radiant with raw, or even awkward sexual energy, such as in "spring omnipotent goddess Thou," in which the aroused, drunken goddess of Spring "dost stuff parks / with overgrown pimply / chevaliers" and their "damosels" (17).

Other poets use the park as a setting for peaceful, even mystical rambles

through lush environments, and therefore emphasize the organic compo-
nents of the parkscape and their influence on the human psyche. For ex-
ample, Harriet Monroe's immensely influential literary journal *Poetry* fre-
quently featured park pieces, whether violet-tinged, generic parkscapes or
local Chicago pieces. *Poetry*'s park verse, such as Max Michelson's "In the
Park" or Dorothy Dudley's "November in the Park," often accentuates the
affective qualities and primitive pull of locales in which "The trees reach
outward upward / Long dark arms / In tearful dancing and in prayer" (Dud-
ley 67). In her own works, Monroe would also consider the parks as spring-
time islands of innocence, such as in "A Play Festival in Ogden Park," which
presents the June-time delight of dancing children ringed round by flowers
and spectators (*You and I* 122). As the mention of Monroe here suggests,
modern poets, along with their editors and publishers, did not work in iso-
lation. The circulation of park literature occurs in the formal and informal
networks of modernism, from Monroe's active investment in publishing
Chicago park pieces to the casual fondness for a park stroll shared by friends
(and ersatz enemies) like Pound, H. D., and Williams. And beyond parks,
many modern poets fostered what we would now consider environmental
concerns, from Monroe's interest in the preservation of national parks to
Eliot's concerns about urban development and soil erosion.

And this is only a quick nod to a few examples. Indeed, one would be
hard-pressed to find a modern poet who did not pen at least one park piece.
My analysis here does not propose to be an exhaustive one, though such a
work would be a valuable and needed addition to our understanding of the
topography of modern poetry, as would a wide study of the development
of a shared, albeit varied, environmental ethic among modernists. Rather,
I have selected four poets whose work not only exemplifies the modernist
park poem but also demonstrates a holism and aesthetic awareness unique
among typical park pieces. While most poets focus on one or two elements
of parkscapes, usually the social or the organic, the poets here considered
treat the organic and the social as necessarily entwined elements of an ar-
chitecture that many writers and readers regard as unadulterated nature.
Sandburg, Stevens, Williams, and Moore display a rare ability to peel back
the veneer of American green spaces for their readers in their explorations
of nature as a crafted art object.

Unearthing the buried history of the modernist involvement with these
architectures occurs across four broad fields: aesthetics, natures, politics,
and professions. None of these categories is distinct: the aesthetics are in-

formed by national imaginings of natures; those fantasies and art forms are enacted by professional designers and managers; the vision of nature they materialize has political implications; the politics of community use in turn physically reinforces or reshapes the architectures; the disciplines respond by training communities in the proper use of the architecture, and so on. And while all four elements are necessarily connected, different poets emphasize different aspects of those connections based on their experiences of local spaces, as well as their own political and artistic investments. If, as Kimmelman suggests, parks are a kind of Rorschach test, what American poets see in these verdant inkblots tell us at least as much about the poets' acts of perception as it does about the development of modern urbanism. And like inkblot tests for aberrant perceptional habits, what all four poets share is their uncommon ability to see beyond the successful erasures of green architecture as they foreground the artistic interventions of the architect and the consequences for the American public.

Just as landscape architecture, city planning, and parks management combine aesthetics and social vision, so too do the following readings investigate how the poets encounter the aesthetic principles and political lives of the spaces under consideration. Unlike the early lineage traced by Sweeting, in which writers largely work to benefit the parks movement, this project shows how later poets practice often ambivalent forms of intra-action. It is insufficient to say that the poets celebrate the aesthetics and lament the failed social ideals that played out in these spaces. Each poet responds to the braided artistic and political lives of their local environments in nuanced ways that stem from the uniqueness of the site and the community that used it. To that end, I examine four poets, planning schools, and places: Carl Sandburg, Daniel Burnham, and Chicago; Wallace Stevens and the parks of Frederick Law Olmsted, Calvert Vaux, and Theodore Wirth; William Carlos Williams, the Society for Useful Manufactures, and Paterson, New Jersey; Marianne Moore, the National Park System, and Mount Rainier National Park. The project ranges from east to west, from a large midwestern metropolis to smaller East Coast cities, from prairies to mountaintops (including one volcano), from city centers to national parks. As I argue, each poet's distinctive park poetics must be prefaced by an understanding of how the particular social, historical, and physical details of nature are experienced as a built topography in each location. This case-study organization allows me to honor the specifics of the poems by attending to the details of both the architectural theories and the site. My tight focus on the local is, in each case, tied into larger national movements, and so expresses in miniature spatial trends in America as a whole.

It is impossible to begin this study without pausing over the vexed use of the word "nature," particularly in the planning documents and in our own readerly assumptions. Beyond the natures performed in the spaces I study here, we also bring natures with us as readers of these texts, both poetic and architectural. Despite calls to do without it, from Timothy Morton's *Ecology without Nature* (2007) to the climatologist Paul Crutzen's claim that, in the age of the Anthropocene, "Nature" is over, nature's weedy tenacity keeps it at the forefront of environmentally situated literary scholarship. Scholars of environmental literature and ecocritical theorists have spilt much ink over the word, from its embeddedness in often environmentally unhealthy cultural systems to its deixic drive out of the text and back to a material world in real peril. This project teases apart these two positions: nature as cultural construct and material fact. The poets I read respond to a prior material reality (a park, a mountain, a city street), and, as a result, I attend to real physicality and spatiality in my readings. However, this project follows the artists I study by not treating matter as the antithesis of culture. In the case of landscape architecture, prior material reality, the space the poets enter, is a cultural construct in the most literal sense of the phrase: a zone constructed and maintained according to culturally shaped notions of what nature should be. This approach thus balances both materialist and social constructionist concerns by revealing the ways in which they are fundamentally interdependent. What a community imagines nature to be directly influences how we sculpt and manage our environment, and our managed environment, in turn, reflects our shared image of nature.

More specifically, my contextualization of nature as primarily a disciplinary term follows similar gestures made by such critics as Joshua Schuster, Dana Phillips, and David Harvey. Whereas Phillips and Schuster largely define nature as the object of ecology, and Harvey focuses on real estate and law, my approach situates nature at the junction of several disciplinary forces and social movements: city planning, landscape architecture, parks management, public health discourses, social reform and the City Beautiful movements, legislation regulating land use, and the travel and tourism industries, to name a few. If this list bewilders, it captures a similarly bewildering cultural moment when the definition of American nature was being cocreated among proliferating fields and practices, along with the publics that consumed these spaces. Such an approach is inevitably and necessarily messy, as these zones arise from and dwell within a complex network of professional discourses. To accommodate that productive mess, I let "nature," as used by poet, planner, and public, emerge through the analysis of linguistic and spatial texts in each chapter. Readers should therefore assume that nature always carries about with it a set of implied scare quotes.

The natures created by early landscape architects, city planners, and park managers are all emphatically modern and American. This move to build natures takes on a special urgency in a nation transitioning from a frontier experience into a modernity characterized by rapid urban expansion. As the era of the frontier came to a close and the century of the city began, planners and designers realized that, if American city dwellers were to have contact with nature, nature must be either built into the city or carefully preserved outside of it. The way modernity was experienced as a spatial shift for what was once a frontier nation distinguishes the American park movement from park use and design in England and Europe. American parkscapes express particularly American myths and politics, ones that are tied to threatened chronotopes associated with the nation's past: the pastoral, figured as a lost, laborless American agrarianism, and the frontier, mixed with a transcendental emphasis on sublime scenic values. One of the major political concerns that architects, planners, and managers addressed was the perceived threat to American character with the loss of these landscapes, particularly the frontier. Much of the language justifying city and national parks echoes that of Frederick Jackson Turner's frontier thesis: the pioneer's homesteading work in the wilderness removed the last vestiges of European culture from an immigrant population, resulting in a distinctively American citizen. Contemporary scholars, such as Annette Kolodny and Patricia Nelson Limerick, have ably critiqued the imperial, masculine fantasies that shape the frontier thesis. I discuss the frontier and the pastoral throughout not in order to reify that fantasy but to show the real hold these imagined spaces had on the minds of a modern public struggling with questions of national identity and landscape. If these vanishing vistas made one American, how could they be simulated? And would those simulations work to create wholesome, healthy, well-behaved citizens?

Hence my use of "natures" rather than "nature." Multiple aesthetics inform American landscape architecture, each of which realizes a different kind of nature loaded with slightly different nationalist and political freight. Olmsted's aesthetic is distinctly pastoral and appeals to a fantasy of colonial agrarianism. And, while influenced by his experiences in parks abroad,

Olmsted's influential designs are largely reactions against a British aesthetic that he found to be effete and classist. His emphasis on green lawns without statuary or exotic flowerbeds expresses democratic desires defined largely against British style. American parks have no place for grand statues of aristocratic individuals, nor room for the upper-class, exotic horticultural samples one could find in London's parks. The unity of Olmsted's greens, unpocked by sculpture or boxes of foreign cuttings, invite and model a vision of a unified American polis. Similarly, designs for the NPS draw from frontier visions of nature that intersect with transcendental landscape ideals. As William Cronon has argued, this mix of the wild frontier and a weekend-vacation version of transcendentalism results in places where misty mountaintops and waterfalls are emphasized for their scenic value. The goal is to design spaces that re-create both the pioneer's robust trek into wilderness and the transcendental hiker's brush with the sublime. Unlike city parks that are scaped for sociability, national parks induce feelings of isolation by placing trails in ways that obscure the throngs of tourists before and behind us, all while safely leading us to an elevated outlook of scenic grandeur. These natures are designed to maximize feelings of scape, scope, wildness, and individualism.

While these same features give our most iconic American parks an always-been-there aura, they were some of the first creations of modern disciplines in the early process of articulation. The phrase "landscape architecture" was still relatively new in the 1870s. When Horace Cleveland introduced his 1873 collection *Landscape Architecture as Applied to the Wants of the West,* he could barely bring himself to use the term: "The term 'Landscape Architecture' is objectionable, as being only figuratively expressive of the art it is used to designate. I make use of it, under protest, as the readiest means of making myself understood, in the absence of a more appropriate term" (preface). The entire collection testifies to these disciplinary fears, as in such essays as "Inadequate Ideas of the Scope of Landscape Architecture." Regardless of the tentative nature of the phrase, Cleveland underscored the importance of the practice: "By whatever name it may be called, the subdivision and arrangement of land for the occupation of civilized men, is an art demanding the exercise of ingenuity, judgment and taste." Although designers sought to mask their interventions in the zones they built, their early theories and public documents emphasize the role of discernment, taste, and craft behind the details of every city and national park.

The attempt to delimit the disciplinary ethos of these new fields extended into the 1900s—it is not until the 1930s that city-planning periodicals like the *Century* appear or that one could obtain professional degrees in city planning or landscape architecture. By then, nature, in one of its many forms, had fallen under the professional purview of the landscape architect and park manager. It was both medium and message. Designers referred to the organic components of their plans as artistic materials: hostas, box-woods, and lily pads became the green paint, the lawn a canvas on which the artist composed his piece. These natural materials were then used to compose a picture of nature, whether the pastoral or the frontier, that obscured the careful interventions of the painter. (And yet, dealing with green media was often more like working with fussy child actors than with docile pigments. Early manuals testify to the constant difficulties of disciplining organic materials into the correct arrangement.)

However hard it was to get one's hepatica growing just so, designers and managers had even greater challenges when faced with a public constantly moving against the architecture of the space. In redefining nature as architecture, these new professional fields also created a new subject: the park goer. This is not to say that bodies had not been lolling on park greens before, but the park goer was a new agent, both consumer of a new kind of public space and a constant threat to it. Regulating unruly bodies in parkscapes became an ongoing concern for designers, managers, public officials, and law enforcement. If parks embodied fantasies of idealized natures, they also contained anxieties about urban corruption: crime, hypersexuality, vagrancy, disease were all similarly evoked by the architecture, particularly after dark. The quiet nooks designed for contemplation and refreshment lent themselves to undercover trysts and clandestine dealings. Or such was the fear. The middle-class perception of working-class misbehavior in parks, often laced with racial and sexual undertones, has always far outstripped the statistical reality of such behavior. Rather than bringing the classes into sociable contact, minute distinctions among the classes were reinscribed into these landscapes, including the literal inscription of rules and regulations meant to discipline blue-collar, immigrant bodies into the proper use of parkscapes: "No drinking or washing in the fountain"; "Stay on the path"; "No dogs allowed"; "No food or drink on the lawn." The modern lyric "I" necessarily carries all of this fraught baggage when inhabiting the new social position of the park goer, as do the many figures who test the line between leisure and vagrancy, play and lawlessness throughout these park poems.

The need for regulation in public parks already hinted at failures in the disciplines that built them. Landscape architects shared a City Beautiful optimism in the morally sanative power of passively consuming spaces. Simply being in a well-ordered space was thought to induce virtue and American spirit in an increasingly multicultural and expanding urban population. The idea that landscape can shape behavior is, as they say, about as old as dirt, but the first generation of city planners and landscape architects was adapting a tradition of Romantic naturalism that argued for the moral and mental benefits of either soothing picturesque scenes or wild, sublime vistas. These landscapes became popularized by Romantic landscape painters such as William Gilpin and John Constable who, in turn, influenced the designers of private estate grounds, like Lancelot "Capability" Brown, who created "gardenless" pastoral retreats for their clients in England. (Ironically, while landscape artists lauded the benefits of happening upon Romantic scenes and painting them *en plein air,* gardeners and designers began shaping private parks to match the composition of those same paintings.) It was landscapes like these that inspired Frederick Law Olmsted during his time abroad, and he subsequently adjusted the tradition to address an American public. But park goers proved stubbornly resistant to the palliative effects of the architecture. Every new attempt to regulate perceived deviance out of park goers through the law signaled another weakness in the landscape's therapeutic goals. Such failures were deeply political and occasioned conversations about the integration of immigrant communities into the American public, the danger of a failed democracy where the sons of factory workers and lawyers still would not play together on the same lawn, and the larger impossibility of sustaining American character and vigor in a nation of cities.

Sandburg, Stevens, Williams, and Moore all react to this shifting sense of American spatiality, with an eye to the social consequences of how community life is lived in modern, architectural greens. For Carl Sandburg, witnessing construction following Daniel Burnham's *Plan of Chicago* results in a poetic sensitivity to the city as a porous organism and receptacle. Whereas Burnham's *Plan* necessarily emphasizes the ultimate product of a complete, holistic urban center, figured as a living organism, Sandburg presents Chicago as a body that is also an ongoing material process. In one sense, Sandburg's depiction of urban ecology is a critique of Burnham's *Plan,* as it celebrates process over product, the chaos of construction over the determining influence of clean, classical design. As a consequence, it also prioritizes laboring bodies at the construction site over the aesthetic work of planners, though they also haunt Sandburg's scenes. However, in another sense, Sandburg plays out Burnham's organismic aesthetic. And like Burnham's design, Sandburg's poetic materiality is entangled in prairie nostalgia, as both artists imagine how the modern city can double as a physical repository for a vanishing midwestern frontier experience. Burnham's solution is a circuit of parks ringing Chicago that reinscribes a natural boundary, a green "out there" within the city, while also imaging Chicago as a vast network of parks walled off from the sprawl beyond by that same circle of green space. Sandburg ultimately downplays such distinctions between indoors and outdoors, within and without, as matter circulates across the seemingly stable boundaries of buildings, parks, neighborhoods, cities, prairies, past, and present. The result is still, however, deeply influenced by Burnham's organismic imaginings and pioneer fantasies. Sandburg's Chicago is a green receptacle, albeit a leaky one, of dreamy prairie dust that materializes the frontier within the ventilation ducts and utility lines that threaten to erase it.

Like Sandburg, Wallace Stevens presents greens that are urban and natural, crafted and organic simultaneously, by focusing on the highly architectural environment of the public park, specifically pastoral-inflected parkscapes in New York City and Hartford, Connecticut. Stevens's depiction of parks and his poetic theory echo the design principles of Olmsted's pastoral school, as well as the more exotic styles found in botanical gardens and formal rose displays. Stevens's poems present the city park as an object shaped by human hands, possessed of often conflicting aesthetics. In treating elements most often associated with nature, like ponds and leaves, as artistic media, Stevens mimics the architectural gestures of the landscape architect while undermining the association of nature with the uncrafted, the nonhuman, and the real. However, Stevens also critiques the failures of Olmsted's democratic ideals through his focus on the park goer as a modern, American subject position. He does so by turning to a reimagined Prospect Park in *Owl's Clover*. Here, he investigates the function of socially and politically engaged art by studying the problems of isolation and oppression within the park context. Stevens uses the artistic excesses of later designers, particularly their imposition of statuary onto Olmsted's architecture, and the lasting class tensions in Prospect Park to think through how the poet must also craft a public art that gives pleasure while redressing the pressures of modernity that threaten the public's imaginative capabilities.

William Carlos Williams diverges from the largely positive visions of urban environments in Stevens and Sandburg to follow currents of toxicity running through Paterson, New Jersey, and its famous Passaic Falls. In his epic poem *Paterson*, Williams presents this contamination as the lasting inheritance of extractive mill-town planning first imposed on the landscape by the Society of Useful Manufactures (SUM). Whereas current studies of SUM in *Paterson* primarily treat the organization as an economic entity, chapter 3 recuperates their role as colonial-era urban designers who import a British model into an American topography. Williams builds his critique of SUM's design on both the macro level, in his large-scale metaphor of Paterson as City-Man and Garret Mountain Park as Nature-Bride, and on the micro scale of individual design elements, like the layout of streets and park paths. While initially suggestive of several of the traditional nature / city divisions, Williams's anthropomorphic metaphors fall apart and into one another when the poem attends to the fine details of toxic architecture. Both metaphorical bodies become one, as it is impossible to separate the materiality of the plan, the park, the Falls, and the creatures who live and labor in this compound environment. The arc of this cocreating romance achieves fullest expression in book 2 as Paterson the City-Man-Poet spends an afternoon in Garret Mountain Reservation, a later creation of the Olmsted firm. In the person of Paterson walking through the park, a representative of both the poet and the subject of the modern park goer, Williams conflates two major literary figures in this similarly conflated urban-natural environment: the flaneur and the nature walker. As the flaneur, Paterson views urban scenes of drinking games, dancing, and courting, as well as admiring the profile of the city, while as a nature walker Paterson also enjoys the contours of the mountain, with all its flora and fauna. Through his dual vision of this parkscape, Williams both criticizes the social malaise arising from the poorly planned industrial city and looks toward the hope of right relationship among urban habitat, local environment, and American poetry.

The study concludes by turning from the poetry of city parks to national parks in order to explore the ways in which Marianne Moore presents these natural zones as highly complex human texts composed for a population of city dwellers. While Moore is most often associated with her New York environs, this "nature" poem is of a piece with her explorations of cityscapes. Whereas she turns city streets back into frontier in "New York," in "An Octopus," she reveals how the apparent wilderness of Mount Rainier National Park is a nature playground built for disaffected urbanites; it is an emphatically urban animal in the rationale and realization of its architecture and in the way it is consumed by the park goer. To capture this strange beast on the page, Moore relies heavily on national park guides and a wide variety of travel literature and mountaineering texts as sources not only for her frequent quotes, but for the very structure of this sprawling poem. The result is an experience of the parkscape never disentangled from the NPS architecture and the literature that shapes and regulates the visitor's experience of the site. Ultimately, Moore eschews any direct experience of Mount Rainier that falls outside of the texts, both written and architectural, that mediate the visitor's interaction with her location. No absolute distinction between human and natural, artificial and originary is possible. The ultimate result is a poem that shifts the many virtues associated with the wilderness experience onto the act of reading both a sprawling landscape and a poem, an act requiring patience, strength, and restraint.

While not quite "dancing about architecture," this study faces several similar difficulties. There is always a gap between the architect's plan and the final site, as well as deviation from the architect's assumed uses for the space by the community (or communities) who use it. In terms of the poetry, each poet's interaction with and representation of the space is inherently unique and therefore not necessarily representative of that community experience or the architect's intent. There is also a temporal lag between when the space is first crafted and the time at which the poet encounters it, with a tangled history of management and additions to the landscape in the interim. In terms of aesthetics, the poet must also negotiate the media shift from the physical art of the space to the experience of that space as captured in poetic language. My focus on the poetry helps me negotiate several of these leaps. I am not trying to resurrect actual uses of these parks and cities, which would be a major undertaking, given the multiple and asymmetrical ways park goers have negotiated these spaces over time. Rather, I investigate how planners' and architects' principles are translated into formal qualities in their spaces and how those formal qualities are, in turn, depicted in the verse.

Given this focus on the poetry, this study at times also necessitates an analysis of the planning documents. This close reading is required, in part, due to disciplinary differences in the approach to such documents, as contemporary planners, architects, and archivists rightly focus on practical design applications. I approach the same documents as cultural texts and professional articulations of what constitutes nature. By questioning the rhetorical and visual gestures planners use in defining their sense of nature, I complicate some of the latent assumptions about the nature/culture divide that contemporary historical discourse often imports into discussions of these texts. What follows, then, is not only a pairing of poetry and landscape documents. Rather, in studying the spatial aesthetics within the verse, I simultaneously perform a reading of the rhetorics of nature at work within the professional dialogues of these disciplines. My hope is that scholars of modernism with an interest in cultural studies or material cultures might greatly expand the analysis of these landscape texts, and others like them, in order to demonstrate how they shape the cultural stage on which modernism plays out.

Understanding modern American natures as built spaces, as these poets do, has consequences for larger conversations about the relationship between the organic and the mechanic in modernism. During the mid-1980s, scholars tended to situate modernism on the chrome-and-piston side of a technological and ecological split, a divide that was subsequently probed and often critiqued. The questions are now *how* do modernists undermine that split, and what are the consequences of their strategies? There are many ways to answer these questions. We might think of the modern body and its sensorium as sites both biological and technological, or consider how the mechanics of trench warfare also entangle the human in hostile environments both organic and crafted. Most recently, Joshua Schuster's *Ecology of Modernism* (2015) has provided a timely study of how ecology, as science and technology, complicates any such distinctions in a modern context. Schuster does so through the disciplinary foci of ecology's quadrat, an approach that emphasizes that "the environs and the representation of the environs cannot be studied apart from each other" (x). In the case of parks, this is doubly true, as the environs *are* the representation. In selecting parks not as setting but as aesthetic and social strategy, American modernists select a vision of represented nature in which there is no outside referent. It is not that their poetry points us to a real nature out there, beyond the city, beyond the text. Instead, it directs us to nature fantasies built of green materials and continually reminds us of the fact of construction. As such, it is not that the poetry blends natural elements on the one hand and technological elements on the other. Rather, in engaging with these architectures, the poets present nature as technical material and aesthetic media.

This text is also a conversation partner in similar renarrativizations of modernity, ones that stretch rather than delimit. For example, my exploration of built natures contributes to a recent environmental shift in modernist studies, from green approaches to the modern novel to reimagining the modern in terms of the rise of ecology as a science or the Anthropocene as a geological epoch. By recuperating natures as designed spaces, I also add to the many studies of literary modernism's fascination with emerging art forms, much like David Spurr, who demonstrates the influence of modern architecture on literature, or Bonnie Costello, who has deftly shown the ways poets write with and against painterly landscaping traditions. However, unlike the architecture of buildings or the principles of landscape painting, the artistic interventions of landscape architects have gone largely ignored, and so their influence on modern poetry has likewise been neglected. At the same time, the sociopolitical consequences of class tensions in these built zones and poems also contribute to a turn (and return) toward labor and class in modernist studies, as in the recent work of John Marsh. Recuperating parks as public art also adds to explorations of popular and material culture in modernist studies, particularly with a focus on urbanism. If modernism is an animal of the dance hall, the skyscraper, the department store, or the penny arcade, it is just as much so a creature of the lawn, the arbor, the pavilion, and the promenade. Indeed, the teeming receptacles of parks serve as uniquely suitable ground for an exploration of the many ways differing approaches to modernism converge.

Parks
  new vistas
  constructed nature w/ allusions to pastoral + frontier
  architectural, social + ecological axis
  containers of "past + present"
  part of holistic urban design
  "art object, nature fantasy and social playground" 3

CHAPTER 1

Carl Sandburg and the Living American City

On 15 June 1896, a young Carl Sandburg made his first trip to Chicago. While overwhelmed and energized by the electric buzz of the city, he was deeply moved upon reaching the sprawling shore of Lake Michigan, the fifth-largest lake in the world: "I walked along Michigan Avenue and looked for hours to where for the first time in my life I saw shimmering water meet the sky. Those born to it don't know what it is for a boy to hear about it for years and then comes a day when for the first time he sees water stretching away before his eyes and running to meet the sky" (*Always the Young Strangers* 379). The contours of the city are embedded in this brief description. From Michigan Avenue, a major and often congested thoroughfare downtown in the 1890s, Sandburg could pivot and see the huge expanse of the lake reaching endlessly eastward. This vantage point captures many contradictions that Sandburg would later explore in his verse, particularly his fascination with Chicago as both urban and natural at once. While readers most often associate Sandburg with the grit of a swiftly industrializing metropolis, his poetry reveals an intertwined preoccupation with the organic matter of the city, such as the sky, mist, waves, and mud most often associated with nature. For Sandburg, the mechanical and built features of Chicago were never to be understood in isolation from its elemental character, nor could the city be clearly distinguished from the prairies and farmlands to the west and the lake stretching out to the east.

This vision of Chicago, one where nature and culture meet in an urban garden on the edge of a shining lake, was promulgated and, in part, realized by Daniel Burnham, the father of American city planning and author of the *Plan of Chicago* (1909). The *Plan* articulates not only Burnham's vision for holistic design in its attempt to meet the needs of Chicagoans through fully integrated urban infrastructure but also voices a persistent concern for the place of nature in this urban context. Increasingly, that context was the defining characteristic of American life as the populations of cities swelled dramatically from 1890 onward. Burnham's *Plan* combines an emphasis on nature's function in healing city dwellers and democracy with an attempt to reconceptualize nature as an urban phenomenon. Specifically, the *Plan* provides several ways of imagining the new natural city of modern America. Burnham presents the city as a living organism, one that breathes with green lungs, thereby emphasizing holism and the interrelation of parts. As a living thing, the city and its components are materially dynamic, as in Burnham's description of a living lakefront. As a space, the city is characterized by permeability achieved by reconsidering the relationship of interiors and exteriors. Just as Sandburg could stand within the busiest district of the city and marvel at the openness of sky and water, Burnham also imagined Chicago as both enclosure and out-of-doors simultaneously. Nature, once associated with a wilderness "out there," beyond the interior of the city, is now imported within city limits through the creation of a large public park system, one that preserved the vistas of Lake Michigan from encroaching sprawl. These parks not only bring the outside in but also make present the past by reconstructing a vanishing frontier experience within city limits.

In one sense, Sandburg's work represents a key moment in the reception of Burnham's *Plan*. He lived in Chicago during an era when the *Plan*, in its various iterations, saturated newspapers, lecture halls, classrooms, movie theaters, and art galleries. As Burnham's philosophy permeated the air of the city, his design began to alter Sandburg's urban landscape bit by bit, and so the poet had to physically negotiate Burnham's aesthetic and social ideals as they materialized as an architectural text. What Burnham dared in concrete, Sandburg attempted in verse. Like the *Plan*, Sandburg's poetry depicts a porous city where organic and inorganic, interiors and exteriors, light, weather, steel, and smoke constantly test and interpenetrate each other's boundaries. In another sense, Sandburg's poetry presents a significant revision of Burnham's aesthetic as it eschews finality and holism in favor of process and heterogeneity. This emphasis on process in the poetry draws from Sandburg's experience of the city as a material text in flux, one constantly written and revised by workers tearing apart streets, welding girders for bridges, and filling in the lakefront with debris. By focusing on labor, Sandburg potently captures the shifting and disintegrating borders between urban and natural environments within the parks, streets, buildings, and utility lines of Chicago. He ultimately presents the city as that continuous act of shifting, rather than imagining a final, stable state, as is expressed in the *Plan*.

Similarly, rather than elevating the figure of the planner, designer, or architect, Sandburg presents working Chicagoans as most intimately involved in the daily material exchanges that create this intricate urban ecosystem. Sandburg's understanding of the city as an ongoing physical process, rather than a finished product, weds with his concerns as a socialist. While Burnham was often criticized for overlooking the details of working-class living environments, Sandburg sees Chicago as an environment everywhere permeated by working-class labor. However, this focus on materialization over conceptualization, concrete and mud over the drafting board, does not wholly undermine city planning. On the contrary, Sandburg praises planning as a uniquely Chicagoan form of work and often blends together architects and laborers, blueprints and bevels, in his depiction of construction work. And yet, while Burnham busily advertised the *Plan,* his design only mattered to Sandburg in its matter: the cycles of sweat, salt, and steel that would embody and yet never perfectly realize Burnham's vision.

That vision had implications far beyond the borders of Chicago. When the *Plan* was made public on 4 July 1909, to much well-orchestrated fanfare, the choice of date communicated the document's broader national importance. With the loss of the frontier, long associated with wilderness and American character, and a corresponding explosion in urban populations, a nationwide environmental and civic crisis faced leaders in city governments and urban reform movements. Between 1800 and 1900, the proportion of the American population living in cities skyrocketed from 3 to 40 percent (Smith xv). And Chicago exemplified these national trends. Within two generations, the city transformed from a frontier town situated on ill-drained prairie, with a population of 4,179 people in 1837, to the second-largest city in the United States by 1890, outdone only by New York. Between 1880 and 1890 alone, the city's population had doubled, totaling 1,100,000. By 1909, it had doubled again, reaching nearly 2 million inhabitants.[1] Sandburg was one of those millions who poured into the city looking for fresh opportunities. Born in the small town of Galesburg, Illinois, Sandburg eventually abandoned a life of piecing together manual labor (as a milk truck driver, coal heaver, and field hand, to name only a few of his positions) in order to explore his options as a writer in the big city. His cry of wonder before Lake Michigan, and his poetic oeuvre as a whole, bears the marks of this emigration from a rural habitat. It is as a newcomer, one not "born to" Chicago but who had "heard of it" throughout his childhood, that Sandburg celebrates the Second City. His perspective as a transplant also allows him to appreciate Chicago as a prairie native like himself: a creature thoroughly modern and yet grounded in a pioneer tradition, made of equal parts macadam and clay, bricklayers and farm boys.

Just as Sandburg attempts to preserve Chicago's frontier heritage and organic character in his depiction of its most modern elements, so too was Burnham anxious to integrate the spirit and texture of the plains into the urban habitat that threatened to destroy it. This anxiety was rooted in a shared national concern over civic virtue, particularly how the loss of nature in its manifestation as frontier would weaken American democratic temperament and result in an enervated population. As Burnham notes, the time for awe over sheer, unordered expansion had come to an end: "The people of Chicago have ceased to be impressed by rapid growth of the great size of the city. What they insist asking now is, How are we living?" (32). The *Plan* contains a litany of harms resulting from poor planning, including pollution and traffic congestion, violence and crime, mortalities due to lack of sanitation, and the general ill health and declining moral character of the working class (32). Nor was the Great Fire of 1871 far from memory. Shortly after the devastating blaze, the nationally acclaimed landscape architect Frederick Law Olmsted argued that the fire might have been prevented entirely if the city had had a better plan (Smith 8). With the overtaxed and outmoded construction of a former trading outpost buckling under its swelling population, Chicago became both emblem and laboratory for the new discipline of city planning. If the first generation of American city planners regarded the poor arrangement of urban centers as the cause of nearly every physical and democratic ill, they simultaneously imagined the well-planned city as a cure-all.[2] Burnham, and the City Beautiful movement in general, assumed that simply dwelling in or moving through lovely spaces would infuse proper feelings in the citizen.[3] In arguing that the loveliness of urban centers resulted in proper civic behavior, city planners moved democratic education from the active homesteading of pioneers to the passive reception of cityscapes crafted by specialist designers. Sandburg also vacillates between deep concerns over the unwholesome, cramped environment of the city and optimism about the restorative effects of its open spaces and wide vistas. He similarly shares Burnham's holistic understanding of urban environments and translates that planning philosophy into ecosystemic and organismic presentations of the city on both the macro and micro scales: from gigantic presentations of the city and its skyscrapers as bodies or watersheds to a tight focus on the particulate materiality of individual moments of exchange, like a girder rusting or flecks of sand drifting in the electric light cast from buildings. In some pieces, such as "The Harbor," Sandburg shares Burnham's ideology about the psychological effects of passively consuming certain kinds of spaces. In others, he shifts the perceived benefits of working the land, the task of the now vanished pioneer, onto the business of working steel and concrete, thereby recuperating the character-building functions of actively shaping one's environment within an urban context.

A close study of the *Plan,* as a series of documents, a public discourse, and a spatial text in the making, elucidates Sandburg's specific engagements with and revisions of *Plan* principles, as well as his negotiation of the actual changes in landscape they precipitated. What follows is a brief history of the *Plan* that explores Burnham's design in order to contextualize how his presentation of the nature/city relationship finds expression within Sandburg's verse. However, reading Burnham alongside Sandburg invites a reconsideration of scholarly assumptions about Burnham's conception of nature as well. This ecocritical and textual approach to the *Plan* exposes Burnham's developing understanding of postfrontier nature as an architectural and deeply human artifice that must be built into American cityscapes.

urban planning rooted in Chicago World's fair

THE *PLAN OF CHICAGO*: THEORIES AND MATERIALIZATIONS

The *Plan of Chicago,* a 164-page document three years in the making, creates not only a proposal for the arrangement of the city but also a nascent history of city planning that takes Chicago as its ground of origin: "The origin of the Plan of Chicago can be traced directly to the World's Columbian Exposition. The World's Fair of 1893 was the beginning, in our day and in this country, of the orderly arrangement of extensive public grounds and buildings" (*Plan* 4). While Burnham might here be accused of immodesty (as he was one of the principal architects of the Chicago World's Fair in 1893), the fairgrounds did serve as a design exemplar for city planners who believed that its popularity would also inspire the nation to address the ramshackle development of its urban centers (Boyer 46). However, providing a start date for city planning as a discipline involves several difficulties. City plans in a global context long predate Burnham's efforts. Within the *Plan,* Burnham acknowledges the influence of the second-century Spartan planner Lycurgus and takes the Paris of Napoleon III as the ideal city. By evoking this long history, Burnham legitimizes his principles by gesturing toward a classical lineage. And yet, on the other end of the timeline, official city-planning periodicals, such as the *Century, World's Work,* and *Journal of the American Institute of Planners,* let alone professional degrees, would not become available until the 1930s (Boyer xi). That being said, when considering city planning as an American movement that culminated in a specific discipline with shared theories, the 1893 World's Fair served as the watershed moment. By 1909, Burnham can already demonstrate the Fair's lasting influence on the national landscape: "From Providence and Hartford in the East, to Kansas City and on to Seattle in the West, city planning is in full progress. The South also has felt the impulse" (28–29). What these individual efforts in urban improvement had in common with each other and with the vision presented at the World's Fair was an underlying principle of unity: "There had arisen the conception of the city as an organic whole, each part having well-defined relations with every other part; and the expression of this idea is now seen to be the highest aim of the city-builder" (29). This foundational principle regards urban environments as organic wholes and set city planning apart from earlier piecemeal municipal improvement plans that failed to address the interconnectedness of city spaces.

Burnham's organic approach and the centrality of nature in his design philosophy is writ large in even the smallest details of the *Plan.* In the handsome and luxuriously expensive first edition, jewel-toned, light-daubed maps of an imagined future Chicago are augmented by ornamental capitals at the start of each of its eight chapters.[4] The word "CHICAGO" begins four chapters, with the imposing *C* at times standing against miniature maps veined with proposed streets and railways. However, in chapters 3 and 6, the *C* fronts images of trees: a stately and shady boulevard in chapter 6, and a botanical example of the American cottonwood in chapter 3. Beneath the cottonwood, Burnham supplies the only note on a capital illustration in the entire volume, turning the word "CHICAGO" into a miniature field guide for native trees: "Cottonwood, near Chicago. Height, 127 ft., diameter 10 ft." (32). This is the first chapter to begin with the name of the city and so graphically announces "CHICAGO" by visually equating it with an icon of nature. The note emphasizes actuality, suggesting a real tree with measureable dimensions and a specific location, while "CHICAGO" hovers between the present and the possible future, referring to both the city in its current, unruly manifestation and the dream of a city yet to be realized. The cottonwood, "near Chicago," exists both inside and outside of the city, visually part of "CHICAGO" while simultaneously located in a vague periphery in

COTTONWOOD, NEAR CHICAGO.
Height, 127 ft.; diameter, 10 ft.

A decorative capital letter C with cottonwood and taxonomic note that begins chapter 3 of Burnham's *Plan of Chicago*. (Courtesy of the Newberry Library of Chicago; call case #fW999.182)

the note, proximate and far at once. This two-way act of writing Chicago onto nature and nature onto Chicago blurs the limits of urban and natural environments.

The presentation of the letter *C*, a minute part of the complex visual and lexical rhetoric of the *Plan*, is emblematic in more ways than one. As a symbol within the *Plan*, it represents Burnham's vision of the city as an organism reliant upon natural spaces and materials, parks and plants. More broadly, Burnham's recurring *C*-for-Chicago, mingled with maps and leaves, performs city planning's attempt to imagine and craft fit places for man and nature. Altering preconceptions about the mechanized character of city life is at the heart of Burnham's philosophy, though Burnham had difficulties letting go of language that emphasized a split between nature and city. While *Plan* scholars, such as Carl Smith, demonstrate how Burnham often falls into traditional conceptions of nature as an anti-urban, preindustrial out-there, the *Plan* simultaneously pushes against this tendency by placing nature within the city and equating that integration with the very essence of city planning. Rather than undermining the *Plan*, this vacillation reveals a larger national reconception of urban spaces in the early process of articulation. If *C* is for Chicago, it must be for cottonwood as well; otherwise, in the minds of the first city planners, they were both in danger of permanent erasure.

Chicago's topography provided a clean page for this new inscription. Just as Sandburg marveled at the wide lakefront, Burnham regarded the flat expanse of Midwest plains meeting the reflective sweep of Lake Michigan as a tabula rasa: "Whatever man undertakes here should be either actually or seemingly without limit" (*Plan* 79). The tension between "actually or seemingly" limitless planning is captured in the preexisting landscape. On the one hand, the openness of land- and waterscapes emphasized the horizon, creating a boundless canvas on which the urban architect might work: "Here the city appears as that portion of illimitable space now occupied by a population capable of indefinite expansion" (80). However, in actual fact, the landscape presented planners with real limitations. Burnham held that any plan must take local topography into account, and thus while it might seem that anything is possible on the prairie, in reality the design must mimic the contours (or lack thereof) of the local environment: "Whatever may be the forms which the treatment of the city shall take, therefore, the effects must of necessity be obtained by repetition of the unit. If the characteristics set forth suggest monotony, nevertheless such are the limitations which nature has imposed" (80). "The unit" here refers to the gridiron pattern of plot division that characterizes most frontier towns. The flat lines of the plains perfectly lent themselves to just such an arrangement. At their worst, they suggested monotony, but at their best, the gridded streets reflected the expansiveness of the site: "Always there must be the feeling of those broad surfaces of water reflecting the clouds of heaven; always the sense of breadth and freedom which are the very spirit of the prairies" (80). Rather than viewing city building as an act of taming nature, Burnham here imagines the city as a reflection of, and limited by, its natural environment. Chicago thus represented the possibilities of city planning for the first generation of urban architects as well as a specifically plains pioneer experience translated into a modern urban reality for the public.

If Chicagoans were to experience nature within city limits, Burnham knew he would have to build nature into their environment. His primary assumption was that humane living and good citizenship are prefaced by contact with nature, and therefore that planners and architects must deconstruct the theoretical split between man-made and natural environments. For Burnham, this meant the creation of a comprehensive park system within the city that would also integrate the lakefront more fully into the urban landscape. Burnham dedicates an entire chapter to the park system, in part responding to a 1904 study of the Chicago Parks Commission that decried the lack of accessible green space for Chicago's laborers. On the theoretical level, Burnham regarded green leisure space as essential to the well-being of city workers and the democratic project.[5] In this, he was inspired by the layout of ancient Rome and cites Lanciani's anatomical description of these spaces: "Parks . . . have been happily compared to the lungs of a city; and if the health and general welfare of a city depend upon the normal and sound function of its respiratory organs, ancient Rome, in this respect, must be considered as the healthiest city which has ever existed on earth" (12). In the organism of the city, Burnham regarded parks as the lungs of the urban animal. Without them, both city and citizen would suffocate.[6] The creation of breathing space, both a space in which to breathe and a space that breathes, requires that the planner treat natural materials as the very stuff of architecture and, therefore, the resultant spaces as highly crafted, man-made products.

The blue jewel in Burnham's green crown of park space was the lakefront. Burnham dedicates lengthy and florid passages to describing the great sweep of Lake Michigan: "The Lake is living water, ever in motion, and ever changing in color and in the form of its waves. . . . In its every aspect it is a living thing, delighting man's eye and refreshing his spirit" (50). Burnham's organismic view of the lake emphasizes dynamism and the play of light and color, the same biotic and shining qualities that would later captivate Sandburg. In the flat, forestless confines of Chicago, the lake also provided the only option for a refreshing vista: "No mountains or high hills enable us to look over broad expanses of the earth's surface; and perforce we must come even to the margin of the Lake for such a survey of nature" (50). As Sandburg would later capture in "The Harbor," Lake Michigan is a place where exhausted laborers can flee from their urban confines while, paradoxically, remaining within them, on the border of city and water. For both the poet and the planner, Lake Michigan is a part of and apart from the organism of the city, representing a living margin at times conceived of within city limits and, at others, imagined as an exterior otherness outside of the city as a natural, prehuman zone.

The success of Burnham's vision rested not only on excellent design principles but also on the ability to implement them, and none of the countless construction projects, let alone changes in zoning law, could begin without the support of the local business community. With the aid of the Commercial Club of Chicago, a society of eminent businessmen who funded and published the *Plan*, Burnham set out on an ambitious advertising campaign. On the day of its unveiling, the *Plan* was published simultaneously in several local newspapers, in multiple languages, with some editions featuring elegant maps created by the artists Jules Guerin and Fernand Janin. When the Club hired Walter L. Moody as their official publicist, his tactics were as sweeping and ambitious as the *Plan* itself.[7] Moody's comprehensive advertising, from classrooms, guild halls, art galleries, movie theaters, newspapers, magazines, pamphlets, and pulpits, saturated the city with Burnham's philosophy and provided a generation of Chicagoans with a new image of urban living. The *Plan* lingered in the public sphere for nearly two decades, as each step forward required a new push for votes, money, and public support. Despite Moody's efforts, the *Plan* was implemented in a patchwork fashion and never reached completion. However, a handful of the *Plan*'s recommendations were eventually enacted and changed the shape of the city.[8] Traffic was successfully reduced in the downtown area known as the Loop, and the park system was significantly expanded and updated. These spaces are themselves texts, or architectures that bear the mark of Burnham's design principles. In living, working, and moving through these spaces, Chicagoans came into intimate contact with the *Plan* in the space of the city. Despite its uneven materialization, the very concept of the *Plan* became a conceptual inheritance for a generation of modern city dwellers. No longer was Chicago imagined as an unregulated mass of streets and people expanding haphazardly from its frontier beginnings. Instead, Chicago was idealized as a unified environment: a civilized and civilizing act of comprehensive, green architecture.

Sandburg's poetic depictions of Chicago mirror Burnham's conception of a living, breathing city that is architectural and natural at once. As in the *Plan*, Sandburg's Chicago is eminently modern while also boasting of its prairie pedigree. Whereas Burnham's prairie aesthetic mimics the land's contours while integrating green space, Sandburg personifies Chicago as an urban creature permanently linked to the memory and materials of the plains. However, unlike Burnham's more teleological approach, Sandburg captures the dynamism of living in the city during its transformation by emphasizing acts of construction rather than completion. While much has been said of Sandburg's political investments in his depictions of labor, reading his poetry alongside Burnham's *Plan* reveals his ecological concerns as well, particularly in how construction makes manifest the elemental, and even agential, character of the city. Tracing Burnham's influence throughout Sandburg's work requires a turn to some understudied, and generally undervalued, pieces, as well as a reconsideration of his frequently anthologized works, particularly "Chicago." This analysis also begins with Sandburg's early work in *Chicago Poems* and concludes with a reading of his later long poem "Windy City" to demonstrate how Burnham's shadow lingers throughout Sandburg's extensive literary career.

SANDBURG: THE *PLAN* AND THE PROCESS

When workers were busy tearing up the streets of Chicago in a two-decade-long effort to realize Burnham's vision, Sandburg was negotiating the business of journalism while walking, working, and living in the changing landscape of the city. By the time he returned in 1912 to make his career as both a journalist and a poet, *Plan* implementation was the hot topic of the day.[9] During his time in the city, Chicagoans witnessed the extension of the lakefront with landfill and creation of the Forest Preserve District, as well as the widening of Michigan Avenue and completion of a double-decker bridge spanning the river. From the beginning of his tenure at the *Daily News* in 1917, debates related to these projects featured prominently in the paper. For example, in November of that year, a large article on the proposed expansion of South Water Street into a boulevard appeared alongside renderings of the suggested alterations. As was typical, the *Daily News* captured the contentiousness of the proposal: "Water Street experienced no thrill of joy to-day when it cocked its eye at the ennobling future outlined for it by the Chicago Plan Commission. A shrewd and disdainful eye it was, an eye not given to the contemplation of Parthenons or boulevards" ("To Turn South Water into Fine Boulevard," 21 Nov. 1917). That "ennobling future" would come under fire many times in the pages of the *Daily News,* especially in the face of limited resources during wartime. Most immediately, Sandburg's life as a journalist also physically situated him near the north branch of the river in the Loop, the epicenter of both presses and *Plan* construction. Sandburg's office at the *Chicago Daily Socialist,* on Randolph not far from State Street in the Loop, was only three blocks away from the heart of the *Plan's* street reforms on Michigan Avenue, which involved massive demolition projects to widen the overcrowded thoroughfares.

Approaching Sandburg's poetry in light of *Plan* aesthetics and implementation invites reconsideration of some often anthologized pieces, as well as a look at often neglected ones. In his iconic poem "Chicago," Sandburg presents the city as it undergoes the cycles of "Shoveling, / Wrecking, / Planning, / Building, breaking, rebuilding" that were integral to *Plan* construction efforts (*Chicago Poems* 4). When *Chicago Poems* appeared in print in 1916, city dwellers near and far would have recognized Chicago as an epicenter for "Planning," and the shoveling, wrecking, and building it required. The seemingly illogical order of this list, as it jumps back and forth from construction and destruction, captures both the history and prominence of planning in Chicago. These verbs stand out in the stanza, the first four printed alone after seven long lines preceding them. The result is a list of muscular activities, each pounded out with the heft of a hammer's blow. However, "Planning" is an abstract, conceptual activity that Sandburg nonetheless incorporates into a kinetic and corporal grouping. By virtue of its placement in this series, "Planning" becomes an activity possessed of the same impact and force as construction work, a quintessentially Chicagoan form of labor. The cycle of "Building, breaking, rebuilding" also captures the necessity of demolishing outmoded construction in order to modernize. In Chicago, this specifically meant Burnham's plan to demolish much of the poor construction implemented after the Great Fire in order to update and expand the cityscape. But what Burnham regarded as a waste of resources due to a lack of foresight, Sandburg celebrates as part of the city's history and cycles of ongoing regeneration. Fittingly, the series does not begin with "Planning," but with "Bareheaded" shoveling, a choice that reflects the actual history of a prairie town first shaped by digging frontiersmen. Nor does "Planning" help the long cycles of construction finally reach a conclusion. The imperfect state of each verb emphasizes process over product. Even the forward motion of the list cannot keep pace with all of this activity; the last line of the section piles up emphatically consonant verbs that reiterate the endless process of "Building, breaking, rebuilding."

Who is the bareheaded shoveler committed to this ongoing task? While Sandburg's personification of the city is most often remembered as the broad-shouldered "tall / bold slugger," immediately following this personification, the images become more complex: "Fierce as a dog with tongue lapping for action, cunning as a savage pitted against the wilderness" (*Chicago Poems* 4). First, the city is figured as an animal, feral in its ferocity and yet domesticated, a dog rather than a wolf, one both actively "lapping" and passively waiting for "action" at once. Chicago here hovers somewhere between stillness and motion, tamed and wild. Similarly, the representation of Chicago's cunning muddles divisions between wildness and civilization: "cunning as a savage pitted against the wilderness." The image seems to link the cunning of city building with an antagonism against nature. The mental agility needed to outsmart the wilderness is the selfsame one needed in acts of shoveling and wrecking, and thus city creation necessitates wilderness destruction. And yet, these acts of cunning naturalize city planning by re-inscribing a homesteading ethos onto acts of urban construction, thereby turning the city into the wilderness against which we are pitted. Similarly, following "pitted against the wilderness," the list begins with "Bareheaded," a descriptor consonant with images of savagery. However, immediately thereafter comes "Shoveling, / Wrecking, / Planning," acts progressively ur-ban in emphasis. Sandburg's readers might imagine a savage shoveling, but the introduction of the tool expands into larger acts of wrecking and the implied machinery needed to demolish preexisting structures. The list cul-minates in "Planning," an act emphatically urban when preceded by the wrecking ball. Yet "cunning" and "Planning" are the only mental activities here evoked. As cunning is to planning, so now wilderness is to city. Chicago here becomes both wilderness and savage, erasing and creating itself in the same motion.

Sandburg's manipulation of the figure of the savage troubles racialized associations with nature that, in turn, have implications for his depiction of Chicago as a diverse and organic habitat. Sandburg's evocation of the savage participates in wider primitivist trends in modern poetry. This in-terest in the perceived vitality of preindustrial cultures sought to redress the deadening qualities of modern society and overlapped with racialist and racist discourse. The figure of the "savage Indian" in particular partici-pates in the primitivist emphasis on strength, vigor, and primal origins while emphasizing a distinctively American tradition. In using these primitivist assumptions, Sandburg also revises them. Rather than reiterating the prob-lematic stereotype that assumes an innate sympathy between "primitive" peoples and the land, Sandburg links the savage with the frontiersman in that both are "pitted against the wilderness." On the historical level, this line gestures back to the original presence of Algonquin tribes in the area, from whom Chicago received its name "wild onion field." In acknowledging this "savage" pedigree, Sandburg presents the city as a native, a new "Player with Railroads" and a preindustrial hunter at the same time. In shifting his depiction away from sympathetic dwelling within wilderness toward the active, even antagonistic reshaping of it, Sandburg also upholds the savage as a prototype of the city planner. Just as Burnham's history of city planning provides a classical heritage and a local grounding for this new discipline, so too does Sandburg justify and nativize city planning by linking it to the figure of the savage. And whereas Burnham's nod to Sparta gives his project the air of a highly Western tradition, Sandburg's savage evokes the distinctly American flavor of Chicago's planning and building efforts.

Sandburg tightly links planning and building, to the point of often blending these acts together. In this instance, he does so by quickly transfiguring the savage into a contemporary construction worker, "dust all over his mouth, laughing with white teeth," within five lines (*Chicago Poems* 4). The speed and ease of this transition troublingly erases a vexed history of violence against indigenous peoples, and so turns a problematic frontier narrative into a story of assimilation as the savage effortlessly becomes pioneer, planner, worker, and the personified city. That the face of the savage becomes the visage of a city in blackface, dust-darkened and punctuated with the white grin characteristic of minstrelsy, also elides differences between Native Americans and African Americans while engaging with primitivist assumptions that often flattened differences among cultures. That being said, this racialized face of Chicago serves as a Janus figure, looking back to Chicago's Algonquin past and forward to the increasingly diverse metropolis shaped by the massive influx of African Americans into Chicago during the Great Migration.[10] As Sandburg noted in his coverage of the Chicago race riots, between 1910 and 1919, Chicago's black community had increased by seventy thousand members. Although troublingly mired in primitivist discourse, Sandburg's presentation of Chicago as a person of color evokes an entire history of changing population trends while framing the current African American community as the icon and apogee of Chicago's citizenry.

For Sandburg, the very act of shoveling, wrecking, and building Chicago reveals the commingling of man and nature. Whereas Burnham imagined the possibilities of a natural city as the product of construction, Sandburg sees man, nature, and city creating each other in the process. In "Muckers," Sandburg describes workers digging a ditch for new gas mains as twenty men stand by and watch: "Stabbing the sides of the ditch / Where clay gleams yellow, / Driving the blades of their shovels / Deeper and deeper for the new gas mains" (*Chicago Poems* 21). There is violence in the work, as shovel blades stab and drive into the earth. However, that earth is surprisingly beautiful, gleaming yellow like unexpected gold, catching light even in the recess of the ditch. Red is the only other color in the poem, "Wiping sweat off their faces / With red bandanas," making the interior of the ditch bold and lively in both natural and man-made materials, in contrast to the nondescript surface-level crowd. The ditch, and the process of digging "Deeper and deeper," push the downward limits of the city beyond cement underfoot to the subterranean utility lines and the miles of clay around them. That clay is also dynamic: "The muckers work on . . . pausing . . . to pull / Their boots out of suckholes where they slosh" (21, ellipses original). The resistant clay of the first lines, requiring vigorous stabbing to give way, becomes a slick, active force by line 9 as it sucks the men down deeper into the earth. As the laborers pause to extricate themselves, the punctuation enacts the counterforce of the mud, and the poem slows as ellipses halt the brisk clip of the first seven lines.

This glimpse into the earth beneath the concrete was available daily to those men and women walking the streets of Chicago during *Plan* implementation. Whereas Burnham imagined a natural city as the result of this labor, Sandburg's depiction of digging, and all the upheaval it produces, emphasizes the act of construction as a kinetic locus where nature and city meet. In "Muckers," tension and difficulty define the relationship between humanity and environment without devolving into outright antagonism or simple victories. It is not that, in sucking the workers down, the clay ultimately triumphs, and therefore that nature is held above the city. Rather, the spatial dynamics of the poem depict the city as a space permeated by human labor, even in its most natural sites. If construction lays bare the organic ground lurking beneath the city, it also places the worker in that ground, so that the very dirt is marked by these human hands and the miles of pipe sending gas throughout the city's bowels. The image is thus both miniature, these men in this bit of ditch, and holistic, suggesting an entire infrastructure running through the earth of all Chicago. Earth is permeated with the human, as the human rests upon, digs, and sinks into the earth.

The intermingling of nature and city takes place not only below ground but also above as borders between human and nonhuman habitats are blurred, as in Sandburg's depiction of the lakefront in "The Harbor." In this piece, Sandburg effectively presents the overcrowded and unwholesome tenements that caused Burnham and urban reformers such concern. In doing so, Sandburg also relies on Burnham's supposition that the shape of one's environment directly affects the shape of one's character. "The Harbor" is broken into two sections, the first of which demonstrates the negative consequences of living in a poorly designed space: "Passing through huddled and ugly walls / By doorways where women / Looked from their hunger-deep eyes" (*Chicago Poems* 8). In the first line, passing "through" these walls creates a moment of spatial confusion: Is the speaker within a building, passing through doorways situated within huddled walls? The speaker then passes "by" doorways, perhaps still within a building but also suggesting a walk down a street where the walls have flipped from a possible interior to a street-side exterior. The confusion between inside and outside here arises from an oppressive monotony. The walls are huddled and ugly, no matter what side of them one is on, so that even walking "out" in the streets feels like walking through the inside of an oppressive building. Sandburg captures that monotony by repeating the entire phrase "huddled and ugly walls" in the next few lines, as the speaker's language similarly cannot escape from drab repetitiveness of this environment. The breathy echo of the lines, in the repetition of the "h" sound, also adds a gasping eeriness to the tight quarters as well as a sense of hush as the speaker passes under the hungry stares of the women.

These cramped conditions lead to stifled lives, specifically those of the women who linger in the doorways. Their position within the doorways, neither within a domestic interior nor out in the public space of the street, creates a sense of entrapment. Although their location suggests a desire for some kind of motion, either an entrance or an exit, they remain frozen in the aperture of the building, not due to constraint but rather because of the homogeneity of the scene; there is no compelling reason for them to move, as the walls are huddled and ugly both inside and out. Just as this space limits the language of the speaker, so too does it constrict the personhood of the women. They look "from" hungry eyes as their bodies become another structure, their eyes another useless doorway. Part of the pathos of this section originates in the speaker's lack of access to the individuals doubly trapped within their doorways and bodies. They are reduced to a nondescript group of "women" as starved and uniform as their urban habitat. While the speaker can acknowledge the deprivation they experience, their glances are ultimately vacant. They look outward, but at nothing specifically, as the gaze of the speaker is met with a wall of unfocused, unmoving starvation.

As the speaker moves on, both the lake and "I" suddenly appear in the middle of the poem: "Out from the huddled and ugly walls, / I came sudden, at the city's edge, / On a blue burst of lake" (8). Only in this second section does Sandburg explicitly mention colors, as the blue stretch of lake and white flutter of seagulls assault the eyes with all the vigor and disorientation of a "burst" that pops with alliteration. The suddenness of this experience does more than highlight the juxtaposition between these two spaces and states of life. It also accurately captures the abrupt transition from dense urban housing to the beach, similar to Sandburg's own experience of glimpsing Lake Michigan from his vantage point on the street downtown.[11] Burnham had intended to soften the transition from housing to lakefront through the creation of the lakefront park system that would provide a green space leading up to the beaches. However, as with so many elements of the *Plan,* that design was only partially realized, and some neighborhoods still run right up to the sand of the lakefront.

North Callahan argues that the lake in "The Harbor" "mirrored for [Sandburg] the local human misery" (58). This reading perfectly captures the sentiment in the first half of the poem, but in the second section, Sandburg shares Burnham's understanding of the salutatory effects of environment. Whereas the miserable women are like their miserable surroundings, the lake presents the speaker with a vision of light and movement that enables personhood, an "I" in relief against the blue sky. Once the "I" emerges in this spatial transition, the sound and palette of the lines also stretches out and brightens when the speaker describes "Long lake waves breaking under the sun / On a spray-flung curve of shore" (8). The rounded "curve" of the shore contrasts with the implied boxiness of the repetitive tenements, arranged geometrically on the gridiron pattern that Burnham had cautiously praised. The assonant "lake waves breaking" replaces the huffing of earlier lines with an undulant roundness that enacts the openness of the shore. The presentation of the lakefront also emphasizes freedom and health, as seen in the image of seagulls flying overhead: "Masses of great gray wings / And flying white bellies / Veering and wheeling free in the open." Like the women, the birds are depicted en masse, just as both groups are reduced to body parts: hands, eyes, bellies, wings. However, unlike the women whose decomposition into starving pieces plays out in a static environment, the gulls are experienced only as impressionistic swishes of color because of their freedom to move. And yet, while the gulls enjoy the lakefront, the women continue to lead unwholesome lives only steps away from the shore. As seen in these lines, although the poem shares Burnham's vision of the lake as vital and therapeutic, it also undermines that therapeutic effect through the stark contrast between the spaces and their inhabitants. The lake, suddenly near for the speaker, remains a distant reality for the women he passes. Sandburg demonstrates how spatial proximity is not synonymous with ease of access, especially for these working-class women who find themselves tethered to domestic portals.[12]

And yet, there are some Chicagoans, like the speaker and Sandburg, whose social position allows them to move easily through both kinds of zones. Like the seagull, a creature of both land and lake, the speaker can negotiate this edge environment, poised as he is between "a fluttering storm of gulls" before him and the "shadows of hunger-hands" to his back. While the poem may initially seem to draw a sharp border between city and lake, the speaker's shoreline experience situates the lake as both separate from and integral to the city simultaneously. In many respects, the lake here functions as the out-of-doors against which the interiority of the city is defined, as well as a regenerative zone for those capable of accessing it. At the same time, the swiftness of the transition between these two spaces also situates the lake as an element of the city, an amenity abutting even its most compact quarters. The poem's title, "The Harbor," points to the dual character of this space as both urban and extra-urban, as harbors provide a point of safe contact between land and water. In Sandburg's context, these harbors are primarily not naturally occurring inlets but are rather built structures. A major component of Burnham's *Plan* was an extensive harbor system designed to accommodate heavy water traffic, such as the creation of what is now called Navy Pier. Thus, on the literal level, the title prevents readers from regarding the shore as uncrafted, ante- or anti-urban nature. However, the poem never mentions the harbor structure explicitly beyond the title. Rather, Sandburg follows Burnham's sanative understanding of the lake by presenting it metaphorically as a psychological harbor for the privileged speaker as he flees from the claustrophobic maze of tenements.

Whereas Sandburg subtly nods to the built qualities of natural environments in "The Harbor," he foregrounds the natural characteristics of built environments in his presentation of skyscrapers. In doing so, he celebrates a quintessentially modern and Chicagoan form of architecture, one that Burnham praised and practiced.[13] Before undertaking the *Plan*, Burnham worked with the architect John Wellborn Root and designed several of Chicago's most famous skyscrapers, including the Montauk Block (1882), the Rookery Building (1888), and the Monadnock Building (1891), thereby radically changing the profile of the city. Once he began drafting his *Plan* proposal, Burnham placed his office atop the towering Railway Exchange

Building to take advantage of panoramic views of the city. He drew on this prior architectural experience when crafting the *Plan*. While not mentioned explicitly, skyscrapers serve as a key architectural feature of Burnham's *Plan* throughout its maps and illustrations. On the practical level, by taking advantage of vertical space, skyscrapers alleviated urban crowding by allowing thousands of people to live and work on a modest parcel of land. On the theoretical and aesthetic level, the vistas provided from these skyscrapers enabled a holistic vision of the city. While Bostonians had long enjoyed hilltop vantages on their urban environment, Chicagoans were limited by their flat terrain until the arrival of this soaring architecture. The publication and dissemination of Guerin and Janin's crepuscular, perspectival *Plan* illustrations presented Chicagoans, and the nation at large, with some of the first bird's-eye depictions of this prairie city. Their images emphasize the interconnectedness of roadways and park space, as well as prominently featuring the vastness of the lake stretching beyond the city.

While Chicago became known for its daring skyline, it was also participating in a larger national trend. As the architectural historian George H. Douglas has argued, the skyscraper, and the resultant changes to city skylines, came to represent the heart of modern American urbanism (2). Sandburg's depiction of the skyscraper thus strikes both a local and a national chord while his emphasis on the building as a natural habitat casts American urbanism in an emphatically ecological light. As with Guerin and Janin's illustrations, Sandburg's poetry achieves this in part by taking advantage of the wide, panoramic views afforded one at the top of a skyscraper. Sandburg stretches that perspective out into the plains and even into a global landscape in order to capture the skyscraper's embeddedness in ever-widening cycles of material exchange. As seen in the poems above, Sandburg also complicates *Plan* aesthetics through his emphasis on process and labor. Rather than presenting skyscrapers as finished, static architectural objects, he frames them as breathing, decaying, growing, porous habitats that constantly enact their own design. That architectural and material activity is never separable from the lives of the workers who both built and maintain the skyscraper, as well as those who labor in its halls and offices.

Sandburg concludes *Chicago Poems* with "Skyscraper," a piece that captures the twenty-four-hour life cycle of a structure with deep connections to the Chicago skyline. Sandburg's "Skyscraper" presents a building that is both ecosystem and organism, whose permeable glass-and-steel membrane connects it to the air, the earth, and the people it shelters. He begins: "By day the skyscraper looms in the smoke and sun and has a soul" (65). This ensouled structure dominates an urban atmosphere in which light and pollution mingle to create a backdrop for its mammoth silhouette. The proportions of the skyscraper expand even further in the next line, as its sphere of attraction extends beyond the limits of Chicago: "Prairie and valley, streets of the city, pour people into it / and they mingle among its twenty floors and are / poured out again back to the streets, prairies and / valleys." This pouring of people suggests a kind of human watershed that flows directly into the skyscraper, which, in turn, circulates the fluid of humanity back into a broader environment. "Prairies and valleys" constitute part of the building's wide habitat as Sandburg stretches the limits of the city and imagines the wider effect of urbanism on small Midwest towns like his own Galesburg. And yet, while the skyscraper's magnetism extends beyond the city proper, it nonetheless has a soul because of its fixed location: "(Dumped in the sea or fixed in a desert, who would care / for the building or speak its name or ask a policeman / the way to it?)" (65). It is a native organism of the city, incapable of transplantation into different habitats, precisely because its life depends upon masses of people: "It is the men and women, boys and girls so poured in and / out all day that give the building a soul."

Sandburg presents the skyscraper as kinetic and fluid in its material exchanges and in even the seeming solidity of its structure. Within the building, "Elevators slide on their cables and tubes catch letters and / parcels," uniting different offices and floors, while "iron pipes carry gas and water in and / sewage out," connecting the skyscraper to wider utility infrastructures outside its walls. "Wires climb with secrets, carry light and carry words" as an architectural nervous system in which human communication becomes the electrical life of the building. Sandburg then drastically widens this vision in the next stanza: "Hour by hour the caissons reach down to the rock of the / earth and hold the building to a turning planet" (65). The vista presented by this sketch telescopes out to a global ecosystem, where root-like caissons grip the earth of not just a plot or even the city, but of the planet. Activity characterizes the relation of building to earth: the apparently stable earth turns, the apparently finished, static building reaches and holds "Hour by hour." The solid building is positioned precariously, as if about to spin off of a spinning world, and so becomes surprisingly delicate in its material relation to the earth. At the same moment, the skyscraper stands out as an international symbol of American urbanism, like a robust spike radiating out from the crust of North America as its girders hold it "to a turning planet."

Just as with Sandburg's presentations of Chicago as a whole, the building is not an object as much as it is a process of engagement: "Hour by hour the girders play as ribs reach out and / hold together the stone walls and floors" (65). The steel frame that characterizes skyscraper construction both dynamically "plays" as it holds the building together while it also functions as "ribs" in the skeletal system of this living construction. The ongoing activity of the building playfully maintaining its own heft then extends to the builders and architects who made the structure: "Hour by hour the hand of the mason and the stuff of the / mortar clinch the pieces and parts to the shape an / architect voted." In its completion, the ongoing presence of the skyscraper's creators somehow continuously plans and spackles the building, thereby emphasizing process. Whereas Sandburg began the stanza by stretching along a spatial axis, he concludes by sliding along a temporal one: "Hour by hour the sun and the rain, the air and the rust, / and the press of time running into centuries, play / on the building inside and out and use it" (65). The building's internal play of cohesion among its parts is matched by an entropic play of elements and time that tease boundaries by weaving "inside and out." While rain and air lead to rust, threatening the structure over a long "press of time," Sandburg captures the activity of oxidation with the same verb used to describe the girders' playful act of holding the skyscraper together. The essential playfulness of material exchange holds generation and decay together in a single act of cheerful activity, a process that defines the building as the living, dynamic thing Sandburg believes it to be.

As is characteristic of Sandburg's oeuvre, "Skyscraper" both lauds the efforts of working-class Chicagoans and laments the economic inequities they suffer. The skyscraper thus stands metonymically for Chicago in particular and the American city in general, capturing Sandburg's social vision in which the "Smiles and tears of each office girl go into the soul of / the building just the same as the master-men who / rule the building" (67).[14] The poem proceeds to describe the daily activity of those working in the skyscraper, celebrating the lives of "the hod carrier," "Ten-dollar-a-week stenographers," and "Scrubbers . . . talking in foreign tongues." The poem concludes with one such working-class laborer, "A young watchman" who "leans at a window and sees the lights / of barges butting their way across a harbor, nets of / red and white lanterns in a railroad yard, and a span / of glooms splashed with lines of white and blurs of / crosses and clusters over the sleeping city." Sandburg privileges this point of view, as the working-class watchman is one of the few people who enjoy a nighttime vantage of the city, along with the cleaners who "mop and clean from the floors human dust and spit, / and machine grime of the day." However, as the cleaners direct their gaze downward, wiping away mingled biological and mechanistic detritus, the watchman leisurely gazes out on the electrified grid of the city. The "nets of . . . lanterns" and "crosses" of white light describe the gridiron layout of streets described in Burnham's *Plan*. The "lights of barges" in the harbor mesh with the netting of lights on the railroads and streets, optically uniting the water and the land in a nighttime light show. These lights bleed in an impressionistic haze of smoke and fog, as "a span of glooms . . . blurs" the grill of streetlights below. This scene is reminiscent of Guerin and Janin's illustrations of the city in the *Plan*, where networked dots of pale yellow light smear the distinction between water and land over a long aerial view of Chicago. In both the *Plan* and "Skyscraper," the interaction of electric lights and atmospheric conditions reveals the man-made planned environment below while causing it to extend and disappear into the dark lake beyond. The perspective from the skyscraper, both organism and habitat, is of the wider cityscape, whose regulated streets melt into a mist where nature and the city continually coalesce.

Sandburg returns to atmospheric effects in a shorter poem from *Smoke and Steel* (1921), "The Skyscraper Loves Night," in which the amorous pair of skyscraper and sky cocreate each other. Whereas "Skyscraper" concludes with a vision of night and the city from a skyscraper vantage, in this later piece the building bizarrely becomes part of the atmosphere. The poem begins: "One by one lights of a skyscraper fling their checkering cross work on the velvet gown of night" (*Smoke* 257). Here, Sandburg likens the night sky to a plush dress, with the lights from the skyscraper creating luminous embroidery. The apparent straightforwardness of this image becomes confused at "fling." "Fling" suggests that light is cast out of the building onto the surface of the sky, with the night mirroring the light of the building. However, the image evoked is that of lit windows in a skyscraper at night, where the pattern of light is in the building itself, the frame of which seems to disappear in the darkness. The building is therefore part of the dress of night while represented as apart from it, at a distance from which it "flings" the gold checkering that it actually is.

The relationship between building and atmosphere grows increasingly complicated as the poem continues: "I believe the skyscraper loves night as a woman and brings her playthings she asks for, brings her a velvet gown, /

A nighttime view of Lake Michigan dotted with lights, from the *Plan of Chicago* as illustrated by Jules Guerin and Fernand Janin. (Courtesy of the Newberry Library of Chicago; call case #fW999.182)

And loves the white of her shoulders hidden under the dark feel of it all" (257). The romance between skyscraper and nighttime sky acquires layers of fabric and distance as the lines progress. Whereas in the first line the velvet gown seemed to be the night, in the second line night morphs into a woman, and the gown transmutes into a dark gift from the skyscraper. The rich blackness of the night sky becomes a phenomenon somehow generated by the skyscraper, a present he offers her, while the body of night becomes a hidden whiteness, clothed by the building while also undressed in his imagination. Sky and structure here create each other: the sky upholding the checkered lights of the skyscraper, the skyscraper offering the garment the sky both wears and is.

The cocreating intimacy in these compounding metaphors suddenly breaks in the final lines: "The masonry of steel looks to the night for some-body it loves, / He is a little dizzy and almost dances . . . waiting . . . dark . . ." (ellipses in original). The building now looks "for" a lover to emerge from night, no longer treating the night "as" the somebody it loves. She is both terribly near and tantalizingly far, as night is the dress, the woman in the dress, and now the horizon looked to in the hope of seeing the woman emerge in her gown. Distance creates tension, as the solid "masonry of steel" turns giddy in anticipation. The building becomes tipsy, on the verge of a tumble. The final words maintain that potential motion while further complicating the image: "waiting . . . dark . . ." The skyscraper waits as el-lipses perform the passage of time and the teetering anticipation of the building. Has he waited so long for his paramour that morning arrives and the skyscraper goes dark? Or perhaps the darkness is the lover, the night, just slightly out of reach? "Dark" reels between identification with the building and the night, capturing in miniature the vertiginous tension between sky and structure that characterizes the poem as a whole. Sandburg ultimately sidesteps a final, stable state of relationship between man-made and natu-ral, construction and atmosphere by leaving the poem suspended between consummation and anticipation.

While Sandburg's engagement with Burnham's aesthetics, architectures, and the construction they required influences his early work in *Chicago Poems,* Sandburg's vision of Chicago as a natural city reaches full expression in his later *Slabs of the Sunburnt West* (1922), in which his emblematic sky-scrapers arise from the very stuff of the wilderness they displace. In linking prairie and city, Sandburg plays with a historical-spatial dynamic. As Hazel Durnell has argued, "The prairie country is for Sandburg the symbol of the pioneering spirit that built America; it represents also the visible signs of American origins and permanence and the creative power of human labor and enterprise in a democratic community" (75). Sandburg's frontier nostalgia and modern urban enthusiasm find a balance in this longer piece that frames the current physical arrangement of the city as an extension and even preservation of the vanishing prairie. In this, he shares Burham's paradoxical answer to concerns over the loss of a distinctive midwestern landscape: the prairie must be built into the city that overtakes it. Burnham regarded the expansion of Chicago's park system as a fulfillment of the city's motto, *urbs in horto,* a city in a garden. That motto expresses both a lost frontier experience of unspoiled prairie and a present call to reimagine ways of fulfilling its mandate:

> Chicago, on becoming a city, chose for its motto *Urbs in horto*—a city set in a garden. Such indeed it then was, with the opalescent waters of the Lake at its front, and on its three sides the boundless prairie carpeted with waving grass bedecked with brilliant wild flowers. The quick advance of commerce and manufactures, the rapid building of railroads and factories, and the hastily constructed homes of operatives crowded out nature's parterres of flowers. Still the motto lingered in the minds of men. (*Plan* 43)

The idea of a "prairie garden" evokes both the nonhuman and the human, as a natural prairie that is also a cultivated garden space confounds the boundaries between natural and architectural spaces. The phrase "nature's parterres" similarly presents a provocative mixing of wilderness rhetoric and landscape gardening. Parterres, flat formal gardens bounded by stone walkways or clipped hedges, were often featured in Burnham's designs, including the *Plan* and his World's Fair layout. Parterres evoke the flatness of prairie space while prefiguring a now lost wilderness as a planned garden in one of Burnham's favorite styles. Nature, even as the pre-urban prairie, is here imagined as an architectural space, thus naturalizing Burnham's architectural intervention. In "Windy City," Sandburg similarly deconstructs the boundary between architecture and nature in the attempt to make the chronotope of the plains, both a space and a moment in the past, physically present. As seen in *Chicago Poems*, Sandburg again achieves this by focusing on process, whereas Burnham emphasizes the final architectural result of such processes. If Burnham attempted to literalize *urbs in horto* in his designs, Sandburg goes one step further in "Windy City" by presenting the city as a garden, the garden as the city, as both are wrapped together in another act of personification.

Slabs of the Sunburnt West begins with "Windy City," a lengthy ten-section history of Chicago that begins with "The lean hands of wagon men" pointing to a "homelike spot" where the railroads eventually meet: "this corner with a mesh of rails, shuttling / people, shunting cars, shaping the junk of / the earth to a new city" (*Slabs* 3). "Junk," a noun suggesting superfluous man-made materials, here signifies the raw materials of the surrounding area used in constructing Chicago. Sandburg here turns building into an act of recycling the waste of the prairie as its tough clay, a foe to farmers, becomes brick. The history continues, paralleling the Judeo-Christian creation myth: "And the breaths of men went into the junk / And the junk stood up into skyscrapers and asked: / Who am I? Am I a city? And if I am what is my name?" (3). In this urban Genesis, men stand in for God, who enlivens the clay-made Adam with his breath. The skyscraper represents the Adam of the prairie, the first sentient creature of the wilderness endowed with the life of its creators. But while the skyscraper breathes the breath of man, it is also living prairie "junk," embodying the wilderness it overtakes in its very materiality.

Sandburg positions the skyscraper, the living spokesman of Chicago, between past and present, nature and man. Its newborn cry for a name receives a reply first from the past:

> Long ago we laughed and said: You? Your name is Chicago.
> Early the red men gave a name to a river,
>   the place of the skunk,
>   the river of the wild onion smell,
>   Shee-caw-go. (3)

The name "Chicago" summons a native past that voiced environmental characteristics of the location, pointing to the onion that once grew wild in the Chicago River's floodplain. The "we" here also reaches to the past, in linking Chicago's current inhabitants and the pioneer generation who breathed life into the city. The naming cry of the past then merges with the "payday songs of steam shovels" as "The living lighted skyscrapers tell it now as a name" (4). In saying its own name, Chicago proclaims both a prairie heritage and its ongoing creation in "the breaths of working men" who build, destroy, and rebuild in the modern moment. Sandburg then returns to the image of a lit, living skyscraper: "Spotting the blue dusk with checkers of yellow, / streamers of smoke and silver, / parallelograms of night-gray watchmen." The substantial buildings again daub the sky with light, then transform into wisps of curling gray smoke that belie their solidity, before again hardening into geometric solids and watchful sentries. Such is the mercurial quality of prairie junk.

Section 2 presents snapshots of city living, from children taking the train to school, to "the respectable taxpayers" reading their papers, and the "haberdasher customers" chatting mindlessly with each other (5). The children are bundled off for geography lessons as they ride "through a tunnel under a river running backward" (4). The Chicago River's flow was reversed in

1900 to prevent the waste choking its banks from flowing out into the lake, still used today as the city's primary source of drinking water.[15] The rerouting of transportation rails was also a major component of Burnham's *Plan* in its attempt to relieve congestion in the downtown Loop area. The backward flow of the river and downward trajectory of the train follow the students' lesson, as they turn back to the past and down to the earth to learn "how now the roofs and smokestacks cover miles / where the deerfoot left its writing / and the foxpaw its initials / in the snow" (5). Sandburg here expresses nostalgia for a wilderness already memorialized in textbooks while also marveling at the ingenuity of engineering that speeds the children on to school. While their function as urban thoroughfares contributes to the loss of deerfoot and foxpaw, the back-flowing river and downward-running trains facilitate and symbolize this historical glance backward to the imprint of a vanished wilderness.

In section 5, Sandburg moves to street level to consider the relationship between the city's net of thoroughfares and the environment beyond. Section 5 offers a list of apologies for the apparent faults of Chicago. These apologies balance between sincerity and sneer, particularly after following the effete description of other cities in section 4. If "Venice is a dream of soft waters" and "Paris is a thought in Monet gray on scabbards, fabrics, facades," Chicago, in contrast, is "Independent as a hog on ice" (8). Whereas Burnham anxiously defended Chicago as the "Paris of the Prairie," capable of comparison with any city abroad, Sandburg locates the glory of Chicago in its difference from those locations. While the description of "brick chimneys" coughing in "Each other's faces" is worthy of an urban reformer's scorn, the liveliness of the "jazz timebeats / Of these clumsy mass shadows" hardly needs forgiveness. Sandburg begins a list of "Forgive us" with Chicago's flat terrain: "Forgive us if the monotonous houses go mile on mile / Along the monotonous streets out to the prairies" (8). Sandburg's condemnation of this urban monotony, a receding boundary bleeding out into the prairie, doubles as praise. Burnham too had apologized for the monotony of Chicago's gridiron layout but yet also lauded its conformity with its native environment. Similarly, Sandburg laments the repetition typical of that layout and simultaneously presents a huge city whose silhouette blends effortlessly into the habitat that surrounds it as the streets run out to the prairies. He further juxtaposes the horizontal stretch of the city, almost without vanishing point, against the cramped living arrangements of the working class whose "lumber porches and doorsteps / Snarl at each other" (9). In its contours, Chicago paradoxically stands as both vertical, crushed, built-up interior and horizontal, airy, prairie exterior, embodying the combined pessimism and optimism that characterizes Sandburg's verse as a whole.

Section 6 returns to the iconic skyscraper and the city as process rather than product. Here, the "stone shanks" of the buildings "stand up and scrape / at the sky," as structures become masons tooling away at the atmosphere above (11). Sandburg moves from generic consideration of skyscrapers to an epic list of specific Chicago buildings, including the Monadnock Block and People's Gas Building, concluding with the Crerar Library. The Crerar Library was designed by the firm of Holabird and Roche, a Chicago-based architecture firm whose name was nationally recognized for their skyscraper construction.[16] The Crerar Library opened its doors in 1921, after a decade of planning and delays, at the corner of Randolph Street and Michigan Avenue downtown. Sandburg captures the sleekness of this skyscraper in terms both mechanical and organic: "The library building named after Crerar, naked / as a stock farm silo, light as a single eagle / feather, stripped like an airplane propeller / takes a path up" (12). Between propeller and feather, the image of the silo mediates between the natural and the constructed, turning the Chicago cityscape into a prairie farmyard marked by human labor and natural abundance. In turn, the propeller and the feather push against the static quality of the silo, turning nouns into verbs as the solid structure becomes a flight path up to the sky. Through these images, this quintessentially urban building becomes naturalized and fundamentally dynamic.

So too is the city as a whole presented as a process, "made, forgotten, and made again" every day, as "The bevels and the blueprints talk it over" (12). The city is thus a constant negotiation between its plan and its materials, a dialogue that requires ongoing demolition and construction:

> Put the city up; tear the city down;
>   put it up again; let us find a city.
> Let us remember the little violet-eyed
>   man who gave all, praying, "Dig and
>   dream, dream and hammer, till your
>   city comes." (12)

The up and down of ongoing creation is necessitated by the "dream" of the city, part and parcel of the hammering and digging needed for its own realization. The motto given here is not a direct quote, but in both its philosophy

The Crerar Library, designed by Holabird and Roche. Photograph by William J. Lynch, 1920. (Courtesy of the Special Collections Research Center, University of Chicago)

and urgency captures the spirit of John Wellborn Root, Burnham's early collaborator and a founder of the Chicago School of architecture. In her adoring biography of her brother-in-law Root, Harriet Monroe, who would later publish Sandburg's works, describes Root's eyes as "of a rare color— dark violet-blue, bluer than blue" (26). Monroe's biography captures the shock and grief in the citywide mourning following Root's death at the age of forty-one after he "gave all," as Sandburg says, by contracting pneumonia while working on the World's Columbian Exposition. Sandburg's evocation of Root foregrounds the ongoing realization of the city in continuous cycles of construction. Unlike Burnham's vision of Chicago, Sandburg's urbanism is a process without end, in which "every day the people shake loose, awake and / build the city again" (*Slabs* 12). Here, Root's imagined prayer for an ideal realized in labor contributes to Sandburg's presentation of Chicago as process: an ongoing negotiation of bevel and blueprint, the dream and the hammer.

Night falls in section 9, and, as in "The Skyscraper Loves the Night," the play of light and darkness makes porous clear boundaries between the natural and the man-made. "The lookouts from the shore of Lake Michigan," lighthouses signaling to boats across the dark water, bevel their heads from lakeshore to city. They both mark a boundary of city and lake while confusing that distinction with a blur of circling light as "Mixed light shafts stack their bayonets, / pledge with crossed handles" (15). It is unclear whether this radiant militaristic display, a stacking of protective beams, comes from the signal lights of the boats, the lighthouse, or the lit skyscrapers, resulting in an unmoored, luminous field. When the lookouts turn to face Chicago's interior, their perspective renders the city natural: "The canyons swarm with red sand lights / of the sunset." The red-washed canyons, flecked with a light that mimics the sand of the lakeshore, are in fact the great gulfs between the buildings downtown. These structures are in turn imagined as a natural environment: "mountain language / Of skyscrapers in dusk." Distinctions degrade even further as Sandburg transitions from the mountainous to the miniscule by presenting an atomic view of the sunset lightshow: "The atoms drop and sift, blues cross over, / yellows plunge." Identifiable locations and buildings soften into granular impressionism where even colors "cross over" boundaries, dropping and sifting like blown sand. Those colors then actively plunge into unidentifiable planes as lake and city dazzle into a singular field of vision.

The play of light eventually gives over to the play of wind as the poem comes to a close. The wind picks up through section 7 and breezes through the poem to its conclusion, at times the threat of entropy and at others the robust breath of the city. Without the lives of its inhabitants, the "city would fall to pieces / and die / and be dust in the wind" (14). The enlivening breath of the city dwellers in the creation myth of section 1 gives way momentarily to this threat of an apocalyptic posthuman wind. However, in the tenth and final section of the poem, the wind expands beyond human breath without presenting a threat to human habitation. Rather, the "Winds of the Windy City" cross from prairie to lake, lake to prairie, in seasonal cycles that incorporate Chicago into a larger national landscape and broader flatland ecosystem. "Corn wind in the fall" flows west to east "off the black lands," as "Blue water wind in summer" flows east to west "off the blue miles / of lake" (17). Just as the autumnal wind brings the scent of ripeness into the city, the summer wind cools the human habitation within, as the speaker begs: "carry your blue to our homes." Land and lake mingle in the city that mediates between both as homes are tinted with cool air off the blue water. The winds, defined by season, location, and history, are called back to Chicago: "Winds of corn and sea blue, / Spring wind white and fighting winter gray, / Come home here—they nickname a city for you." Chicago, city of the skyscraper, is also a home of seasons, weather, and air. It is not simply an edge between prairie and water, lost wilderness and electric urbanism, but a dynamic, liminal environment in its own right. The poem ends as the "wind of the lake shore waits and wanders." Sandburg prevents closure in favor of roaming motion as the wind defies clean borders between lake, city, household, plains, past, and present.

Ultimately, both Sandburg and Burnham understand such boundaries to be soft and kinetic. However, while Burnham's *Plan* emphasizes completion and stability in a way that Sandburg's verse does not, both the architect and the poet incorporate nature into their vision of the urban environment. In conceiving of the city as both a livable and living environment, Burnham and Sandburg materialize a frontier ethos in even the most modern and mechanistic corners of Chicago. In writing nature onto Chicago and Chicago onto nature, Burnham and Sandburg also present a midwestern space with serious national ramifications. If *C* is for Chicago and Cottonwood, it must also be for the City at large. For the first generation of American city planners, landscape architects, and urbanites, the health of the nation hinged on the success of this palimpsest.

CHAPTER 2

Wallace Stevens and the American Park

In a 1950 letter to his friend Barbara Church, Wallace Stevens described his state of mind during one of his habitual strolls through Elizabeth Park in Hartford, only a few blocks from his home: "On my Sunday morning walk . . . I tried to pretend that everything in nature is artificial and every-thing artificial is natural, as, for example, that the roses in Elizabeth Park are placed there daily by some lover of mankind" (*Letters* 684).[1] This botanical thought experiment was far from pure fantasy. When Stevens reflects on the chimerical quality of nature and artifice in the public rose garden, he does so in a space that complicates any sharp division between the natural world and human aesthetics. The grounds of Elizabeth Park were originally "placed" there by Hartford's first park superintendent, Theodore Wirth, a Swiss horticulturalist and park planner who would later gain acclaim for the Minneapolis park system. The paths, lawns, arbors, plantings, and even the pond in the park were all intentionally positioned by Wirth and "daily" maintained by later superintendents and staff. Even the roses are the prod-uct of horticultural breeding. Fittingly, Elizabeth Park, and American public parks more broadly, served as felicitous ground for the poet's lifelong study of the relationships among art, reality, and society. Parks function as poetic loci throughout Stevens's oeuvre, appearing in collections as early as *Har-monium* (1923) and as late as *The Rock* (1954). In this recurrent use of public parks, Stevens presents seemingly natural locations as man-made spatial compositions. While they are green environments sensitive to the changes of the seasons, these spaces are also works of art planned by "some lover of mankind" for emphatically civic ends. The artistic principles and political goals that shaped American parks at the turn of the century arose from the new profession of landscape architecture, a field whose styles would evolve through the 1930s and 1950s, just as its social idealism would be tested by the communities who used these public greens. Stevens's works attest to

Theodore Wirth [handwritten margin note]

his long engagement with American landscape architecture and the zones crafted by its practitioners. As spatial sculptures expressive of seasonal and stylistic mutability, Stevens's parks, both those he visited and those he poetically constructs, are the ideal scene for a supreme fiction: they give pleasure, they change, and, as pastoral fantasy or botanical playground, the muddy particulars of their design originate in abstraction and imagination.

In the American parks movement at the turn of the century, that imagination was still in formation, and the green worlds crafted by early landscape architects often materialized competing aesthetic values. Elizabeth Park exemplifies the uneven designs and social uses that characterize many American parkscapes. In Hartford, Wirth collaborated with the renowned firm of Frederick Law Olmsted. Olmsted, the father of American landscape architecture, is best known for the iconic pastoral style that characterizes his major works, like Central Park, another of Stevens's favorite green rambles. Olmsted's firm eschewed the geometric horticultural displays and statuary associated with the British aristocracy in favor of rolling green lawns and curving paths where all classes were invited to mingle and refresh themselves. Olmsted's American parks sought to alleviate the overtaxed faculties of city dwellers through holistic swaths of verdant landscaping and calming water features. Elizabeth Park's rough-hewn bridges, its open lawns, and pond system perform this aesthetic vision. However, British and European landscaping models still had their charms for a public intrigued by exotic plants, the likes of which dazzled viewers at botanical gardens, many of which were often nestled within the borders of public parks. These botanical styles, ones that emphasize the native landscape and lineage of exotic floral samples, ranged from symmetrical, geometric displays to miniature re-creations of the plants' foreign habitat. If Olmsted's greensward relaxed and renewed the senses, botanical styles excited the curiosity while nodding to design precedents associated with the English and French upper classes.

Elizabeth Park, like many other American parkscapes, combines these competing styles. The rose garden features varietal displays arranged in boxy plots and regular, concentric rows labeled with each plant's name, while at its center stands a highly pastoral rustic arbor. Wirth designed the rose beds to invite the walker's intellectual engagement and admiration, while the arbor at the heart of the garden serves as a shaded, dreamy retreat designed for rest and stillness. The mix of pastoral and botanical styles in the rose garden, and American parks in general, lent itself to Stevens's fascination with aesthetic extremes: the plain and the ornate, the local and the exotic, the scope of the maximalist and the attention of the miniaturist, and, ultimately, reality and imagination. However, while Stevens celebrates elements of these botanical and pastoral architectures, even when in conflict, he criticized the work of later-generation landscape architects and park managers, whose tastes veered toward neoclassical styles. Many later park managers abandoned the holism characteristic of Olmsted's style and included triumphal arches, ornate fountains, and memorial statuary in the 1920s and 1930s, such as the late addition of large monuments in Olmsted and Vaux's masterpiece, Prospect Park. Stevens presents these later amendments to American parks as frothy, imaginative excess, particularly in *Owl's Clover* (1936). While contemporary park goers hardly notice the stylistic conflict in these parks—accustomed as we are to these spaces decades later—they initially embodied competing public appetites, class valences, and imagined natures that were far from harmonious.

If parks serve as a fit analogue for a supreme fiction, they also reveal the ways this fiction can fail. The democratic ideals of the American parks movement buckled under the pressure of the Great Depression, as seen in the Hoovervilles erected on the Great Lawn of Central Park in the early 1930s. Stevens casts the neoclassical flourishes of second-generation park managers as untenable, encumbering ornament by contrasting them with the grim realities of urban life during the Depression, as homeless women are overshadowed by equestrian statuary. But even before the economic crash, parks more often framed class divisions than alleviated them, as green lawns fractured into ever smaller spaces claimed by individual class and immigrant groups. Appropriately, even the Olmstedian lawns and rustic structures of Stevens's verse attest to failures in park sociability. As such, parks marry Stevens's artistic investments with his social concerns; that "lover of mankind," the landscape architect and park manager, may succeed in realizing his artistic vision in the landscape and yet still fall short of achieving its social ends, a danger that plagued the poet as well.

Both Stevens and Olmsted understand their art forms as a palliative to the social stresses each found in his respective historical context. In his Princeton lecture, "The Noble Rider and the Sound of Words," Stevens uses the word "real" to describe different external pressures on the mind: the natural, physical world, but also history and society. In the first sense, Stevens posits that good art has the "strength of reality or none at all" (*Collected Poetry and Prose* [*CPP*] 646). The mind's adherence to the real, material world

shanty towns

beyond us allows for a healthy imagination that is vibrant without being indulgent. However, in the latter sense of the real as sociohistorical pressures, Frank Lentricchia argues that Stevens presents these "twin forces of gravity" as "powers of determination almost irresistible" (137). The "real," in this sense, crushes the public's imaginative capabilities. Whereas Olmsted identified the working conditions and poorly planned urban habitats of his era as the major realities that harmed the American public, Stevens sees the "pressure of reality" arising from the atmosphere of dread and scarcity lingering during and after the two world wars (*CPP* 655). Olmsted thought that the very sight of his pastoral landscapes would heal these overstressed mental faculties: "The enjoyment of scenery employs the mind without fatigue and yet exercises it, tranquilizes it and yet enlivens it" ("Yosemite Valley" 13). Similarly, Stevens held that the poet "fulfills himself" by allowing "his imagination to become the light in the minds of others" dispossessed of active imagination (*CPP* 661). Both poet and landscape architect work as cognitive therapists for an overwhelmed American public.

Given the park's role as a healing space for the mind, it is not surprising that Stevens's speakers, and Stevens himself, indulge in aesthetic contemplation in park settings. And yet, one of the difficulties in tracing Elizabeth Park's influence on Stevens's later poems, and the prominence of parks in his works in general, is how successful landscape architects were in masking their own interventions, especially in the pastoral style. This naturalization of park artifice colors the critical discourse surrounding Stevens's park poems. Often, his park settings are treated as unalloyed nature and, by extension, a touchstone of reality. Nature, the physical world, and the real often collapse into a single term in these analyses, one presented as the antithesis of humanity, the mind, and imagination. For example, the dichotomy traced by J. Hillis Miller typifies this dualistic reading of Stevens's philosophy: "Nature is the physical world, visible, audible, tangible, present to all the senses, and man is consciousness, the nothing which receives nature and transforms it into something unreal" (221). Alan Perlis also argues that "[Stevens's] point of origin is external nature, the font to which we come seeking inspiration for our fictions" (117). Such readings deftly identify Stevens's continued fascination with the green world beyond the mind. The difficulty lies in the problematic term "nature," as Bonnie Costello notes: "The idea of Nature with its lure of metaphysical presence, its promised totality, is something else, a term Stevens almost never uses" (*Shifting Ground* 56). Particularly in the case of parkscapes, Stevens's evocation of nature cannot be situated as an oppositional term to the human or the imagination since these locations are already the work of an artistic mind. To rephrase Miller's language, in a park context, nature is both the physical, tangible world *and* the artwork created by the transformative power of consciousness.

It was on the paths of several different American parks that Stevens would directly engage with the artistry and ideals of American landscape architecture. A study of Stevens's personal use of parks as captured in his journals and letters reveals the poet's observant interactions with the specific architectures and communities at play in American public parks. They also serve as an introduction to the design and social life of some of the most influential American green spaces, such as Central Park and the New York Botanical Garden. This study of Stevens as a modern park goer then turns to his park poetics, as well as the major landscape texts that he draws from in the creation of his verdant worlds, particularly Elizabeth and Prospect Parks. In his use and depiction of America parkscapes, Stevens combines admiration with critique, all while foregrounding the artifice of these apparently natural spaces.

WALKING WITH WALLACE: CENTRAL PARK AND THE BOTANICAL GARDENS

If one followed a young Wallace Stevens through New York City in the oughts and teens, she could trace a map through the foundational texts of American landscape architecture, as well as uncover the seams between the competing styles of the day. His letters to his future wife, Elsie Viola Kachel, provide lush details of his park rambles in Central Park, often referred to authoritatively as "the Park," as well as his horticultural adventures at the Botanical Garden in the Bronx. The former green zone was Olmsted's inaugural work, and the latter, one of the major designs of his partner and mentor, Calvert Vaux. While Vaux's style was also influenced by the holistic ideals he shared with Olmsted, the Botanical Garden was a different sort of creature, one that inevitably pushed against Olmsted's valorization of unified landscapes to be taken in at a glance. Vaux's design also drew from major British precedents, a nod back to England the likes of which Olmsted largely tried to avoid in his American styles. Stevens's letters and journals testify to his intimate engagement with the aesthetics and civics (or lack thereof) materialized in these major American park texts in ways that sometimes align with the goals of the architects and, at others, hint at an early ambivalence that would later ripen into criticism.

The collaboration between Vaux and Olmsted was both felicitous and unlikely: the former, a British-born architect with styles influenced by English manorial estates, the Gothic revival, and botanical gardens in London; the latter, an American gentleman-farmer and journalist, whose book *Walks and Talks of an American Farmer in England* (1852) brought him to the attention of designers like Vaux, despite Olmsted's lack of formal architectural training. Nonetheless, Vaux's rustic sensibilities married well with Olmsted's pastoral tastes. Both designers also shared an urgent sense of the social need for parks, as well as the lack of proper theorization about how architecture could meet those needs. To redress these issues, Vaux and Olmsted created the profession into which they entered. The title "landscape architect" that the partners agreed upon positioned their work as an aesthetic, with artistic principles, and a profession, with disciplinary mandates directed to democratic ends. As the landscape historians Charles Beveridge and Paul Rocheleau demonstrate, the title revealed anxieties about ethos: "[Olmsted] finally accepted the term 'landscape architecture.' Awkward though it was, it helped to 'establish the idea of the distinction of my [Olmsted's] profession from that of gardening—as that of architecture from building—the distinction of an art of design'" (37). Olmsted always understood parkscapes, even his effortless pastorals, to be works of high artifice: "What artist so noble as he who, with far-reaching conception of beauty and designing power, sketches the outlines, writes the colors, and directs the shadows, of a picture so great that Nature shall be employed upon it for generations" (*Landscape* 247). Here, rather than nature providing the basis of park planning, the landscape architect deploys nature as the material of composition; art is prior to and shapes nature.

The partners understood this aesthetic to be fundamentally political in its aims. Olmsted went so far as to describe Central Park as a "democratic development of the highest significance" (qtd. in Fein 26). The democratic nature of this development arose largely as a response to the pressures of urbanism. While Olmsted was enthusiastic about American cities, he was also keenly aware that they had yet to live up to their potential. Those most harmed by their urban environs were members of the working class, and Olmsted and Vaux positioned them as the chief beneficiaries of park systems. Olmsted specifically argued that exposure to these green spaces was

directly restorative to not only the minds but also the bodies of overstimu-
lated factory workers and tenement dwellers. His hope was that individuals
healed in his parks could then indulge an innate human inclination toward
sociability, particularly across class lines. The reawakening of this "neigh-
borly instinct" was the central social concern of early landscape architec-
ture, and Olmsted anticipated that stimulating and strengthening sociability
among the classes would likewise strengthen American democracy (Olm-
sted, "Parks" 75).

It was Vaux, already well known for his work on the grounds of the
Smithsonian and the White House, who invited the untested Olmsted to
help with the "Greensward Plan" for Central Park. The new partners won
the commission, with Vaux focusing his efforts on many of the park's built
stone structures and Olmsted creating his hallmark lawns and waterscapes.
Vaux's rustic bridges melted into the curvilinear paths that quietly snaked
around Olmsted's greens and ponds. Such integration was key, as Olmsted
believed that the act of viewing this uninterrupted "clean greensward" ther-
apeutically stimulated the unconscious: "The chief end of a large park is
an effect on the human organism by an action of what it presents to view,
which action, like that of music, is of a kind that goes back of thought, and
cannot be fully given the form of words" (*Landscape* 31). This effect was
achieved through holistic design, specifically the use of uninterrupted roll-
ing green lawn: "What we most want is a simple, broad, open space of clean
greensward, with sufficient play of surface and a sufficient number of trees
about it to supply a variety of light and shade. This we want as a central
feature" ("Parks" 80).[2] Notably, the central feature of the park is the totality
of the park itself, not a single point of architectural interest. By visually
consuming this refreshing, unbroken green palette, park goers would be
rejuvenated mentally and physically, finally able to then enjoy one another's
company. Or such was the hope of the park's architects.

Stevens's journal entries and letters from 1900 through the mid-teens
demonstrate his appreciative participation with Vaux and Olmsted's archi-
tecture, while they also demonstrate his awareness of the park as artifice,
fantasy, and rocky social terrain. In an early February journal entry in 1901,
Stevens describes an enchanting evening stroll through the snow-clad park
in terms that highlight the construction and fiction of the space: "The park
was deserted yet I felt royal in my empty palace. . . . I stumbled about over
little bridges that creaked under my step, up hills, and through trees" (*Let-
ters* 50). With Vaux's bridges leading him on through Olmsted's carefully

situated trees, Stevens envisions the park as icy fairy-tale palace, building, and daydream, rather than natural retreat. But it is a palace in which nature dwells, as his walk induces a brief transcendental moment, before the city crashes into Stevens's sight again: "I stopped and suddenly felt the mysterious spirit of nature—a very mysterious spirit, one I thought never to have met with again. I breathed in the air and shook off the lethargy that has controlled me for so long a time." Such mental reinvigoration was exactly the therapeutic goal Vaux and Olmsted hoped their design would achieve. However, Stevens's frosty moment of minor sublimity ends as "the spirit slipped away and left me looking with amusement at the extremely unmysterious and not at all spiritual hotels and apartment houses that were lined up like elegant factories on the West side of the Park." Stevens's view cannot avoid the New York skyline, a much taller and denser feature than when the park was first designed. This urban frame not only delimits his experience of the park but punctures it with disenchanting architectures. The poet's attitude toward this rough transition, from organic winter palace to lines of "elegant factories," is one not of displeasure or disdain, but amusement. The word hovers as a gentle commentary on both city and park: amusingly, the hotels look like so many factories in comparison to the park palace. But this park vantage also cannot guarantee a lasting hold on that "spirit of nature," embedded as it is in the city, and so its magic is amusingly fleeting.

If Stevens enjoyed Vaux and Olmsted's aesthetic while also realizing its limits, he also indulged in park sociability while noting the ways it faltered. In letters to Elsie in 1909, Stevens spends as much time detailing his people watching as he does describing the local flora. On one afternoon, he meets a "Dutchman with a red beard exercising his little girl, and we sat down on the grass and talked" (*Letters* 155). On another, the park "seemed to be the scene of a universal picnic": "The trees were as full of voices as a bush is full of leaves—thousands of children everywhere—the children of the Irish slums, largely" (*Letters* 173). In one sense, these vignettes present civic successes: the poet-cum-insurance-man strikes up a chat with a Dutchman, the children of the working class enjoy the "universal picnic." Vaux and Olmsted regarded such moments of shared conversation and recreation as the social contact zone where real democratic spirit would be fostered. At the same time, Stevens's language hints that this picnic is far from universal. While the park teems with children, they are "largely" low-class, Irish immigrants. Rather than inviting a mingling of classes and ethnic groups, the park divides into class-encoded zones where only a little contact beyond one's social milieu is possible.[3]

The park also becomes a zone of behaviors that fall outside middle-class expectations of proper comportment, which leads to a constant policing of the space. In a 1906 journal entry, Stevens's attempt to flee into the healing green world of the park is thwarted by such behavior: "To-night—I fled to the Park. . . . [M]y feet crunched on the pebbles and there were young men and women in erotic grips. Well I tried to think whether or not life was worth living—I cannot think" (*Letters* 119). Early park regulations testify to anxieties about how Vaux's bridges and Olmsted's secluded pockets of trees would encourage such illicit behavior after dark, as well as creating shelter for tramps and vagabonds. Here, Stevens's encounter with the "erotic grips" of others leads him into dark meditations and, eventually, the end of thought itself. "I cannot think" captures the mind's inability to rise above the pressures of reality in the park precisely because the space enables the play of unseemly social acts. As the architecture failed to infuse a civil, polite character into its users, police were needed to enforce the rules of proper park behavior, from the more serious infractions of sexual misconduct to the minor, though much fretted-over trespasses across the lawn. Stevens once found himself on the receiving end of such enforcement, as an excited chase accidently led him across protected grass: "Wild ducks! We followed them. A policeman shouted and we came meekly back to the walk. The police are as thick as trees and as reasonable. But you must obey them" (*Letters* 144).[4] Stevens here naturalizes the police as park elements. They are as expected, numerous, and unreasonable as Olmsted's trees, while they must also be obeyed, even when their demands interrupt one's engagement with the wildlife of the parkscape. The free movement of the wild birds starkly contrasts with the restricted movement of the poet who follows them, as the police must domesticate aberrant park users.

If Central Park at times failed the peripatetic poet, there was always the Botanical Garden. In 1891, Vaux and his new partner Samuel Parsons Jr. were invited to develop a botanical garden in the Bronx that would incorporate one of the last patches of native, old-growth forest in New York City. Unlike Olmsted's greensward, the preserved forest functions as a protected botanical sample rather than a pastoral retreat. Although Vaux and Parsons collaborated with the Olmsted firm in designing the circulating paths through the park, the very telos of the space jarred against Olmsted's aesthetic. He was concerned to see exotic displays growing in frequency during his trips abroad to England, particularly in Hyde Park and Kew Gardens, the latter of which Vaux took as the inspiration for his designs in the Bronx.[5] Olmsted's exclusion of flowerbeds and other "distracting" elements also had classed and nationalistic overtones. In a 1915 lecture for an American horticultural society, Arthur W. Mill, the assistant director of the Royal Botanic Gardens at Kew, linked the rise of botanical gardens, both ancient and modern, to economics, medicine, and empire: "Gold, spices and drugs. It is to the two latter of these universal needs of man that we may trace the origin and foundation of botanic gardens" (185).[6] While horticultural gardens long predate the British Empire, the particular character of the Victorian-era botanical garden is entwined with colonialism. If spices, tea, and opium were to be had from China and the Indies, so too were larkspur and coleus. For Olmsted, the botanical garden was thus heavily encoded as British in its curatorial character, one that tended toward oriental and tropical curiosities. And if Olmsted's American lawns relaxed the psyche, botanical gardens sparked the intellect. As a combination of research institution and organic bijouterie, botanical gardens like Vaux's were designed to stimulate the rational, scientific mind while also enticing imaginative re-creations of the foreign landscapes from whence the samples were plucked. Growing these imports often required the construction of large rockscapes, shade houses, or hothouses, especially in colder American climates. The design of the grand, lacey greenhouse, now called the Haupt Conservatory, in the Bronx was inspired by both the Palm House at Kew and the Crystal Palace of Hyde Park. Significant built structures punctuate botanical spaces, along with clearly segmented zones meant to display the taxonomic and cultural significance of different plants, such as alpine rock gardens for succulents or medicinal herb displays for physic gardens.

Stevens uses the language of study, discovery, and exoticism when writing of his visits to Vaux's creations. Unlike his descriptions of Central Park that emphasize larger landscapes, rambles, and the social life of the space, Stevens's portrayal of the botanical garden involves both catalogues of flowers and focused, sustained investigations of single plants: "Then I went over to the Botanical Garden where I spent several hours in studying the most charming things. I was able to impress on myself that larkspur comes from China. Was there ever anything more Chinese when you stop to think of it? And coleus comes from Java. Good Heavens, how that helps one to understand coleus—or Java" (*Letters* 195). And while a 1915 trip to the greenhouse was "dismal" ("The rain leaked through the glass roof and the few people there walked around under the palms and banana trees with their umbrellas up"), he lists the discovery of "some in't'resting things": "papyrus, carious crotons, water-lilies, and one or two orchids. Afterwards, I came down town [*sic*] to the library and read more or less about orchids" (*Letters* 197). The first passage typifies the attitude Vaux anticipated his visitors would have. Stevens is both curious and charmed. He links each plant with its Eastern clime, even doubling his imaginative efforts as the coleus opens up Java, just as Java makes sense of the coleus. His catalogue of "in't'resting things" climaxes in a trip to the library. Such study (more or less) was the kind of mental work Vaux designed his botanical garden to induce, the kind of solitary effort, with one's mind directed away from his local landscape, that Olmsted reacted against in his pastoral aesthetics.

While the botanical and pastoral natures built by Vaux and Olmsted often seem antithetical, they both intrigued Stevens and appear in different guises throughout his poetic career. One of his earliest published pieces, "Tea" (1915), exhibits Stevens's thoughtful participation with botanical styles.[7] The poem, written during the height of Stevens's Central Park rambles and Botanical Garden studies, has the greatest affinity with Vaux's Bronx creation. While it is difficult to specify a clear park referent in this lean piece, the gaze and imaginative leaps of the speaker align the poem with a horticultural tradition associated with the Botanical Garden. The botanical focus of the poem centers on a dead leaf of elephant's ear in a park, and around the time Stevens composed the piece, the Botanical Garden boasted at least seven different varietals of elephant's ear.[8] However, at face value, the statement of this eight-line piece is simple: in late autumn, your lamp-light fell on pillows. Stevens temporally grounds this reminiscence with a reference to autumn in the park: "When the elephant's-ear in the park / Shrivelled in frost, / And the leaves on the paths / Ran like rats" (*CPP* 77). Stevens divides the poem in two, with the description of the chilly park giving way to one of "your" bedroom. He then divides the bedroom scene in half, with the last two lines associatively moving from the pillows to umbrellas in Java: "Your lamp-light fell / On shining pillows, / Of sea-shades and sky-shades / Like umbrellas in Java." Thus the piece progresses from outdoors to indoors, cool to warm, here to an imagined there, as the sibilance of the penultimate line echoes the whisper of the seaside tide. So too do the umbrellas of this tropical fantasy stretch open with the bright assonance in "umbrellas in Java," as the parasols shade the mind from the very sky they evoke.

Given these contrasts, Robert Buttel argues that the poem sets "the world of civilized order" against "outdoor coldness" (29). While Stevens does draw heavily on this series of opposing pairs, the poem entangles the reader in odd chains of likeness. The leaves are like rats; the pillows are like the sea and sky; the sea and sky are like Javanese umbrellas. The foliage is also metaphorically named: elephant's ear is a kind of caladium that grows massive, elephant-ear-shaped leaves. The play of animal-plants in the first lines also hints at the shared traditions of botanical gardens and zoos, the latter also an architecture designed to present living samples of exotic creatures to the public. In large American parkscapes, like those in New York, botanical and zoological spaces are often found side by side. Stevens's letter to Elsie about the Botanical Garden actually begins with a slip that reveals his tight association of the space with the zoo: "I went up to the Botanical— no: the Zoological Garden this morning to see a collection of birds . . . just brought up from Brazil" (*Letters* 195). In "Tea," just as the plants are like animals, so too is the park like a zoo. Similarly, the domestic interior becomes like Java, which then in turn becomes another kind of interior as we are tucked under the shelter of umbrellas. The piece moves forward due to these associations, and they make porous many of the apparent divisions they simultaneously describe. Insides and outsides, chilly climes and Javanese beaches, slip effortlessly from one to the other. The evocation of Java suggests a here-and-exotic-there, but then the "there" of the first half of the poem is already here-and-there, bedroom-and-park. Distinctions among places slide away, as the park serves largely to mark the season in relation to the bedroom, which then transports us to Java, though a quick impressionistic play of light and color.

At first glance, it may seem that the park and bedroom are oppositional spaces, where the bedroom represents an aestheticized interior and the park functions as a zone of the natural and the seasonal. Stevens often relies on heavily decorated interiors, and Elisabeth Oliver has explored the relationship of these spaces to the wider social discourse on aestheticism, home décor, and "decorative" poetry. She argues that "aestheticism's decorative theories and practices were a source of both inspiration and anxiety for Stevens" (529). Though the description is minimal, "Tea" presents a decorated interior composed according to Wilde's house-beautiful ideals as described by Oliver. There is a lamp close enough to the bed or sofa to cast light on the blue-hued pillows. They shine, indicating a reflective fabric such as satin or silk. Instead of presenting exotic artwork on the walls, such as the masks, Chinese prints, and traveler's bric-a-brac that Oliver notes were then highly in vogue, the Javanese umbrellas hang in the associating mind, suspended on a hook of simile by the aesthetic decorator-poet. Eleanor Cook adds that, besides its association with the tea trade, Java also "once had a sophisticated court culture; its subtleties and appreciation of artists made it the kind of culture that Stevens especially liked" (86). Java as locale of an artisan culture also then associates it further with the artistically arranged scenes in the poem. The glory of the umbrellas and pillows against the cold, shriveled exterior appears to represent a triumph of artifice and imagination over a fading nature or a cooling reality.

The park setting, however, undercuts any rift between the natural and the crafted. Just as viewing the coleus at the Botanical Garden sent Stevens's mind to Java, a material gateway to an exotic (and colonized) elsewhere, the elephant's ear also functions as an aesthetically arranged sampling of foreign culture integrated into the park architecture. Elephant's ear originates in tropical climate zones.[9] Their appearance in the park therefore signals the intervention of a landscaper, just as the pillows signal the activity of an interior decorator; neither the plants nor the pillows would be where they are unless an artistic agent had arranged them just so. Furthermore, the park as planned space also resists any designation as unmediated reality. It is a space complete with paths ("And the leaves on the paths" [*CPP* 77]), landscaped to include exotic groundcover, and so is just as much artifice as is the bedroom. As a sample of exotic flora in a local park environment, Stevens also links the leaves to the pillows. The blue fabric functions as a well-situated sample of the exotic sky-umbrella, much like the tropical samples found in botanical gardens. Although at first the piece appears to be a progression of similes that leaves the park behind, it is actually a closed circuit that ends where it began. The poem becomes like the cup of tea that occasions it: a mix of artfully selected dry leaves steeped in the hot waters of Java, resulting in a complex brew of both.[10] Elephant's ear and the park setting, when considered as artifice, cast the poem not as a contrast between cold, dying nature and warm, vibrant aestheticism, but as a case study in mixing types of artifice, the one pliable to seasonal change, the other an immutable tropic. Significantly, Stevens brews these two forms of artifice together, thereby preventing us making easy assumptions about the artificial and the natural.

ELIZABETH PARK

When the Stevenses moved to Hartford in 1916, they put down roots in Olmsted's hometown and made sure they would be within walking distance of Elizabeth Park when they settled on a house in 1917. Elizabeth Park was the landscape text with which Stevens had most intimate contact during his later years. As Peter Brazeau notes, Stevens "detoured through some portion of [Elizabeth Park's] one hundred acres most mornings on his two mile walk to work and spent hours there on weekends, composing his poetry" (231).[11] Helen Vendler argues that the park even functioned as a kind of stand-in for the poet's home: "Stevens was a man without a home; he made a home instead from Elizabeth Park and the Connecticut River, those local objects" (6). Elizabeth Park began as the private estate of Charles and Elizabeth Pond, who bequeathed their property to the city upon their deaths with directions that it be a gift to the public. When Theodore Wirth was hired as park superintendent for Hartford, he transformed the grounds, which already boasted some horticultural displays, into an admixture of traditional Victorian botanical plots and pastoral country-scape (Cornelio 19). In the latter style, Wirth was influenced by the aesthetic of the Olmsted firm and collaborated with them throughout his tenure in Hartford on the entirety of the city's park system.[12] However, Wirth's stylistic alloy of pastoral and botanical styles did not sit well with his collaborators. In his report to the annual meeting of park superintendents in 1901, John Charles Olmsted, in his capacity as a consultant, described Elizabeth Park as a "gentleman's suburban residence playground" (37). Coming from an Olmsted, this was far from a compliment. The firm disapproved of Wirth's "eclectic assemblage of styles" and demoted his efforts to mere "gardening" (37).

If Wirth's architecture offended Olmsted's tastes, it nonetheless delighted the public and became famous for the acre-and-a-half rose garden that opened to the public in 1904. While the park began with roughly 190 rose varieties, its designation as the first test garden for the American Rose Society in 1912 helped the collection expand to more than a thousand specimens by the 1950s ("Rose Garden"). Wirth's symmetrical design for the rose garden included a rustic, cedar-wood gazebo at the center of eight paths that radiate out from its base, each of which boasts arched trellises covered with climbing roses. More than a hundred rectangular plots for different rose samples were then arranged between the paths. Wirth also included

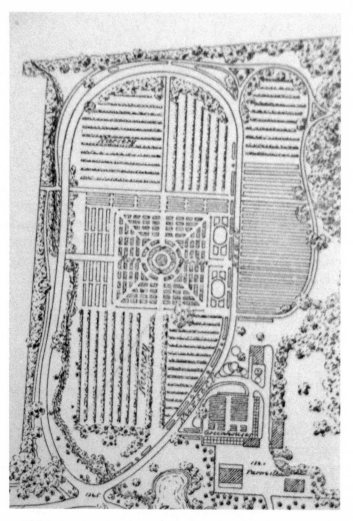

A detail from the schematics of the *Elizabeth Park General Plan* (1900), Theodore Wirth's plan for Elizabeth Park that showcases his combination of styles. The square figure with paths radiating out from a circular center is the rose garden with the arbor in the middle. The rose garden and nurseries are surrounded by elliptical paths and arboreal plantings typical of Olmsted's style. (Courtesy of the Hartford History Center)

Elizabeth Park's rustic arbor with rose trellis in the foreground. From the *40th Annual Report of the Board of Park Commissioners of the City of Hartford for the Year Ending 1900*. (Courtesy of the Hartford History Center)

two large greenhouses, designed by the same architects responsible for the conservatory in the Bronx Botanical Garden, a shade garden, and the Lily and Laurel Ponds, man-made water structures ringed with trees, paths, and benches. Below the rose garden, an Olmstedian lawn stretched out toward the ponds, and gently curving paths invited park goers to ramble under miles of shade.[13] The final product was a layering of different landscape aesthetics, one totalizing and integrated, the other focused on differentiated zones for botanical collecting.

Whereas the Olmsted firm balked at the use of these contrasting styles, Stevens enjoyed them both, just as he did in his earlier walks in New York City. The Stevenses' interest in the park was partially an outgrowth of their own efforts as gardeners, as their daughter Holly Stevens notes: "[The Stevenses] had lived within walking distance of the park since the early twenties and enjoyed the rose garden there particularly, as both were very interested in horticulture" (255). As a frequent and contemplative park user, Stevens thoughtfully meditates on his experiences in Elizabeth Park when writing letters. He often comments on what was in bloom in the park, as in his 1948 letter to Wilson Taylor: "And finally, on the subject of sweet peas:

do you realize that they are just beginning to bloom here? I looked at a long row of them in Elizabeth Park last Sunday morning" (*Letters* 604). As in Central Park, Stevens also delighted in people watching: "This little park is almost all there is in Hartford and I like it especially on Sundays when people go there. The very fat woman who exercises her dog had a new dress on yesterday. The tennis courts were full" (*Letters* 761). Most importantly, Elizabeth Park served as a site for the poet's mental acts of composition. In his later years, he identified the restful benches of the park as the very well-spring of his poetic inspiration: "The feelings, the great source of poetry, become largely the feeling of + desire to sit under the trees on a bench in the park" (*Letters* 928).

Beyond providing a space for composition, the park also features in several of Stevens's poems, though his spatial referent is often veiled. For example, "The Plain Sense of Things" makes reference to both "The green-house" which "never so badly needed paint" and "The great pond and its waste of the lilies," both of which are found in Elizabeth Park (*CPP* 428). Similarly, "Nuns Painting Water-Lilies" arose from Stevens's observation of a group of nuns who had taken up open-air painting by the pond: "Until quite lately a group of nuns came there each morning to paint water colors especially of the water lilies. Whenever I saw them I thought of the chaste-ness of the thing like the chasteness of the girl in Oscar Wilde who spent her time looking at photographs of the Alps" (*Letters* 610). Yet "Nuns Paint-ing Water-Lilies" bears no obvious marks of its park setting, emphasizing as it does the relationship between the vegetation and the act of painting within the narrow scope of the painting itself. And Stevens's letter likens the lily pond not to nature, but to photographs of alpine landscapes, another curated collection of exotic natural scapes. While that information is available only to a reader of Stevens's letters, it serves as a caution against assum-ing that any of his natural landscapes is not potentially also an artificial one.

In contrast, "Vacancy in the Park" (1954) explicitly takes Elizabeth Park as the setting for its extended meditation on the social aspect of park aesthetics. Unlike "Tea," which concentrates on vegetation, here Stevens stresses the presence, absence, and errancy of park goers. His park setting dramatizes both the desire for sociability and the opacity of those chance encounters in public places. Within the poem, the architectural features of Elizabeth Park impel and impede human connections in this midseason world. The poem begins: "March . . . Someone has walked across the snow, / Someone looking for he knows not what" (*CPP* 434, ellipses in original).

The play of presence and absence informs these first lines, as the tracks left in the spring snow testify to a human presence and to the vacancy that person leaves behind. Stevens casts "Someone" primarily as a landscape feature and then must imaginatively work backward to a fictional person, even as that fiction keeps breaking down. The ellipses following "March" signal the beginning of that imaginative act while also mimicking the footprints that inspire it. They suggest both words not said and a time-elapse made present by the little trail of periods across the field of the page. The graphic representation of the speaker's quiet ruminations parallels the errant footsteps of the wandering, absent Someone, as thought, trail, landscape, and page overlap.

Stevens highlights the deviance of Someone's walk by foregrounding the park setting. To walk "across" the snow, rather than through it or in it, suggests a wide lawn to be traversed. When considered in the park, this implies footsteps that have strayed from planned paths. Leaving the path is to absent one's self from the social intent of the landscape architecture, where Someone might have run across the speaker. It is also to act against the guiding influence of the architecture and so enacts a small moment of spatial rebelliousness. All of these elements combine to create a minor mood of discomfort. Like the absent park goer, Someone who looks for something but "knows not what," the midseason, marked lawn, and mimetic punctuation all generate an air of frustrated longing. And yet, the speaker remains captivated by the space's invitation to sociability even when it is frustrated. While the title "Someone" emphasizes the anonymity of this park encounter, the speaker immediately fantasizes an intimacy with the mind of Someone in the second line. The capitalization of "Someone" underscores that anonymity, as the Platonic form of the unknown other, while inviting familiarity, capitalized like the name of an acquaintance. However, just as the footprints enact a here-but-not-here dynamic, so too is this sympathy between speaker and Someone both substantive and contentless: the speaker *knows* that Someone does *not* know what he seeks, as the poet wraps the two in a shared unknowing.

Specifically, the speaker's knowledge of nonknowledge leads into an extended series of similes, and, as with "Tea," the poem manifests a forward momentum largely through this list of associations. The crafting of likenesses here turns Someone into aesthetic impetus and artistic media at once; his materiality remains a trace landscape element, an inspiring, if confounding, line across a lawn. These similes dramatize opacity-in-revelation as each subsequent stanza adds another layer of likeness that often deepens ambiguity rather than providing clarity:

> It is like a boat that has pulled away
> From a shore at night and disappeared.
>
> It is like a guitar left on a table
> By a woman, who has forgotten it.
>
> It is like the feeling of a man
> Come back to see a certain house. (*CPP* 434)

The stanzas share some structural likenesses of their own. They all play with subject/object relations: the implied navigator and the boat, the woman and the guitar, the man and the house. The subjective human experience grows in prominence as the poem develops. The boat masks the rower within it, while the curved ergonomics of the guitar hints at the body of the woman who has forgotten it. The fourth stanza progresses more fully toward the subjective pole, as "It" is likened to "the feeling of a man." The interior emotions of the man serve as the tenor of the simile, while the object, "a certain house," functions as a causal explication of the man's feelings. Unlike either the boat or the guitar, here it is the house that lurks as a nonpresence, a location that the man "comes back to see" rather than to enter, a source of feeling more than an actual location.

The frustrated hope of social connection within the park is enacted in the ambiguous and repetitive use of "it": "It is like a boat," "It is like a guitar," "It is like the feeling" (511). Is "It" the thing Someone is looking for, or is "It" the trail Someone leaves behind in the snow? "It" becomes laden with suggestive and withheld meaning through the play of places and similes. George Lensing argues: "All the couplets contain images of enclosure: park, boat, table (within a house), house, and arbor. Absence (or presence) is therefore defined in terms of specified human habitation" (153). However, while these couplets do evoke habitation, they also constantly frustrate any sense of dwelling. Just as in "Tea," where similes keep insides and outsides linked in chains of likeness, "Vacancy in the Park" toys with the boundaries that constitute in and out. Stevens generates restlessness by promising and then foreclosing abodes. The boat, possessed of its own interior, has disappeared from view, shifting the image from one of a human craft to one of wide, dark waters. And while the table where the guitar rests suggests an interior, the poem withholds any description of that place. Is it her home?

Is it a home at all? The lack of spatial specificity mirrors the woman's act of forgetting, as even she cannot call the place to mind. And the last "it" links not to the house primarily, but to the feeling, one that remains contentless as the speaker fails in his attempt to inhabit Someone's imagination, just as Someone approaches, but does not enter, the building.

The speaker's inability to locate real dwelling spaces and settled inhabitants underlines the character of the park at large. Beyond his analysis of these metaphorical spaces, Lensing's argument that the park, and specifically the rustic arbor that appears in the last lines of the poem, constitute human habitats works only if those habitats are understood as essentially temporary. Although they are zones crafted by and for people, the park and its arbor are not permanent dwellings. They are like abodes, but only in the tentative relation of the simile. The arbor is only truly inhabited by the winds that run through it: "The four winds blow through the rustic arbor, / Under its mattresses of vines" (*CPP* 435). Brazeau has identified this structure as the gazebo in Elizabeth Park (232). This "elevated rustic summer house" is located in the middle of Elizabeth Park's rose garden and is constructed with a series of pillars and lattices overgrown with vines that offer "views of the entire Rose Garden from all directions" (Cornelio 36). Like its referent, the arbor in the poem is also dense, composed of "mattresses of vines," which have presumably not yet broken leaf, given the snowy weather. Mattress vine is a common name for *Muehlenbeckia complexa,* also known as wire vine or maidenhair, an ornamental species often used in topiaries and so named for its tendency to form thick mats of climbing vines. As with the elephant's ear in "Tea," Stevens here nods to the intervening hand of the landscaper by hinting at the planned use of this ornamental species. And yet, however thick the mattress vines, the arbor remains a highly permeable structure, open on each side, with the "four winds" blowing through it. In the poem, this openness allows the arbor to function as a structure of totality and holism; winds from each of the cardinal directions meet under the same roof. If the poem cannot figure human connection, it does present an image of elemental meeting and balance in exactly the spot left vacant by those human presences.

Stevens does not ground this sense of elemental totality in an ante- or antihuman natural environment. Rather, he emblematizes it with a centrally placed structural element in a landscape text, one that functions as a shelter for both the winds and, ideally, the park goer. In the final stanza, the winds testify to the architect's successful aesthetic unification of organic elements while dramatically marking the failure of his social ideals. Whereas the footprints in the snow suggest the absent Someone, the winds in the arbor make present the vacancy that mar this meeting place. The park remains a space that both promises and withholds contact between people, a zone hospitable and inhospitable at once. Yet, while it is a locus of social breakdown, the force of that breakdown is blunted by the aesthetic efforts of the speaker. After all, his imaginative understanding of Someone has been facilitated by the architectures of the park, from snowy lawn to drafty arbor. The landscape architecture evokes an empathetic sociability that spins into poetic ruminations, thereby fulfilling its role in refreshing the contemplative mind even as it fails to create community.

Stevens did not limit his park poetics to his smaller pieces, as two of his major long works, *Notes Toward a Supreme Fiction* (1942) and *Owl's Clover* (1936), turn to parks as the ground for extended meditations on the relationships among aesthetics, the public, and green media. The shaping influence of Elizabeth Park in "It Must Change" colors respective landscapes throughout *Notes,* calling attention to the relationship between the real and the imagined. Foregrounding the park setting of *Notes* requires a shift in traditional approaches to the poem achieved by emphasizing Stevens's reliance on a pre-aestheticized green world. For example, while Costello compellingly argues that "'Notes Toward a Supreme Fiction' is not a pastoral or aesthetic retreat from the dimension in which we live," "the dimension in which we live" is already presented as "a pastoral or aesthetic retreat" within the poem in its reliance on Elizabeth Park (67).

Part of the difficulty in discussing particular landscapes in *Notes* is the poem's tendency to shift locations. Several segments of the piece resist clear emplacement as a result. In section 10 of "It Must Change," nearly halfway through the poem, we suddenly find ourselves in a park:

> A bench was his catalepsy, Theatre
> Of Trope. He sat in the park. The water of
> The lake was full of artificial things,
>
> Like a page of music, like an upper air,
> Like a momentary color, in which swans
> Were seraphs, were saints, were changing essences. (*CPP* 343)

The plain statement "He sat in the park" follows an ambiguous description of the bench and, by extension, the parkscape. The "he" is presumably "the poet" from the preceding section. To say that "A bench was his catalepsy" has several possible meanings. In medicine, catalepsy refers to a state of suspended consciousness, due to either a violent seizure or an immobilizing trance. In philosophical parlance, it means the act of comprehension. The bench serves as the place where the poet both enters into a deep, trance-like meditation and a spot where he stops to think, a catalepsy of catalepsy.[14] What he comprehends is the scene before him, the lake full of swans. However, the relationship between park bench and park poet rises up beyond simile and into metaphor: the bench *is* the catalepsy, as Stevens conflates the park location where thought occurs and the experience of thought itself.

The poet's thought is aesthetic, providing the "freshness of transformation" through, yet again, a series of similes, as he transforms the park into a "Theatre of Trope" (*CPP* 343, 344). The lake that he observes is "full of artificial things," a surprising phrase, given that one usually equates pond ecosystems with the natural, not the artificial. However, just as Stevens imagined the artifice of roses placed in the park by a lover of mankind, the lake is also placed there by the architect who scaped the space. In Elizabeth Park, Wirth drained much of the land and then installed Laurel Pond, a "manmade pond . . . [r]inged with spruce, hemlock, and pine trees," that was frequented by swans and Canada geese (Cornelio 73). Therefore, it is perfectly true to say that the pond is "full of artificial things," as everything here, down to the placement of the water, is artifice. Stevens then likens the lake, dotted with waterfowl, to a page of music covered with notes, and those birds in turn become the very stuff of transformation: "swans / Were seraphs, were saints, were changing essences" (*CPP* 343). Similes give way to metaphor, as the swans glide from angels, to saints, to "changing essences," embodying the artistic act of change in transformation that this section lauds. The emphasis on change reveals the mutable quality of the elements in the park. Just as the dead leaves in "Tea" testify to the seasonal sensitivities of landscaping elements, so too is this pond-side vision grounded in time and mutability. Stevens likens the swan-flecked lake to both "a momentary color" and the temporal unfolding of music: "The west wind was the music, the motion, the force" (343). Part of the beauty of this park scene is its mercurial character, one that lends itself to the imaginative acts of the viewer. Elizabeth Park provides the locus of aesthetic change as the artificial land gives itself over to subsequent acts of scaping by the poet, providing him with a space for contemplation and the matter to inform that meditation, as Wirth had hoped the space would do.

Section 10 of "It Must Change" echoes a previous passage in "It Must Be Abstract." In section 7, Stevens locates another contemplative person at the border of a lake, and just as in the "Theatre of Trope," understanding is here linked to the relationship one has with one's environment:

> The truth depends on a walk around a lake,
>
> A composing as the body tires, a stop
> To see hepatica, a stop to watch
> A definition growing certain and
>
> A wait within that certainty, a rest
> In the swags of the pine-trees bordering the lake. (*CPP* 333–34)

It is this walk around the lake that replaces "the giant, / A thinker of the first idea." The primacy of ideas here shifts off of his mythic shoulders and onto the landscape where one walks (333). Arguably, this scene is also set in a park, one similar to Elizabeth Park with its pond ringed round by evergreens. Just as the poet rests on his cataleptic bench to observe the lake, here he walks around that same lake, not simply discovering truths, but "composing as the body tires." The act of composition suggests Stevens's own habit of composing poetry during his park walks. As with the later section, the park here also provides a place of rest that facilitates cognitive acts: "a stop to watch / A definition growing certain." Just as the bench is catalepsy, the poet's mind becomes a kind of park. Definition grows, much like the hepatica the speaker observes a line earlier. Stevens here weds the defining, contemplating mind of the poet to the parkscape he observes, equating definition growing in the human mind with the vegetative ground-cover around the lake. The speaker here composes in a place itself already composed to facilitate his creative acts. The opportunity to rest and reflect under these swags of pine is precisely what Wirth's design was meant to create.

Section 7 does not pronounce itself as having a park setting in the direct manner of section 10 and is only identifiable as a park in retrospect. This later specificity of location follows a general movement throughout *Notes*, where Stevens begins by stripping concepts bare and then slowly allows them to accrue layers of reality-rooted artifice. For example, *Notes* begins with the raw, unthinkable sun and being itself in "It Must Change," and then progresses toward the new-come bee-ings arriving in seasonal waves that manifest being in flux. Likewise, the earlier lakescape is unveiled later as a parkscape, allowing artifice to develop around and through the green materials the poet turns to for inspiration. As a result, it becomes increasingly difficult to point to any scape as a natural one as the poem progresses, as it may in retrospect be understood as artifice. For example, Adam and Eve's habitation of "a very varnished green" suggests a kind of nature in which they find themselves reflected, as in a varnished surface (331). However, it may also, or simultaneously, mean a "green," as in a planned lawn, that is "varnished," or artificial, thus making of our first world a kind of divine park and the Creator the first landscape architect. This does not mean that every landscape is necessarily an artificial one, only that Stevens makes such distinctions difficult, if not at times impossible. In doing so, he forces his readers to suspend to any assumptions about the aesthetic character of the environments he presents, a fitting difficulty in this long meditation on the relationships among aesthetics, mutability, imagination, and reality.

OWL'S CLOVER AND PROSPECT PARK

In his later long poem, *Owl's Clover,* Stevens emphatically brings the park's architecture and social character to the fore. *Owl's Clover* in many ways exemplifies Stevens's balancing act among the social, the aesthetic, and the green, with a special emphasis on the first term.[15] A typical afternoon in the park in 1936, when *Owl's Clover* first appeared, had changed significantly from when Stevens first penned his reflections on Central Park in the winter of 1909. Calling upon a park setting in the 1930s evokes an anxiously classed environment undergoing extensive alterations. Changes in park use and regulation during the Depression and World War II typify the failure of Olmsted's democratic ideals. Park funding was heavily cut during this period, resulting in a drastic decrease in the upkeep of public park spaces. As the park historian Galen Cranz demonstrates, even as parks deteriorated, they were still imagined as democratic leisure sites needed more than ever in difficult times: "During the Depression, despite talk that parks were necessary to sustain morale, park expenditures and income evaporated" (176). Parks were placed in an even more acute crisis following the outbreak of World War II, as managers had to demonstrate the social utility of their spaces in order to get even a small portion of ever-dwindling funds: "Under war-time conditions, if park and recreation commissioners did not justify park activities as absolutely essential to the welfare of citizens, their budgets would be cut" (110). And so American public greenswards became sites for Red

Cross activities and military drills. Alan Filreis situates the Hartford Public Park System, specifically Elizabeth Park, within this historical context: "Hartford's public spaces were improved by various underemployed arms of the WPA, beginning in June 1935. These were Italian-Americans from Hartford's East Side" (*Modernism* 236). As Filreis notes, these working-class immigrants who maintained the parks were the same citizens who relied upon it as a free leisure space. Working-class usage of public parks boomed during the Depression as people experiencing unemployment often loitered in parks. Homeless populations also increased in parks, as in the case of Central Park, where shantytowns were erected in the 1930s (Cranz 111). Parks were thus doubly class-encoded, as spaces both maintained and utilized by the urban poor. Rather than fostering democratic zones for class mingling, park managers and social uplift groups tried to use these zones as spaces to distract or simply contain dissatisfied working-class citizens.

Stevens turned to the decaying, contested greens of the American park during the Great Depression when penning his most politically invested piece, *Owl's Clover*. This long poem served as a response to the criticism of the right-wing critic and writer Stanley Burnshaw, who held that Stevens's baroque poetry failed to address a readership crushed by wartime realities and political turmoil. While Filreis's helpful history of American park usage provides an excellent general background to the politics of these spaces, he draws largely from an Elizabeth Park context. However, the location described in *Owl's Clover* does not match the architectural features of Elizabeth Park. Rather, as the poet tells us at the beginning of the piece, it is "Another evening in another park" (*CPP* 567). The opening lines of *Owl's Clover* describe a statue of horses, ringed round with trees. None of these features can be found in Elizabeth Park, especially the prominent statuary. It is possible that Stevens here acts as his own landscape architect in creating a fictive representation of a common American park. However, there are several features mentioned in the poem that suggest Stevens may here be drawing from Prospect Park as his specific inspiration, another major Olmsted and Vaux collaboration in New York City.

Park historians often refer to Prospect Park as the "masterpiece" of Olmsted and Vaux's collaborative efforts (DeMause 26).[16] The pair was hired in 1866 to design the 580-acre parkscape that opened to the public in the following year. The site aesthetically tended toward the pastoral, with the huge Long Meadow area, an aquatic system replete with waterfalls, and several miles of curving trail through gently sloping lawns. However,

A neoclassical decorative urn
at the Park Circle entrance of
Prospect Park, next to Frederick
MacMonnies's sculpture *The
Horse Tamers*. (Photo by author)

Vaux's rustic arbors and sandstone bridges would later be supplanted by the
neoclassical additions of the architectural firm of McKim, Mead & White.
Stanford White's firm replaced the pastoral wooden fences Olmsted and
Vaux had used at the park entrances with stone walls, classical urns, tower-
ing pillars, and prominent statuary. Stevens nods to these specific elements
in his description of "some gigantic, solitary urn" (*CPP* 572) reduced to a
doomsday park trash can, as well as the shining columns in section 5 of
"Mr. Burnshaw and the Statue." The horse statues and ring of trees in the
poem's opening aptly describe the Park Circle entrance that features Fred-
erick MacMonnies's paired statues *The Horse Tamers*. In the background of
the poem, one also hears "The clank of the carousel" (583). Prospect Park's
carousel was installed in 1874 and was removed only as late as 1952. These
markers, along with Stevens's specific mention of waterfalls, yew trees, and
elms, and the sculptor's inclusion of himself in a war memorial at the other
end of the park, make this landscape text the most likely candidate for Ste-
vens's spatial referent, as there were no other parks in New York or Hartford
that combined all of these unique features during the time Stevens com-
posed the poem.[17] As one of the most didactic of Stevens's pieces, the poem
presents conflicting perspectives on the aesthetic and the social within, or

sometimes against, the park context. In particular, the civic and imaginative failures of the horse statuary entwine with the larger failure of the park's purportedly democratizing topography. At the same time, Stevens presents the mutable, green matter of the parkscape as potentially fertile ground for aesthetic success within a warlike world.

White's firm was hired shortly after Brooklyn was incorporated into New York City in 1898, and their emendations over the next thirty years drew from the City Beautiful movement and Beaux-Arts style, particularly in the firm's Greco-Roman flourishes. White's designs relied on statuary to create a sense of grandeur and patriotism, the failures of which Stevens explicitly investigates within the poem.[18] White's firm hired the Brooklyn sculptor Frederick MacMonnies to contribute large pieces throughout Prospect Park, including the sculptures for the Soldiers and Sailors Memorial Arch in Grand Army Plaza and *The Horse Tamers,* an allegorical representation of the mind triumphing over sheer force. Such sculptural additions were emphatically against the style of the original park design. Olmsted argued that large statuary marred the unity of the greensward and slavishly mimicked European traditions in a distinctive American landscape. Just as White modeled his Prospect Park designs on Parisian precedents, MacMonnies also looked to the kind of European traditions that Olmsted so heavily criticized. In his selection of horse tamers as a subject, MacMonnies participated in an equestrian statuary genre with roots reaching as far back as the reign of Constantine.[19] Similar pieces can be found on the Champs-Élysées and Anichkov Bridge in St. Petersburg.

Stevens criticizes the MacMonnies sculptures for their derivative nature. They are "not beautiful / As sequels without thought" (*CPP* 570). Even worse, these thoughtless iterations of a bourgeois statuary form fail to achieve even the relative success of their predecessors. Stevens demotes Mac-Monnies's horses as "not even Russian animals," a reference to the forceful pair on the Anichkov Bridge. More generally, Stevens echoes Olmsted's concerns about aping a vacuous, imported tradition as "The heaven of Europe is empty" (575). In section 2 of "A Duck for Dinner," Stevens contrasts the overly effete MacMonnies piece with the cowboy, that archetypal American horse tamer: "Buckskins and broad-brims, crossers of divides . . . O free, O bold / That rode your horses straight away" (582). The cowboy maintains a straightforward, bold control over his mounts, unlike the nude youths precariously trying to rein in their horses in the MacMonnies sculpture. And yet, just as the classical statues fail, the cowboy remains a hopelessly remote figure, riding away on horseback into a past and a landscape now as foreign to the common park goer as the Russian figures. They live in a world where "the cities [breed] as the mountains bred." Whereas Olmsted attempted to reinscribe an American pastoral ethos into the city park, at this moment in the poem, such an attempt seems doomed to nostalgia and failure.

For all of the difficulties embedded in *The Horse Tamers*, Stevens cannot long imagine a park without them, and his alterations to the MacMonnies horses in the early sections of the poem signal the poet's critique of the artistic and social character of the wider parkscape. Stevens here does not simply mimic the park but indulges in architectural interventions of his own, particularly in his slight alterations to MacMonnies's sculpture, in order to further his investigation of art's relationship to the everyday. The ways in which Prospect Park, both in actual fact and poetic fiction, deviates from Olmsted and Vaux's early ideals play a major role in how Stevens builds his reply to Mr. Burnshaw's critique of socially disengaged art. In "The Old Woman and the Statue," Stevens describes "A group of marble horses . . . on wings / In the midst of a circle of trees," whereas *The Horse Tamers* is a wingless, rearing pair cast in bronze, with a nude youth restraining them (567). The shift from bronze to marble allows Stevens to build a high-contrast symbolic palette of light and darkness throughout the work to explore tensions between idealism and realism, the mind and the body, the immutable and the mutable, all of which is heightened by the inclusion of the Platonic wings. For example, the blackness of the old woman's dark mind overwhelms the attempted flight of the white statue, just as the very nature of the marble is undermined when splashed with dark blood in section 5 of "The Greenest Continent." Stevens preserves the bronze of the original by casting it onto the environment as the landscape also becomes statuary: "clouds of bronze imposed / On clouds of gold, and green engulfing bronze." As the day lengthens, even the "golden clouds . . . turned to bronze" (568). The scenic natural vistas of open sky and clear greensward morph into multimedia bas-relief artwork: metallic clouds layer under the green media that all combine to frame the horses. Later, when the mind of the park goer infects the scene with its black thoughts, the entire composition, not just the sculpture, changes: "The clouds of bronze / Slowly submerging in flatness disappeared" (569). Here, a literal and metaphorical night descends, flattening the green-on-bronze-on-gold layering of the earlier composition into a monochrome palette before vanishing completely as the woman's mind momentarily destroys the art of statue and parkscape.

Detail of a nude youth
restraining horses
in *The Horse Tamers.*
(Photo by author)

As Filreis demonstrates, the darkness of the old woman's mind results
from the pressures of her sociohistorical context: "'she' is a woman of the
depression . . . a 'vagabond' in the old sense, a 'bag lady' in the new" (*Mod-
ernism* 224). The woman remains in the park through "all an afternoon" in
section 3 and into the night in section 4, which situates her as one of the
countless New Yorkers experiencing homelessness during the Depression.
Beyond her confinement to the park on this literal level, she is also concep-
tually trapped within the landscape: "What path could lead apart from what
she was / And was to be? Could it happen to be this, / This atmosphere in
which the horses rose" (568). Here, the speaker directly questions the very
philosophy of American landscape architecture: Is there any park environ-
ment that could possibly alter the character or even mood of a woman ex-
periencing such hardship? Just as her wounded mental state reduces the pas-
toral ramble into a claustrophobic maze, so too does it threaten the horses.
Stevens first describes the statue as dynamic, "marble leaping in storms of

light" (567), but against the "naked" mind of the "destitute" woman, the artifice fails. In this poetic revision of the original, Stevens replaces the naked youths who hold back the horses with the naked mind of the woman. The weakness of her imagination causes her to fail as an allegorical horse tamer, incapable as she is of imaginatively taming the force of the world, and so the horses tumble into artistic destruction, "collapsed to marble hulk" (568). Stevens positions the statue between two opposing forces: the ascending rush of the ideal, the beautiful, the unchanging, and the gravitational tether of the real, the grimly social, and the mutable. To succeed as a work of art, neither an airy confection nor mass of crushed stone, the composition must achieve perfect equipoise between these competing pulls.

That balance must also include integration within the larger art piece of the park. Even before introducing the woman, Stevens connects the horses to the earth through their aesthetic relationship to the park: "A group of marble horses rose on wings / In the midst of a circle of trees, from which the leaves / Raced with the horses in bright hurricanes" (567). This interplay of statue and leaves was part of the artificer's plan: "So much the sculptor had foreseen." The circle of trees that frames the statue becomes part of the piece, which lends the static horses a sense of motion as the autumnal leaves briskly swirl about them. The arrangement of the horses also mimics their setting. Their "heads held high and gathered in a ring" mirror the circle of the trees, and like those trees, the horses are rooted in the ground: "staggering from the thrust against / The earth" (568). This description concludes by returning to the hurricanes of leaves: "The rotten leaves / Swirled round them in immense autumnal sounds." Joseph Riddel argues that this dead foliage casts aspersion on the static past the statue represents and the decay of the present: "Yet [the statue] now stands among the 'rotten leaves' of the present, which swirl about it and detract from its beauty" (121). However, the kinetic force of the immobile statue comes in part from its interaction with its environment, an interaction the sculptor held in mind when composing his piece, including the dead leaves that tie the art to the realm of mutability. The park, down to whirling bits of autumnal detritus, is part of that art, becoming both monumental and mythic in its association with the statue.

The sculptor fails not because his horses cannot take flight in the autumn leaves but rather because he "had not foreseen" the massive downward pull of "the bitter mind" of the old woman, "that tortured one" who "walked along the paths / Of the park," which reduces his composition to a stiff "marble hulk" (568). By the end of section 4, the woman replaces the statue as park focal point and center of gravity:

> A woman walking in the autumn leaves,
> Thinking of heaven and earth and of herself
> And looking at the place in which she walked,
> As a place in which each thing was motionless
> Except the thing she felt but did not know. (569)

The leaves now surround her, and she mentally replaces the statue with "the thing she felt but did not know" as the heart of motion within the setting. She also supersedes the horses as a truly mobile subject, moving through the stillness as the statue once seemed to move through the light air of day. As she walks in the park with the churning "thing she felt but did not know," she anticipates Someone from "Vacancy in the Park," who walked off looking for "he knew not what." But unlike Someone, the woman achieves a limited form of self-awareness about her own state of dissociation through her stroll in Olmsted and Vaux's contemplative landscape. As she walks, she can think of heaven and earth and, to some extent, herself, if not her feelings. What she lacks is the language or poetic sensitivity to name her experience. The entropic power of this mute suffering spreads beyond the failed statue to the green materials of the larger park architecture, as her presence keeps evening from becoming "brilliant" like "a budding yew" (569). As the green matter of the park was entangled with the art of the statue, here too it shares the statue's fate, as Stevens creates a bizarre park cosmos in which stars and trees freeze in the face of the woman's pain. Oppressive reality here overwhelms the artwork in its entire media, from marble to petal to starlight.

In the last section of "The Old Woman and the Statue," the speaker attempts to rehabilitate the static parkscape by imaginatively removing the woman. To have a park "Without her" may imply a straightforward act of expulsion, and many parks during this time began instituting sundown or midnight curfews to prevent people from loitering overnight. This imagined expulsion helps the speaker elevate the park and statue back up to the aesthetic realm, "Untroubled by suffering." But conceiving of the park "without her" is a doomed imaginative act unmoored from reality. The fanciful cry for "dark-belted sorcerers / Dazzling by simplest beams" manifests the rarefied imagination that treats the working-class public as an inconvenient, unromantic problem to be resolved rather than as the primary consumers of park architecture (570). To show the park's actual connection to the urban poor, in opposition to the speaker's approach, Stevens presents the very elements as sympathetic to the cries of the woman, as her "desolate syllables" become one with "The tortured wind" to cry "against a need that pressed like cold" (569). He casts the possibility of a socially disengaged park as a landscape without air, as the cries of the poor and the wind are one. At the same time, the wind is part of what tortures her, as her need is likened to the chill of a life lived out-of-doors. Here, the park's social failings are rendered not as vacancy, but as tragic habitation. The very space designed to lighten her mental anguish becomes the stage where it is performed, an ersatz home open to the biting winds.

In section 4 of "Mr. Burnshaw and the Statue," the pendulum swings to the other extreme, as the Burnshawesque speaker indulges in a dream of a postapocalyptic park in which all the facile sculptures, and effete pretentions associated with them, topple over. In the Prospect Park context, Stevens's characterization of the ruined sculptures in section 4 as "the hopeless waste of the past" where "the dead / Give up dead things" may specifically refer-ence the sculpture at the park's opposite end: the triumphal arch memorial to the Union dead in Grand Army Plaza (573, 572). In the fallen pile of "heads / Severed and tumbled," there lies also "the head of the sculptor" (572). These lines may point to MacMonnies's insertion of his own like-ness into the Grand Army Plaza war memorial as the officer leading the battalion in the army group. Similarly, the classical pillars White inserted into the parkscape, once upright and parallel, now form a cross as they fall: "columns intercrossed, / White slapped on white." Stevens reduces White's careful arrangement into a sloppy slapping of white here and there like paint on the futurist canvas of the landscape. The repetition of whiteness underscores the blanched palette of White's neoclassical style, if not quietly suggesting the architect's name. The waste of blasted monuments mocks the attempt at decorum and permanence made by the later artists who intervened in Olmsted and Vaux's creation. Even as rubble, the extravagant statuary fails to engage with the natural elements of the scene. The debris is "Motionless, knowing neither dew nor frost," just as the destroyed horses are now "beyond / The help of any wind or any sky" (573). Here is artifice overcome by its own artificiality to the point of rejecting any connection with the organic components of the parkscape.

In "A Duck for Dinner," the Bulgar voices an opposing view of the park by criticizing its successful use in placating and deadening the working

Detail of MacMonnies's army battalion group on the triumphal arch in Grand Army Plaza. MacMonnies is the figure to the left with his arm raised and face in profile. (Photo by author)

classes who use it. Whereas Mr. Burnshaw's social critique in the second section of the poem emphasizes the pretension of the statue and, by extension, the failure of socially unengaged art, the Bulgar criticizes sociopolitical powers that sustain both park and statue precisely for how dangerously engaging they can be. In section 1, he describes a Sunday stroll through the park where "The workers do not rise, as Venus rose," but rather "rise a bit / On summer Sundays in the park" (582). The rise of the working class is not achieved with the splash, pomp, and suddenness of the goddess Venus's appearance from the sea, but "an inch at a time, and inch / By inch, Sunday by Sunday," as befits their less-than-epic surroundings and limited leisure time. The Bulgar then foregrounds the urbanism that defines the faux pastoral of the park: "They rise to the muddy, metropolitan elms." Their diminutive revolution is contained by the park, as they even cannot rise above the line of dirty city trees. Much as the elms try to mask the city skyline as an idyllic screen, the workers beneath the elms are "Forgetting work," a momentary leisure that masks the reality of their lives as urban laborers.

The park also serves as a meeting place where "hands from Sweden," "English noses," and "edged, Italian eyes" come together as a group, "Massed for a head they mean to make for themselves" (582). Whereas the woman suffered the extremity of isolation, here the park goers suffer the loss of individuality as their faces are dismantled to create a giant patchwork visage. This is a new bust to replace that of the decapitated sculptor, through which "their grizzled voice will speak" (582). Just as the nameless thing the woman feels replaces the central position of the horses, here the monstrous head of the masses momentarily becomes a living monument within the parkscape. This vision of a united monument is ultimately fleeting. While the Bulgar, himself a member of this ethnically diverse population, insists upon this common voice in section 1, by section 3 he comes to question the seeming unity of the park masses: "Is each man thinking his separate thoughts" (164). Likewise, rather than providing a possible location of minor uprising, the park is now blamed for the failure to form a collective: "They keep to the paths of the skeleton architect / Of the park" (583). Here, the Bulgar links the deadening effects of the park's controlling architecture to the skeletal body of the dead architect who planned it. In "The Old Woman and the Statue," the horses were similarly depicted as "matchless skeletons" with "marble skulls" (569). Bare, bony artifice connects park and statue, while the skeleton of the architect haunts his landscape, controlling the populace from beyond the grave. The Bulgar ultimately realizes that "Apocalypse was not contrived for parks":

> Geranium budgets, pay-roll water-falls,
> The clank of the carrousel and, under the trees,
> The sheep-like falling-in of distances,
> Converging on the statue, white and high. (584)

The apocalypse of a socialist uprising cannot take place in the park, whose very bones are budgeted materials designed to create a "sheep-like" attitude in its working-class users by creating a similarly sheeplike pastoral landscape centered on the aristocratic form of the statue. Rather than the park framing the statue, the statue now stands as epicenter, acting as the hub to which lines of sight fall in like spokes. The passivity of the people finds a corollary in the oddly passive architecture, as the "distances" of the park's limits docilely "fall" into the statue.

If the character of the landscape mirrors its users, it also testifies to the presence of its managers. The Bulgar's hostile lament over "Geranium

budgets, pay-roll water-falls" reflects a common concern about park man-
agement during the Depression. The rationale for many park budget cuts
was that spending funds on geraniums or water features, like the extensive
system of waterfalls, ponds, and lakes in Prospect Park, seemed an expense
less worthy than supporting hospitals or orphanages. "Pay-roll water-falls"
may also suggest the mismanagement of park funds and practices of graft,
as money poured out of park management offices. More likely, it may refer
to WPA efforts, where constructing or maintaining landscape water fea-
tures placed needy workers on the payroll, thus providing them with just
enough support to keep them from accomplishing the Bulgar's revolution.
During the Depression, the new park superintendent Robert Moses took
advantage of WPA funds by constructing a band shell, several children's
playgrounds, and by expanding the menagerie into a full-fledged zoo in
Prospect Park.[20] From the stance of the Bulgar, the kind of social control
lauded by park designers and managers, from Olmsted to White to Moses,
is not only effective but ultimately coercive and harmful.

In the final section of the poem, "Sombre Figuration," Stevens tries to
achieve the balancing act between imagination and reality, poet and popu-
lace that has to this point eluded him. To place the aesthetic and the social
back into some form of balance, thereby rebuking the apocalyptic desires
of the Bulgar while also answering Mr. Burnshaw's critique, Stevens lit-
erally resorts to a bird's-eye view: "The statue in a crow's perspective of
trees / Stands brimming white, chiaroscuro scaled / To space" (590). Stevens
returns to the green matter of the park to negotiate the question of perspec-
tive. The crows observe the statue from the trees that surround it, acting
as the eyes of the park's greensward, from which perspective the statue is
well scaled to the space it inhabits. It is no longer the reduced pile in the old
woman's mind, nor is it the looming white center of the Bulgar's pastoral
rotunda. It is after considering the crow's vision that the speaker can reclaim
a human perspective that, like the crow's, is grounded in the circumference
of an earthly, immediate environment:

> in camera of the man below,
> Immeasurable, the space in which he knows
> The locust's titter and the turtle's sob.
> The statue stands in true perspective. (590)

What makes the human perspective different from that of the crow is a
sense of immeasurability. But this is a sense of the immeasurable that does

not depart from the park world in which the sounds of turtle doves and crickets fill the dusk. The circle of men in the park combine with the sounds of animals and insects to express and delimit this human-scale comprehension of what exceeds limits. "True perspective" is attained by marrying the immeasurable human capacity for conceiving of the immeasurable, our imaginative faculties, with the limited, material space that circumscribes and facilitates our acts of knowing, the park at nightfall.

Stevens personifies the middle view in "The medium man among medium men" (591). This man, the hoped-for poet, is "medium" both in his sympathy with the "medium" or everyday men in whose company he finds himself, and in his ability to attain a happy medium between the extremes of the imagination and the pressures of daily life. He is also a medium, or intermediary in whom the community may recognize their own desires and through whom those desires might be communicated. This medium man, who balances the individual, the social, and the aesthetic, is dressed in a "clipped" cloak "Adorned for a multitude." North argues that the "clipped" cloak suggests that the poet must necessarily sacrifice some aspect of his imaginative abilities in order to be faithful to the masses and the social pressures of his moment. This causes North to read the final line of the poem as a surrender: "[The poet's] aspiration causes the 'cloak to be clipped,' to be reduced, as the land-breath of night is 'stifled.' 'Night and the imagination being one' is an expression of defeat" (219). However, Stevens's attempt to hem his poetic mantel and the very onset of night are cast in terms of artistic intervention. The cloak is "to be clipped" as "the night is to be re-designed," thus tailoring both the "flapping cloak" of the old woman and the nighttime parkscape she haunted in the first section into an artistically viable costume and set for the poet. Whereas before the old woman's mind could not admit of imagination, here the poem ends with the medium man landscaping or "re-designing" the night in which she walked, transforming that darkness from bleakness into a fertile dreamscape as night and the imagination become one. As North states earlier in his argument: "Night, which was indicative of a special mental bleakness in 'The Old Woman and the Statue,' becomes the means of reconciliation for imagination and reality, poet and people" (217). Stevens does not conclude by returning to the white statue in daylight but rather repurposes the once oppressive darkness in the park into the very stuff of imaginative composition.

While it is therefore not necessary to read the comingling of night and the imagination as a negative reduction of both into unproductive darkness,

Stevens can only articulate the desire for balance and then wrap that long-ing up in a short cloak. *Owl's Clover* does not clearly state how the poet is to attain that middle ground, only that he must. However, Stevens writes the possibility of true balance into the medium man's park environment. It is the park, when viewed and used correctly, that can provide a safe road: "Green is the path we take / Between chimeras and garlanded the way" (588). The park does more than facilitate the poet's investigation of the aesthetic and the social, the imagined and the real. In its green materials, the park embodies the potential marriage of these extremes and offers a safe path between them. At the same time, the lived experience of the space demonstrates the dangers of failing to achieve this aesthetic balancing act. The chimeras that line the way, whether the fantastical equine beasts of rarefied art or the compound monster of the oppressed masses, constantly threaten those who would stray from the middle way of the green trail.

The interplay of the aesthetic, the social, and the green informed both Olmsted and Vaux's creation of an American school of landscape architec-ture and Stevens's depiction of these planned, public, and verdant spaces. His park pieces present landscape architecture as an art form that utilizes green material in order to build different visions of nature, as Stevens frus-trates attempts to discover a radically prior natural world by framing that green matter as part of a pre-aestheticized environment. Stevens also breaks with the park movement's utopian democratic ideals by presenting a more troubled vision of parks as social spaces, marked by both the hope of con-nection and the reality of isolation. In the case of *Owl's Clover*, that break in park sociability occurs due to the hardships of the Depression. The fail-ure of realizing the democratic telos of the American city park mirrors wider failures in the democratic and environmental ideals that characterize American city planning at large. As the twentieth century wore on, park goers, poets, and the American public became increasingly aware of how misguided planning attempts continued to generate social and ecological woes. In the thorny tangle of those weeds, managers, architects, publics, and poets found it difficult to cut a path back to the garlanded way.

CHAPTER 3

William Carlos Williams and the Failures of Planning

On 4 July 1932, Garret Mountain Park opened for the people of Passaic County. This new green space was designed by none other than the prolific Olmsted firm. Unlike Wallace Stevens's relatively flat Elizabeth Park, this parkscape combined the firm's characteristic greensward and pastoral lawns with sweeping mountaintop vistas of Paterson, New Jersey, and the Passaic Falls and River below. The choice of date communicated the national import and civic idealism long associated with Olmsted's creations. For William Carlos Williams, who enjoyed walks through this park, the perspective from the top of Garret Mountain was "beautiful but expensive!" (*Paterson* 44). While celebrating the elemental beauty and force of the Passaic Falls and River, Williams mourned the great human and environmental cost of harnessing their power. Specifically, Williams linked this ongoing environmental harm with the planning efforts of the Society for Useful Manufactures.[1] In 1792, the Society, known as SUM, was created at the behest of Alexander Hamilton in order to build the first true company city in America. Paterson was financed, founded, and planned around the energy of the Passaic Falls, which would drive new mill industries like textiles and ironworks. Like Burnham's Chicago, Hamilton's Paterson stood out as an emblem of the possibilities of the American city and, by extension, the promise of the nation. SUM's plan predates city planning as a distinct discipline and treats the urban environment more as a massive manufactory than a human and natural habitat. Unlike the organic plan of Burnham, which would revolve around questions of human flourishing, this early experiment in American city design was focused exclusively on industrialization and profit. The basic shape of that original plan had lasting consequences for both the local environment and generations of Patersonians, long after the mills closed and SUM disintegrated.

In his long poem *Paterson*, Williams conveys the history and landscape of the city in his quest to discover a distinctively American poetics. That history, as presented by Williams, is a process of imposing foreign mill-town schematics on an exceptional American locality. The result is the contamination of the Passaic Falls, polluted by industry, as well as a lasting sense of isolation and brokenness in the working population of the city. Later attempts to mend the relationship among city, citizen, and landscape, particularly the creation of Garret Mountain Park, moved the community in the right direction but never fully repaired the damage done by SUM's initial design. Williams viewed the resultant situation as a poetic crisis. Just as SUM failed by importing English, extractive models into an American environment, so too is the failure of American language the imposition of foreign precedents that do not adequately voice the new, dynamic relationship of person and place in the American context. This crisis takes on a distinctive form in a city with equally unique contours. Williams studs *Paterson* with long prose passages throughout, several of which recount the discovery and various uses of the Passaic Falls. At different moments a primal elemental power, a kind of curiosity in nature's freak show, and an energy source for industry, the Falls continue to voice a roar that promises the poet hope for discovering a genuine American language. But it is an anxious hope, and here the loss of wilderness to city sprawl represents the potential loss of that idiom. Williams's answer is not, however, a regression to a pre-urban state of reclaiming wilderness but rather a call for a healthy union between nature and city.

Whereas Stevens focuses on the aesthetics of the city park and its immediate Depression-era context, Williams dedicates long passages in *Paterson* to exploring the historical and economic pressures that resulted in both the physical shape of the city and the experiences of the working class living along the Passaic River. In doing so, Williams presents an amalgam of the human and the natural, the landscape and the city, while never wholly valorizing or lamenting the dynamic interplay he witnesses. He does so by keeping the beauty and the expense in constant tension. While Williams hopes for a balanced relationship between citizen and site, a relationship he characterizes as a marriage, he most often finds the fissures of divorce scarring both the land and the lives lived within it. This balancing act of city and nature, person and place reaches a peak in book 2 as the speaker, Mr. Paterson, spends a Sunday afternoon at Garret Mountain Park. Here, Williams uses the sculpted terrain to explore both the beauty and the expense of life in and as Paterson. Just as Stevens had experienced in Elizabeth Park,

Garret Mountain failed to live up to the palliative and democratic ideals of its architects. Instead, it provided new grounds for enacting the social and environmental tensions that Hamilton initiated when the city was first designed.

PLANNING PATERSON

The Society for Useful Manufactures was the first of its kind in America, and Paterson was a similarly distinctive creation. In all things, especially its factory town plan, SUM emphasized thrift in construction and overall profitability. Paterson promised to be the realization of Hamilton's industrial plans for America, as laid out in his famous *Report on Manufactures*. As the historians John C. Miller and Broadus Mitchell demonstrate, Hamilton saw the shift from agriculture to industry as the solution for many national ills. An industrial America, by Hamilton's logic, would be independent from European imports, thereby positioning itself for greatness on the world stage: "National wealth and power, he perceived, were passing rapidly into the hands of those countries that devoted their energies to commerce and manufacturing: here, he believed, was the wave of the future upon which nations would rise to greatness" (Miller 284).[2] Hamilton established the Society for Useful Manufactures and set his sights on Paterson.[3] The location seemed ideal. With a wealth of natural resources, including waterpower and mineral deposits, a location close to both New York and Philadelphia to attract investors, and a population already thickly settled along the Passaic River, Paterson offered "the closest approximation to ideal conditions that were to be found in the United States" (Miller 300). Much as the nation would later watch Burnham's Chicago as a local project with national implications, the new republic kept its eye on Paterson as the representative of American industry and, in Hamilton's equation, the future of the nation.

What Hamilton envisioned was an American Manchester, a city patterned on successful British company towns centered on a mill as the primary source of power. The architectural historian John S. Garner defines the company town as "a settlement built and operated by a single business enterprise," specifically those constructed during the "early industrial age" (3).[4] While there is no one design for a company town, the unifying principle of all its architectural features is industrial utility, and so factories loom large in this industrial landscape: "Factories or mines, 'the works' to which the

British refer, dominated the site, and there was a sameness to the houses and other ancillary buildings" (4).[5] Planning, in these instances, often progressed haltingly, depending on the current state of the business and the number of workers the settlement needed to accommodate. The plan's relationship to its environment was extractive, as the site provided either the raw materials or the power source for creating the company's product. As such, these locations came to be equated with environmental exploitation and unchecked pollution, to the point that "the company town came to symbolize the wrecking of the environment" (3).[6] By February 1793, the task of planning Paterson was handed off to the businessman and Connecticut state treasurer Peter Colt, who completed the plan "with the least possible cost, to secure immediate results" (Nelson and Shriner 330). Even the trees of the city, which Williams would later praise, were selected with industry in mind: "The superintendent was also instructed to purchase a number of white mulberry trees for the purpose of fostering the growing of silk worms" (331). A cotton mill, carding works, and printing press were built, along with a block of fifty structures for workers, each on a quarter-acre lot. Space was left vacant for four mill owners to design their own homes (Mitchell 184). The subsequent history of planning in Paterson is a series of often haphazard additions and subtractions from the boxy mill-town layout, frequently completed only after long debate and at a modest cost. As in Burnham's Chicago, both local politics and a few key affluent citizens were heavily responsible for shaping the city, especially in the inclusion of green space. Eventually, the people of Paterson sought to create common park spaces of their own, but urban crowding and debates among aldermen about the exact locations of the parks significantly stalled the project until the late 1880s.[7] It was not until 1911, in the wake of park planning successes like those in Chicago and New York, that the City of Paterson tried, yet again, to incorporate more parkscape within the city's environs.

The uniqueness of Paterson's environment owes much to the Passaic Falls that would later serve as the central feature of Williams's major poetic work. Beyond attracting businessmen, the Passaic Falls became a popular tourist destination praised for their force and beauty. The 1834 *Traveller's Guide through the Middle and Northern States* told tourists to make a special stop in Paterson to admire this natural wonder: "The perpendicular pitch is 70 feet into a narrow rocky chasm. The scenery is wild and imposing; and the falls are among the greatest natural curiosities of this country" (Davison 112).[8] The literary journal the *Casket* provided greater detail, offering the

The Passaic Falls, with the Great Falls Generating Station on the left. (Photo by author)

following description to accompany Washington Irving's poem "The Falls of the Passaic":

> The Passaic River at the Falls . . . is truly remarkable; it is about forty yards wide, and flowers [*sic*] with a very rapid current till it comes within a small distance from the edge of the Fall, when it suddenly empties itself in one entire sheet over a ledge of rocks nearly eighty feet in perpendicular height. The river winds in the form of a Z, and the falls are at the upper angle. Further below it runs on through a chasm formed of immense rocks on each side, into which the water has worn large fissures for a distance of one hundred yards. (68)[9]

The Falls enjoyed a reputation as the motor for Paterson's booming industry and as a natural wonder. No other town in America could boast such a massive waterfall at its center, and thus Paterson earned the dual distinction of housing one of the nation's most notable "natural curiosities" and serving as the model American corporate town.

However, as Williams dramatizes in *Paterson*, this split personality as natural and industrial wonder was ultimately unstable. In an 1888 survey, the New Jersey Geological Committee noted: "This leap [of the Passaic Falls] is now only occasionally made . . . for usually the stream is led away into the race of the Society for the Encouragement of Useful Manufactures, and harnessed to the wheels which have done so much to raise Paterson to the front rank of manufacturing cities" (G. Cook 154). It was only when industry languished that the Falls returned to their full power, and mercantile success in Paterson came in unpredictable waves before eventually drying out. Textiles faltered when forced to compete with the New England mills, so Paterson shifted to steel and rail components until that venture collapsed after the Civil War. Silk then became the commodity of the day, enjoying success until labor disputes, strikes, and, eventually, the Great Depression slowed the mills to a halt. Paterson became a new kind of emblematic American city, one of the hundreds of failed industrial centers dotting the nation. SUM grew increasingly anemic as industry slowed in Paterson, but the official Society charter was not purchased by the citizens of Paterson until as late as 1945, only a year before Williams published book 1 of *Paterson*.

Williams lived in the neighboring town of Rutherford and worked in Paterson, tending to its citizens during his tenure as the head of pediatrics at Passaic General Hospital. In his role as school medical inspector for the county, Williams also lobbied for additional parks for the population of working-class schoolchildren in the area. There are records of Williams attending the opening of several parks and playgrounds around 1914 (Leith). In 1910, Williams and his brother Edgar also submitted plans for "The Isle of Safety," a triangle of common space among three intersecting streets, which would serve as open green space for the neighborhood schoolchildren.[10] Williams knew the benefits of green space. His autobiography begins with several stories of long hikes, nature watching, and even some squirrel hunting in the area.[11] Throughout his life, the poet also returned to Paterson's Garret Mountain Park, a site that would feature prominently in book 2 of *Paterson*, such as his visit in December 1950 with his grandson, only two months after the publication of book 4 of *Paterson*.[12]

Despite this contact with the people and topography of Paterson, Williams was later criticized for his portrayal of the city and was labeled an outsider in the process. As Christopher MacGowan has noted, "for his perspective upon local history as demanding a larger context for its full meaning, Williams was himself treated as an outsider," particularly by local historians

William Carlos Williams in Garret Mountain Park, overlooking Paterson, New Jersey, 1957. (Photo by Eve Arnold/Magnum Photos)

who thought the poet's representation of the city was either unflattering or overly lofty ("Paterson" 50). MacGowan cites a 1948 review from the *Passaic Herald News* that claims the poem is only fit for "that firey-eyed young man in a beret, who needs a haircut so badly," whereas "you and you and you" will make neither "head nor tail of it" (50–51). Locality, legitimacy, class, and language all combine in these early reactions to Williams's dense presentation of the city, interactions that Williams takes up in the poem. In choosing Paterson as his poetic ground, Williams made no claims as a native, nor does the success of the poem hang on his ability to provide local credentials. What the poem does draw on is Williams's immediate contact with the city and its park, along with his intensive study of a wide array of historical archives relating to Paterson. More importantly, one of the major themes of the poem is the divorce between person and place. In taking on a modern urban American context, Williams presents an environment where there is no such thing as a native, as all Patersonians, and Americans by extension, are transplants with little sense of their elemental environment. His speakers intentionally, and often falteringly, negotiate this insider-outsider divide.

More broadly, the city of Paterson provided Williams with the rich historical fodder he sought for his long poem. The space embodied harmful habits of land management, and the populace used disengaged habits of speech that Williams thought were endemic to America. From its colonial past to its modern uses, the contours of Paterson would allow Williams to explore the causes of what he understood to be a national crisis. As Walter Scott Peterson notes: "For Williams [Hamilton's] plans ignored the 'local genius' and in trying to reproduce European civilization in this country thwarted the promise latent here" (10). While Williams scholars have investigated Williams's critiques of SUM as a political, industrial, and capitalistic force in suppressing the local genius of the American environment, this analysis takes up Peterson's mention of planning to focus on SUM's urban landscaping, as well as how Williams addresses the minute spatial specifics of the design in his representation of the city.

PLANNING *PATERSON*

The task of poetically plumbing the depths of Paterson's history and topography was a large one, and Williams conceived of several overlapping schematics to structure his poem. Like the city, the composition of *Paterson* spanned several years. Williams began work on this sweeping project in the early 1940s and initially published each book in a separate limited-edition volume in 1946, 1948, 1949, 1951, and 1958 respectively (MacGowan ix).[13] At different moments, Williams articulated a variety of visions for this long exploration of Paterson, though all of them ultimately found a place in the finished work. In a prefatory note to the 1946 edition of book 1, Williams presented the following general schematic: "Paterson is a long poem in four parts—that man in himself is a city, beginning, seeking, achieving and concluding his life in ways which the various aspects of a city may embody. . . . Part One introduces the elemental character of the place. The Second Part comprises the modern replicas. Three will seek a language to make them vocal, and Four, the river below the falls, will be reminiscent of episodes— all that any one man may achieve in a lifetime" (preface xiv). In this imagining, Paterson the city is a vehicle through which Williams can explore the consciousness of "man in himself." Mr. Paterson, the human figure who surfaces throughout the poem as an anthropomorphic miniature of the city in its own dream, a stand-in for Williams the poet-doctor, and a questing, sometimes bumbling Everyman, is the chief node of the man-city complex.

In this first articulation, Williams uses this complex primarily to explore human consciousness, as seen in the lines, "Eternally asleep, / his dreams walk about the city where he persists / incognito" (*Paterson* 6). In book 1, not only is Mr. Paterson an incognito representative of the city-dreamer, but all of the inhabitants of Paterson, "a thousand automatons," are also dream creatures (6).

Yet, in 1951, Williams restated his interest in the "resemblance between the mind of modern man and a city," while shifting his emphasis:

> Thus the city I wanted as my object had to be one that I knew in its most intimate details. . . . Paterson has a definite history associated with the beginnings of the United States. It has besides a central feature, the Passaic Falls, which as I began to think about it became more and more the lucky burden of what I wanted to say. . . . From the beginning I decided there would be four books following the course of the river whose life seemed more and more to resemble my own life as I more and more thought of it: the river above the Falls, the catastrophe of the Falls itself, the river below the Falls and the entrance at the end into the great sea. (preface xiii)

The flow of resemblance now slides from the human to the environmental. Here, the city serves as Williams's primary "object" in the poem, an object that would allow him to focus on local particulars while simultaneously making a statement about "the beginnings of the United States." Williams presents the structural schema here as a topographical map, unlike the more thematic presentation in the 1946 edition, and so the landscape of Paterson and the Passaic River Valley serve as the unifying principle of the poem. In a letter to Henry Wells penned in 1950, Williams slid from the human end of this relationship to the local extreme, describing *Paterson* as "a failing experiment, toward assertion with broken means but an assertion, always, of a new and total culture, the lifting of an environment to expression" (*Selected Letters* 286). In this configuration, lifting an environment to expression deemphasizes the human, making Mr. Paterson a human vehicle by which we better understand our physical place and glimpse the possibility of a "new and total culture" shaped by local geography and language. Williams's conception of the project thus swings from extreme anthropocentrism to a nearly deep ecological stance, whereby the human presence is functionally emptied as the environment is elevated.

By providing a multitude of definitions for this project over the course of its composition, Williams also provided later scholars with a host of differing approaches to the poem. Is it primarily human in its focus, or is it rather a verse treatise on the importance of local environment? While critics tend to emphasize one aspect of the poem to the detriment of the other, Williams ultimately crafts a work that disturbs the margins between man and his environment, civilization and landscape, thus integrating both of his goals for the poem. Book 3, published in 1949, begins with a quote from George Santayana's *The Last Puritan* that criticizes a view of the city that divorces it from either the human person or from nature: "Cities, for Oliver, were not a part of nature. He could hardly feel, he could hardly admit even when it was pointed out to him, that cities are a second body for the human mind, a second organism, more rational, permanent and decorative than the organism of flesh and bone: a work of natural yet moral art" (*Paterson* 94). In this iteration, failing to recognize the humanness of cities is part and parcel of failing to appreciate their naturalness. As "a second body," the city is also an "organism," while it is simultaneously "permanent and decorative," a planned art form that is both natural and moral.

WHO IS PATERSON?

The figure of Paterson is thus both a man who is like a city *and* a city who is like a man. As both city and man, Paterson is never clearly distinguishable from the wider, elemental environment. Book 1 begins with his topographical anatomy: "Paterson lies in the valley under the Passaic Falls / its spent waters forming the outlines of his back" (*Paterson* 6). Williams imagines Paterson as the slumbering husband at the feet of his wife, figured as Garret Mountain and the Falls: "The Park's her head, carved, above the Falls, by the quiet / river . . . / farms and ponds, laurel and the temperate wild cactus, / yellow flowered . . facing him" (8). Williams utilizes the longstanding equation of nature with woman and city with man, and much has been made of the marriage / divorce dynamic here imagined as dissociation between Paterson the city and the primal features of his East Coast landscape. Both Scott Peterson and Benjamin Sankey return to the marriage / divorce dynamic throughout their guides to *Paterson*. Joel Conarroe dedicates an entire chapter to "The Man / City": "The various parts of *Paterson* are fused into a comprehensible whole primarily by three major symbols— man-city, river, and mountain, or feminine principle" (63). Glauco Cambon also links Williams's portrayal of marriage to larger questions of postfrontier American identity: "Is marriage still possible between Americans and

America? Or, to paraphrase it unmythologically: Granted our pioneer start, is real civilization still attainable?" (187).[14]

However, Williams immediately and consistently undermines the male/female, city/nature dichotomy he invokes. Both Paterson and his estranged wife have bodies that are defined and shaped by the river. Oddly, the river makes a unified skeletal system out of both Paterson and his wife, she as the head and he as the torso, while also cocreating them. In serving as the head, the mountain-wife also inverts the tradition of imagining the husband as the head of the marriage. The relatively inactive verb choice of "forming" in reference to the city is replaced by the more muscular "carved" for Garret Mountain, emphasizing an organic act of shaping and growing for Paterson and a more sculptural, architectural shaping for the mount. That rocky head is not a nonhuman, wild mountaintop but is rather a "Park," along with "farms and ponds," "laurel and the temperate wild cactus." Williams dedicates the entirety of book 2 to exploring the urban-natural landscape of Garret Mountain, but even at this early moment in the poem, he presents it as a zone that cannot be equated with a pre-urban ideal of nature, as the hands of farmers and landscapers shape the space along with the crafting force of the river. In the parkscape, it is impossible to tell whether the "laurel" and "wild cactus" are native growths or architectural inclusions in the park.[15]

As a representative of Williams within the poem, Paterson is often linked to the poet. However, Williams first presents the mountain-bride in book 1 as wreathed with laurel trees, the leaves of which traditionally form a garland for the poet. Her crown is also one of thorns, as the cactus mingles with the laurel, suggesting the inherent difficulty of the poetic venture at hand. The roar of the Falls recurs throughout *Paterson* and is often equated with the voice of the wife, a primal language of place that hums with the possibility of a new, vibrant American verse. The sleeping city hears "the thunder / of the waters filling his dreams," and Paterson asks "(What common language to unravel? /   . . combed into straight lines / from that rafter of a rock's lip)" (6, 7). With her laurel crown and murmuring speech, the mountain-wife becomes like her husband, the poet who writes of her. In fact, she becomes somewhat hermaphroditic. Williams imagines the chaos of the water as both hair and poetry: this raw material can be combed into lines, suggesting both an act of grooming and an act of composing verse.[16] However, the image also creates a mustachioed bride with facial hair over her lip, in need of some light styling. In the closing lines of book 1, the nature-woman, city-man dynamic melts into a last moment of confusion as both poetic language and earth become suddenly paternal: "Earth, the chatterer, father of all / speech" (39). In lifting this environment to speech, Williams invites it to speak for itself. But the exact boundaries of that environment remain veiled in the mist rising from the Falls: is it a kind of natural environment that must speak, an elemental bride? Or Paterson the city as both modern environment and modern man? Williams answers with a combination of the two and must merge his allegorical figures in Tiresian twists as a result. He returns to this mother-father combination even more emphatically in book 2: "You are the eternal bride and / father—quid pro quo, / a simple miracle" (75). By the time Williams describes "The giant in whose apertures we / cohabit" late in part 2 of book 1, titled "The Delineaments of the Giants," it has become impossible to delineate which giant he is referencing, the city or the mountain (23). Unlike Santayana's Oliver, who makes the mistake of estranging the city from both nature and man, Williams's giant is an environment, a body, and an organism that is urban and elemental at once, "an / interpenetration, both ways" (4).

This interpenetration finds expression in Williams's first description of the city below the park, a human environment that is surprisingly sylvan: "and cylindrical trees / bent, forked by preconception and accident— / split, furrowed, creased, mottled, stained— / secret—into the body of the light!" (6–7). The city is here an arboreal zone where the trees are shaped by both "preconception and accident," suggesting both the accidental loss or twist of limb, as well as the preconceived acts of pruning to accommodate buildings or utility wires in the city. Given SUM's original mandate to plant trees for silkworms in Paterson, the trees themselves are preconceived elements in the urban landscape. However, their classical cylindrical bases, evocative of the geometrically regular city streets that Williams criticizes in the next stanza, burst into baroque irregularity, "split, furrowed, creased, mottled, stained," as they contort to achieve maximum sun exposure. The marks of that contortion testify to the living dynamism of the trees as more than static landscape elements and also hint at the unwholesomeness of the environment that has furrowed and stained them. Nonetheless, these trees achieve a mystical photosynthetic union with "the body of the light!" In framing this engagement with the sunlight as a kind of corporeal penetration, Williams conjures the image of marital union in miniature. As such, the streets of Paterson, while unclean and ill-planned, can still allow for marriage instead of divorce. And yet, the nature-as-bride, city-as-man designations fall apart as the trees are both natural growth and urban phallus entering into an elemental body of light that is accessible within the city-scape. By introducing Paterson as a kinetic urban forest embracing its atmo-sphere, Williams commences the poem with an integrated human-nature cityscape. In the secret sex act between city tree and sunlight, there are no easy distinctions to be made among the bodies involved.

However, this is not to say that *Paterson* simply lauds the reunion of man, city, and nature by unproblematically dissolving the triad into a unity. Williams is all too aware that some acts of combination result in imbalance and harm. The end of book 1 details the environmental and social ills that resulted from Hamilton's initial plan for Paterson and subsequent decades of industrial misuse: "Half the river red, half steaming purple / from the factory vents, spewed out hot, / swirling, bubbling. The dead bank, / shin-ing mud ." (36). In 1854, SUM sold its water rights to the newly formed Passaic Water Company, which, by 1868, received permission from the legis-lature to dump industrial and human waste into the Passaic River, initiating nearly forty years of water pollution in the process.[17] The hot, purple waste from industrial grates may specifically allude to the dark by-products of silk dyeing, a booming industry in Paterson following the end of the Civil War. "Half the river red" suggests both a turbulent river chumming up the red clay in its bed and the hint of blood: "Into the sewer they threw the dead horse" (37). Throughout *Paterson*, Williams recounts the biological waste that eventually mingles with the Passaic River, such as the carcass of the horse and the blood of a maimed millworker. He also decries a state he refers to as blockage, referring to the damming up of sexual and poetic powers, as well as to the literal blockage of the river:

> The outward
> masks of the special interests
> that perpetuate the stasis and make it
> profitable.
>   They block the release
> that should cleanse (34)

Williams here equates the damage done by the Passaic Water Company with the kind of static mentality created by "the knowledgeable idiots, the university" who damn up the flow of poetry with a pedantic attachment to dead traditions (34). The "dead bank" of the Passaic River is thus dead both literally, incapable of supporting vegetation because of thermo-chemical pollution, and metaphorically, a kind of Styx where the dead of Paterson are eventually washed ashore as poetry perishes. Nonetheless, Williams finds a moment of beauty in the waste's "shining mud." Much as Sandburg did in "Muckers," Williams pauses over the streak of light reflected by this wet silt, beautiful in the aesthetic surprise of discovering the shining mud beside the bloody river. Yet, unlike Sandburg, Williams finds beauty not in creative acts of labor but in destructive acts of pollution. As with the view from Garret Mountain, or the stained urban trees thrusting into sunlight, the Passaic River still retains some beauty, despite the environmental catastrophe that has made the bare mud visible.

Williams then turns his gaze from the lovely filth of the Passaic to the streets of Paterson: "Tenement windows, sharp edged, in which / no face is seen—though curtainless, into / which no more than birds and insects look or / the moon stares, concerning which they dare / look back, by times" (37). The workers' tenement housing is angular and bare, as the invisible inhabitants lack window coverings. There is also no need for curtains, as "no more than birds or insects" ever try to look into these obscured domestic interiors. The absence of the human spectator is filled by the presence of natural voyeurs who show interest in the present-absent tenement community. Williams then conflates the viewer and the viewed as the grammar of the line tangles both together: "or / the moon stares, concerning which they dare / look back, by times." "They" floats without a clear referent. The line would seem to say that the humans living in the tenements sometimes look back at the moon who looks at them, as their faces finally appear under the cover of night. However, "they" may point back not to real human faces but to the windows that hide them, as the line conflates people with their dwellings. Human visages keep receding, as the windows reflect the curious face of the moon back at itself. Williams captures a sense of impoverishment in this strangely unpeopled neighborhood while finding a natural beauty in the shining moon and fluttering creatures that, like speaker and reader, strain to see a human figure. Fittingly, the natural agents in the scene demonstrate more interest in humanity than the utilitarian architecture that represents and entombs the workers of Paterson.

The bareness of the tenement serves as a synecdoche for the similarly institutionalized and oppressive layout of Paterson: "It is the complement exact of vulgar streets, / a mathematic calm, controlled, the architecture / mete, sinks there, lifts here   . / the same blank and staring eyes" (38).[18] The "vulgar streets" of Paterson are laid out in a modified grid pattern, a design characteristic of many American cities. As the urban historian Kenneth T.

Jackson notes, this ubiquitous grid of right-angled streets became identified with American cityscapes, as opposed to the often curving lines found in the country.[19] The grid not only emphasized precision and cleanliness but made the selling of lots an easier business affair by reducing the landscape to a series of interchangeable square parcels. Architects like Olmsted and Burnham lamented the implementation of the grid over hilly landscapes as an inefficient and inelegant imposition on the site.[20] The mathematical exactness of the grid in Paterson, intersected on occasion by contours of the river, mirrors the measured, or "mete," architecture of the uniform red-brick structures that characterize the original mill and tenement structures in the city. In Williams's poem, this sterile grid "sinks there, lifts here" as it follows the gently hilly topography of the area. While the grid poorly matches its undulant landscape, the landscape adds a kinetic buoyancy to the city's plan, causing the mirage of sinking and lifting as if the whole city were floating on moving water. The overall effect, however, cannot rise above the numbness of the plan, as "the same blank and staring eyes" re-assert themselves. Tenement windows are equated with the vulgar streets, all of which evoke the blank eyes Williams first associates with the staring moon and the invisible human inhabitants. Again, acts of looking and the actual placement of the eyes muddy these relationships. Are the "same blank" eyes found in the streets of Paterson, like eyes hidden in the windows, the eyes of humans, or is the same "staring" moon vacantly shining down on this vacant scene? Or are the streets and buildings themselves the "staring eyes" of Paterson the city-man? It becomes impossible to locate the eye of the beholder, resulting in a tableau characterized by a glazed, cold glance that originates from and falls upon a compound environment.

The next stanza moves from chill, geometric exteriors to hot, violent interiors. Williams begins with a transition that equates failures of city planning with failures of poetic speech: "An incredible / clumsiness of address" (38). The possibilities of reviving American language and verse are a central concern for Williams throughout *Paterson*.[21] In the preface, he warns himself against "turn[ing] to no more / than the writing of stale poems," seeking instead a language that more closely mimics the murmur of the falls in order to answer the question "What common language to unravel?" (4, 7). "Clumsiness of address," like the paltry cry of "Ain't they beautiful!" in response to the glory of the local scene, plagues both the poet Paterson and the people of the man-city Paterson (18). It also troubles Paterson in its physical layout. In immediately following Williams's discussion of streets and buildings, the word "address" first evokes the actual addresses of those buildings. Because the river intersects the city at a sloping, curved angle, several streets have different names on different sides of the Passaic, resulting in some literal clumsiness of address.[22] The layout of the vulgar streets becomes entangled with the vulgarity of poetry as the "roar of the river / forever in our ears" embodies a nascent, unrealized American language (17). The "clumsiness of address" manifests a dual failure of site and speech, neither of which weds with the river and Falls (38). Between the options of the hegemonic Hamiltonian grid and the disorderly loops of European village streets stands the kind of design imagined by Burnham for San Francisco: an orderly and logical layout that accommodates both human movement and the curves of the landscape. This middle ground remains unavailable to Williams and the people of Paterson.

Within these clumsily addressed structures, Williams finds "senseless rapes," "the blood / boiling as though in a vat, where they soak" (38). The sexual violence within the tenements is brought about by boiling blood, described not as fluid within the human body but as contained in a huge environmental cauldron in which humans are scalded whole. This image nods to the boiling vats used to dye silk as it links the interior turmoil of the working class with the material specifics of their labor, while also closing the ecological circuit of fluid exchange: the hot purple dye, red water, blood, the Passaic River, the human body, and the silk mills all form a unified, cocontaminating ecosystem. Williams is again able to criticize this state of affairs while also finding surprising beauty: "the sink with the waste farina in it and / lumps of rancid meat, milk-bottle tops: have / here a tranquility and loveliness" (38). Not only does the domestic mess of wheat, flesh, and milk congeal into a surprising still-life, but this detritus will all find its way to the river through the sink. These natural materials are transformed into human goods and then human waste in the city sink that, in turn, pours more blood and meal out into the water supply, where their odd beauty will meet the similarly odd beauty of the shining mud.

Violence is not restricted to Paterson's interiors but also extends to "the gravel of the ravished park, torn by / the wild workers' children tearing up the grass, / kicking, screaming" (36). The "senseless rape" of women in Paterson grows to gigantic proportions, as the bride-mountain-park is "ravished" by the kicking feet of children either at play or in the middle of a tantrum. The tearing of the ground, whether gravel path or grassy field, results from the recreational escapism parks such as Garret Mountain extended to laborers incapable of making lengthy and expensive trips to the country for clean air and entertainment. While landscape architects like Olmsted hoped parks would provide a democratic zone where all classes would enjoy a healthy environment, parks in actual fact became locations where class differences and difficulties were acted out in miniature. Whereas Wallace Stevens began to explore the sources of those tensions in *Owl's Clover,* Williams rigorously contextualizes the causes by focusing on the particular environmental and human costs of industrialization in the city of Paterson. One of the ways he does so, as in this small passage, is through a focus on the actual act of Patersonians walking through and on the land. The tread of feet throughout the poem can range from a painful blow to a sensual caress as the heels of city children and picnickers become the hands of Paterson the city-husband touching his wife. In book 1, this first glance at kicking, raping feet emphasizes violence while eliding blame. Uncomfortably, the rapists here are children who cannot be held entirely accountable for their heavy romping. Not only are they children, but they are the children of "wild workers," and so Williams situates the wildness of the children as an unhappy inheritance from their parents. Yet the wildness of those same parents comes from their boiling blood and the stifling conditions of city below where "silk spins from the hot drums" of the mill, drowning them in currents of toxicity (36). The mountain's rape by little feet is one node in a systemic web of violence and pollution that combines mountain and city, a web of material exchange in which the workers and their children are inevitably enmeshed. In book 2, Williams follows those feet to investigate other ways the population might tread on the mountain and, by extension, other possibilities for interacting with their environment.

PATERSON IN THE PARK

Book 2, "Sunday in the Park," is characterized by an emphasis on walking that, at times, verges on the comedic. Huffing after his hike up the footpath to Garret Mountain Park, Paterson-as-man interrupts his own strolling meditations with a chunk of clinical prose describing the action of walking: "The body is tilted slightly forward from the basic standing position and the weight is thrown on the ball of the foot, while the other thigh is lifted and the leg and opposite arm are swung forward" (45). As Sankey argues in his companion to *Paterson,* this abrupt insertion "insist[s] that this scene is literally a man walking before it is anything else" (74). If this passage amounts to insistence, the reader is left to ask why the emphatic reminder that Paterson is *walking* through the park? Williams returns to the word "Walking" as a transitional phrase throughout book 2, each time graphically set apart and capitalized. Beyond emphasizing embodiment, this attention to walking raises the figure of other strolling literary speakers. Specifically, in the person of Paterson, Williams achieves the conflation of two iconic walking types: the nature walker and the flaneur. In one sense, Paterson represents the traditional nature walker, as his stroll leads him to witness a transcendent flight of grasshoppers and a vision from the mountaintop. However, that vision is not of sublime wilderness but of the city below. In this other sense, the natural zone of the park is simultaneously an urban zone, as Paterson the flaneur catches glimpses of trysts, dancing, and drinking bouts that the working-class population enjoys during their Sunday off. Not only is Paterson a hybrid walking figure, but he becomes one by virtue of his setting. This planned mountaintop public park is both elemental and architectural, wild and civilized at once. Paterson's walk in the park therefore not only links two seemingly antithetical literary traditions, one organic and the other metropolitan, but also demonstrates the fundamental comingling of natural and human environments in modern American parks.[23]

The flaneur, a strolling urban observer, first walked the streets of nineteenth-century Paris and was later made famous (or infamous) by Walter Benjamin's reading of Charles Baudelaire.[24] As is also true of the nature walker, the flaneur is a genus that admits of a wide variety of species, but a few generalizations can be made of *flânerie*'s literary manifestations. By his very title, the flaneur is a stroller. The idea of a stroll stands in contrast with a goal-oriented walk; the flaneur wanders through urban haunts rather than marching off to a specific location. Witness and voyeur to the urban scene that forms his natural habitat, the flaneur is a creature both of the crowd and apart from it. His detached intimacy with the crowd affords the flaneur special vantage points for observation within the city.[25] In observing these urban spectacles, the flaneur's artistic temperament allows him to unearth special meaning or beauty from what he sees. Sometimes this is achieved through a kind of ecstatic union with the crowd, while at other times it arises by meditating on the fleeting glimpse of a city vignette.

Baudelaire refers to the flaneur as the botanist of the sidewalk, and this figure shares significant similarities with another kind of strolling botanist, the nature walker.[26] Like the flaneur, the nature walker takes a journey that is less about achieving a specific goal than about participating in his land-scape.[27] Whereas the flaneur is an animal of the crowd, the nature walker is typically a solitary figure wandering through an emphatically anti-urban environment. However, like the flaneur, the nature walker also embodies an attached-detached dynamic, at times enjoying sympathetic intimacy with his organic surroundings and then, at others, experiencing the shock of na-ture's radical alterity.[28] As a voyeur of the wilderness, his unique knowledge of and sympathy with his environment affords him a privileged point of view. This special perspective can offer him an experience of transcendence, at times terrifying and at others uplifting, as his sensitive temperament al-lows him to appreciate the particular beauty or even horror of the scene. As these brief overviews suggest, the flaneur and the nature walker share a similar plot: a sensitive speaker, both intimately a part of and yet apart from his surroundings, goes on a stroll and witnesses a spectacle that opens up into a kind of revelation. The fundamental difference between these two walking figures is their environment, zones so apparently opposed that one can hardly imagine the nature walker stumbling upon the flaneur, or vice versa. However, in Williams's modern American landscape, it grew increas-ingly difficult to disentangle natural and urban environments, particularly in the space of the public park.

Would a speaker with a poetic temperament, wandering through an American park, observing masses of trees and people, be a flaneur or a nature walker? In book 2 of *Paterson,* Williams answers this question with an emphatic "Yes." In the walking person of Paterson, Williams combines the flaneur and the nature walker in a manner that expresses both dismay at the unhealthy relationship between city and nature, which Williams calls a state of divorce, and hope in the possibility of a right relationship between the two, a balanced and passionate marriage. Williams does so by taking us on a Sunday stroll through Garret Mountain Park. When Paterson "starts, possessive, through the trees," his sense of possession connects to the larger metaphor of marriage between city and mountain, man and nature (44). There is also, however, a very basic way in which Paterson literally pos-sesses the park: Garret Mountain Reserve became public property in 1929, thus transferring from private ownership to the people of Paterson. In 1926, Passaic County formed a parks commission that hired the prestigious Olm-sted firm to design this public space, which was officially opened on July 4, 1929.[29] In its physical arrangement, the park design memorializes moments of Paterson's industrial past while also simulating an Olmstedian pastoral leisure space for local urbanites. While the elemental force of the location remains a prominent feature throughout book 2, the architectural illusion of untouched nature should not be equated with "nature" in this carefully planned and maintained space made specifically for the city dwellers below.[30]

Book 2 begins with a turn to the outside world: "Outside / outside myself / there is a world, / he rumbled, subject to my incursions" (43). By casting both his musings and his walk as a series of "incursions," Paterson initially presents his engagement with the park as a potential invasion. Paterson's walk through the park, and the tread of the crowd, vacillate between a loving caress of the mountain's body ("she finds what peace there is . . . / stroked / by their clambering feet" [54]) and a kind of thoughtless assault ("scratched by their / boot-nails more than the glacier" [56]). The basic kinetics of both the flaneur and the nature walker are therefore morally ambiguous from the start: the bare fact of walking in the park is no guarantee of right relationship with one's surroundings. Paterson then "goes by the footpath to the cliff (counting: / the proof) / himself among the others" (43–44). This elliptical insertion cuts two ways. The lines may be read as a nature walker ascending by a footpath, counting his own steps as a kind of quantitative proof of his nature hike, then realizing himself part of a crowd. Alternately, they may describe a flaneur counting himself as a member of the crowd, a group membership that proves his sympathy with the urban masses and his role as a poet. Paterson maintains a connection to this crowd while then distancing himself in the next lines: "treads there the same stones / on which their feet slip as they climb" (44). Unlike the clumsy mass, the flaneur is a sure-footed poet. However, that reliable step is not on the pavement of the city, but on the stones of the mountain, thus likening the urbane attached detachment of the flaneur with the tread of the ascending nature walker. Stanley Koehler also notes the careful step of the poet in this section, contrasting it with that of the crowd: "The difference between the poet's response to the environment and that of the crowd is spelled out by their actions; the inconsequential scampering, scattering, charging, loitering, and general filtering . . . in contrast to the situation of the speaker" (65–66). However, the difference here, to argue a fine point, is not found in actions. Indeed, Paterson and the crowd are performing the same action: loitering, strolling, and filtering. There is no clear object to the speaker's walk, other than amassing the observations this leisurely stroll affords him. He explicitly states the pleasant purposelessness of his stroll later in part 1: "Mount. Why not?" (52). It is the artistic remove from the crowd, the sensibility rather than the action, that characterizes Paterson as a previously unknown animal: the mountaintop flaneur.

The first sights and sounds on this park ascent are those of the city crowd "laughing, calling to each other," and their sturdy, working-class limbs: "ugly legs of young girls, / pistons too powerful for delicacy! / the men's arms, red, used to heat and cold" (44). These bodies, raw from life in the city and again equated with its industrial materials, morph into a fluid mass that Williams likens to the waterfall: "—over-riding / the risks: / pouring down!" (44). As the city crowd becomes, for a brief, transcendent moment, like the Passaic Falls, the viewpoint of the flaneur merges with that of the nature walker beholding an overwhelming natural phenomenon. The ability of the crowd to become like their habitat hints at the possibility of right relationship between person and place. Yet this is only a momentary glimpse of such a possibility, as Paterson then "looks back (beautiful but expensive!) to / the pearl-grey towers! Re-turns / and starts, possessive, through the trees" (44). The city is expensive not only monetarily but also in the cost of human labor, suffering, and environmental harm. The two exclamation points, visually punctuating the line as the towers do the skyline, stand in uncomfortable contrast. The one following "expensive" undercuts the beauty of the costly scene while the punctuation following "pearl-grey towers" recaptures the sudden apprehension of their loveliness. In the same breath, the mountaintop park is an idyllic space apart from the mechanized ugliness of the urban world, in the tradition of the nature walker, while it also provides the vantage point from which one can appreciate the unique beauty of that same urban habitat, in the tradition of the flaneur. Paterson then "Re-turns" from this view as he turns back to the trees of the park. He does not, however, "return," but rather turns again. Like the pastoral idyll, the park is not a final, stable place of dwelling, a home one can return to. It is rather a zone of excursion, a location an urban population can turn to again, every Sunday, for momentary refreshment, before returning to the city.[31] By spinning our speaker around, Williams complicates grounds of origin. While the mountain seems to provide a natural state that urban civilization can return to, the city below is the actual place of return, and Paterson will descend back to it in book 3. With the small flourish of a hyphen, Williams undercuts a simple return-to-nature solution for urban ills.

In turning back to the park, Paterson begins his walk in earnest. "Walking" serves as both the binding that holds part 1 together and a transitional break between each distinct episode. In moving on from site to site (and sight to sight), Paterson keeps the poem moving. The walk allows this montage to remain a whole of unique parts. The first use of "Walking—" occurs around forty lines into the book and precedes a description of tree clusters and their root systems. This passage condenses the standard conventions of the nature walk: during his stroll, the walker happens upon a natural phenomenon that leads to profound meditation or an experience of transcendence. Here, sand-pine, cedars, and sumac present "roots, for the most part, writhing / upon the surface," leading Paterson to ruminate: "so close are we to ruin every day!" (45). The exposed roots reveal a tenuous dynamic between struggling plants and stripped, dry soil. When this image is taken with Paterson's exclamation, the root-wracked dirt symbolizes a variety of nearly ruined relationships. The grasping roots in bare dirt suggest the people's inability to root themselves firmly in their local surroundings, as well as the thin cultural soil that prevents Americans from flourishing. The push toward the symbolic also makes of the trees a kind of human community: the cedars are "man-high," and the thickets "gather about in groups" of pine, like members of a crowd. The vision of a natural habitat here bleeds into a vision of human culture, just as the vision of the masses blurred into a vision of the Falls in the lines above.

The second use of "Walking—" follows this passage, serving as a transition into the textbook definition of walking, complete with a reference to an unavailable figure: "the leg and opposite arm are swung forward (fig. 6B)" (45). While the first usage of "Walking—" prepares readers for its implementation as a linking phrase between episodes, here it functions like an encyclopedia entry that points to both the appearance of the word and the mechanics of the action. The discomfort of referencing an unprinted illustration captures the oddity of Paterson himself as a walker. While Williams here emphasizes the physicality of walking, sinews and all, the walker is a speaker both embodied and yet disembodied, one representative citizen in the park and yet a symbolic representation of the city. He is, in other words, an individual walking figure and a representative figure of walking that is both present and abstractly absent at once. This embodied disembodiment functions along similar lines to the flaneur's attached detachment. Paterson is, in one sense, just another man in the crowd, and so is part of the masses. In another sense, he remains apart from them in his very abstraction as a symbol of those masses. The same is true of Paterson as a nature walker. As just another park goer, he remains at a distance from the natural landscape, another pair of shoes scuffing the rocks. But as a miniature of Paterson the city, he is the husband meant to achieve union with the female mountain, though he has trouble doing so, and so represents an attached detachment with the mountain as bride. Furthermore, this detailed kinesthetic description of walking makes the mode of movement as much a subject of the book as are the episodes seen on this Sunday stroll. As the textbook reminds us, walking is essentially a collection of small leaps and falls. Williams equates successful jumps, like that of the waterfall daredevil Sam Patch, with successful poetry, and falls, like that of the tragic Sarah Cumming, with poetic failure. Walking therefore emblematizes in miniature the poetic project of *Paterson,* both in its heroism and its pitfalls.

After an epistolary selection from a fellow poet, Cress, the speaker responds to her complaint of detachment and blockage: "How do I love you? These!" (45). Just as the strolling figure in book 2 struggles to maintain a relationship with the feminized mountain, in his avatar as "Dr. P," the speaker also continually fails to connect with the poetess Cress, whose growing distress punctuates book 2 as her letters interrupt the walk. The speaker here turns away from the letter and toward the landscape as an answer to Cress's accusations of his disinterest. His cry of "These!" hovers without a referent, gesturing outward to a momentary absence, as the line is followed by a blank before the next words: "He hears! Voices . indeterminate! Sees them / moving, in groups" (45). "These!" may cast backward to something prior: these trees in the above passage, these walking limbs in the figure, even as a metagesture to these lines of poetry, each a sign of possible love or connection within place, body, or art. "These!" then also flings forward to these voices in the crowd, a group of city dwellers "filtering / off by the way of the many bypaths" (45). Love is embodied now in the masses that, again, move like water, filtered through the planned landscape of the park. The complaint of divorce and blockage is answered by the union of the flowing human mass and the architectural, organic landscape.

However, these promises of union are temporary, and Williams soon after includes the prose account of the 1880 shooting of John Joseph Van Houten by William Dalzell, a property owner who "claimed that the visitors had in previous years walked over his garden and was determined that this year he would stop them from crossing any part of his grounds" (46). This passage contributes to an investigation of individuals and crowds developed throughout *Paterson,* but it also foregrounds a history of human engagement with this natural location. Land on Garret Mountain went through a variety of private owners before becoming a public park, and on this occasion the tension between private and public resulted in a near riot, as "many had come from the city to join in the conflict" (46). The mountain is therefore not excluded from the violent history of industrialization and class conflict that characterizes the city of Paterson below it. The park cannot serve as a natural tabula rasa, a fresh wilderness on which to write a new American culture, mired as it is in a long narrative of human settlement, industry, and violence.

Williams's inclusion of the detail that Dalzell was protecting his garden links this shooter with the arrival of Priapus, the Roman protector of gardens, later in book 2: "the female of it facing the male, the satyr— / (Priapus!) / with that lonely implication, goatherd" (58). The sexually thwarted Priapus, interrupted during the rape of the nymph Lotis, stands as an instance of blockage and divorce within Garret Mountain Park, "Rejected" from the fertility rites of the mountain (58). However, beyond Priapus's function as a mythic figure for sex and masculinity, he is also known as Garden-Keeper and Fruit-Guard. Roman gardens often boasted a small statue of the phallic Priapus with an inscription threatening sexual violence to any who trespassed or stole fruit (Redfield 1168).[32] Dalzell, like Priapus, violently threatens garden trespassers and, even after the land passes into public ownership, this satyr still lingers as a kind of regional deity. The choice of Priapus as one of the local guardians emphasizes that the park is not a wilderness but is a planned, garden-like space that is verdant, sexualized, and policed. The appearance of Priapus elevates the historical narratives that intersect in the park to the level of mythic fertility rituals while also underlining the ultimate failure of that ritual in the modern scene. The "lonely" Priapus is both "persistent" and "Rejected" at once, much like the lovers in the park and like Paterson the strolling man-city in relation to the mountain-wife (58). However, in place of Dalzell, Priapus functions as a protector of the ravaged parkscape, quietly threatening reprisals by his very presence and thus suggesting negative consequences for the misuse of this common garden.

The history of Dalzell's attack on the crowd is followed by another nature passage: "Signs everywhere of birds nesting, while / in the air, slow, a crow zigzags / with heavy wings before the wasp-thrusts / of smaller birds" (46). By following the account of the shooting, this scene mirrors the dynamic of one against many as the mob of smaller birds assaults the crow. Williams here relies on the technical ornithological term "mobbing," a group-protective behavior whereby many small birds harass a larger predator.[33] By linking human mobbing with avian mobbing, Williams spreads influence in all directions, as the comparison uncomfortably naturalizes human violence, another instance of many small animals attacking a single foe, and also turns nature into a cultural allegory, likening the birds to a mob of people. This moment also evokes augury, specifically divining the future by interpreting the flight patterns of birds, and so this moment also hints at the continuation of cycles of violence, both natural and social, in Paterson's future. The nature walker sees how red in tooth and claw the local fauna can be; the flaneur sees the sordid dark side of the crowd. The historically thick backdrop of the park, urban and natural, past and present, holds these views together in tandem.

"Walking—" again transitions from this section to Paterson's adventures off the beaten path: "finds hard going / across-field, stubble and matted brambles / seeming a pasture—but no pasture . / —old furrows, to say labor sweated or / had sweated here" (47). Sankey reads this passage as contrasting the crowd of humanity with a pre- or antihuman environment: "The people as a disorganized 'mass' is one key term in this stretch; uncultivated nature is another. Paterson's walk brings him into an uncultivated field, 'stubble and matted brambles'" (77). However, this adventure across the field, while off the common walkway, is not a diversion into unkempt wilderness. Rather, the field of matted brambles is only a "seeming" pasture as part of a pastoral-inflected parkscape. The reminder of human labor, whether the sweating agrarian work the pastoral style erases or the designs the landscape architect crafts, prevents this location from becoming a stand-in wilderness or unproblematic bucolic backdrop. It is in this compound space that Paterson beholds a vision of epiphanic grasshoppers: "When! from before his feet, half tripping, / picking a way, there starts . / a flight of empurpled wings!" (47). Here, the nature walker literally stumbles upon an epiphanic vision of grasshoppers "from the dust kindled / to sudden ardor!" (47). This revelation, "livening the mind" of the walker, is in part his own creation. It is Paterson's tripping, picking feet that actually disturb the insects and send them into flight. Here, the nature walker does not so much happen upon a transcendent vista that exists apart from him as he participates in its generation. His tread also sustains it: "Before his feet, at each step, the flight / is renewed . . . / couriers to the ceremonial of love!" (48). The "churring" purple mass is an erotic response to the presence of Paterson, the city-as-lover, moving through the body of "the Park . . . female to the city" (43). While the passage at first blush seems rooted in a nature-writing tradition, the occasion is created by the excursion of the personified city entering into his beloved. The vision of love, seen by the nature walker, spreads out and colors later, more urban scenes of attempted human connection in the park. Furthermore, the "churring" love song of the grasshoppers reappears throughout the book, as this cloud converges around a couple during their awkward embraces in the lines following.[34] After all, the park is, as Williams reminds us, a "—park devoted to pleasure : devoted to . grasshoppers!" (50). The punctuation evokes the relationship of an analogy and links human acts of pleasure and recreation to the insect inhabitants of the mountain. "Devoted" balances between a sense of ownership, invoking a space set aside and devoted to certain kinds of activity, and a sense of love, invoking the female park amorously devoted to both pleasure and grasshoppers at once.[35]

Paterson then pulls back from a meditation on the crowd, "The 'great beast' come to sun himself" (54), the better to consider his surroundings: "limited by the escarpment, eastward; to / the west abutting on the old road : recreation / with a view!" (55). This lookout point is limited by both natural and man-made barriers as the escarpment and the road frame the view. In the tradition of the nature walker, mountaintop views typically provide a privileged vantage onto a sublime natural landscape below. However, what Paterson here sees is a panorama of the city in the gorge. The reader achieves that urban vision with him, as the speaker commands us in the rhetoric of a travel guide: "Stand at the rampart," "look away north by east where the church / spires still spend their wits against the sky" (55). The reader is here placed next to Paterson as he guides our eyes on a quick walk about town while also firmly locating us on the mountain at the same time, like tourists looking through the binoculars "chained / to anchored stanchions along the east wall" (55). The Baedeker-like command of these lines makes earlier uses of "Walking" retroactively feel like a hiker's guide through the park. The style is also reminiscent of early travel guides to Paterson and the Falls, such as the 1834 *Traveller's Guide through the Middle and Northern States* discussed above. This modern act of tourism on the mountain is linked to the longer history of Paterson as a tourist destination for those seeking exposure to natural wonders.

Williams resists resolving this scene into a dichotomy of natural mountaintop and urban waste below as the view of the "churches and factories" in the valley transforms into a meshed urban-natural sublime vision. As the eye moves downward into the gorge, the "imagination soars" upward. Yet

The current view from the top of Mount Garret. The neo-Gothic spires seen here, "spend[ing] their wits against the sky," belong to the Cathedral of St. John the Baptist, which was dedicated in 1870. (Photo by author)

this rise of imagination does not lift Paterson away from the cityscape but rather sends him back into the gorge as he hears the "thunderous voice" of the Falls somehow "summon[ing]" the "churches and factories" "from the pit." In a literal sense, the force of the Falls did occasion the creation of this mill town that relied upon the river for energy and the transportation of goods. Yet this mountaintop vision transcends bare history by presenting the city as a creature summoned by the environment, rather than a construct imposed upon it: "a voice / beckons / . . . the voice / that has ineluctably called them— / . . . summoned them from the pit" (55). A natural summit becomes a city outlook, as the city looked at becomes a natural wonder. As both man and city, Paterson maintains this doubled vision as both nature walker and flaneur.

Yet this vision is not, as it may seem, the culminating moment of part 1. After this spectacle, Paterson melts back into the crowd and takes up his wandering walk again: "So during the early afternoon, from place / to place he moves, / his voice mingling with other voices" (56). Nor, as it turns out,

is the lookout point the final summit: "At last he comes to the idlers' favor-
ite / haunts, the picturesque summit" (56). This structure of dual climax
prevents the walk from having a clear teleology. Paterson also does not de-
scribe the view *from* this summit, but the view *of* it, moving from a descrip-
tion of the soil and plant life ("ferns rife among the stones") to the activities
of "Loiterers in groups" (56). The view from the lookout is here replaced
by the more humble act of looking around, and the scenes on these "rough
terraces" are of city folks enjoying a moment of "gaiety" (56): a young
man playing guitar, "eating and drinking," Mary's wild call for a dance, and
the lovers tucked away in their "grassy den" (58). These observations and
voyeuristic peeks into how the crowd is "celebrating / the varied Sunday of
their loves" are achieved by the continued *flânerie* of Paterson, who walks
through and watches this urban population at play on the "blue-stone" of
the mountain (58, 56).

The move from city to park has not, however, enabled the crowd to
achieve union with either their landscape or one another. Rather, the same
difficulties of dissociation that mar life in the city are transplanted into this
green environment. A teenaged guitar player performs "dead pan," suggest-
ing both his link to the faun-god and his inability to fill his ritual role (56).
In his flat affect, he represents a dead Pan in what should be a mountaintop
saturnalia, just as the Italian immigrant Mary bemoans the lethargy of her
group: "Everybody too damn / lazy" (57). Only Mary, whose Italian heri-
tage links her to "the air of the Midi" and "the old cultures," strikes "the
cymbals / of her thoughts, cocks her old head / and dances!" (57). While
the modern Sunday festivities, "the hand holding the cup, the wine / spill-
ing, the arm stained by it" are supposed to reenact "the very old, old upon
old, / the undying" saturnalia, the result is only a fatigued pantomime (58).
The Sunday feasting results in lethargy as the picnickers are "too full to
move," resulting in a stasis that afflicts the majority of the crowd. For ex-
ample, a young modern Aphrodite attempts to woo Mars, "beer bottle still
grasped spear-like / in his hand" in a little temple-like nook with "columnar
rocks" around them (59). However, her lover "moves in his sleep" "and does
not waken," as the "sexless" spying boys, representatives of peeking Cupid,
"go charging off," "bored equally" (59).

Similarly, in part 2, the nymph-turned-laurel-tree Daphne is reduced to
a bathroom placard: "The cop points. / A sign nailed / to a tree: Women"
(63). As the conservation historian Karl Jacoby has demonstrated, the spaces
most Americans associate with nature and wilderness are among the most

heavily regulated zones in the nation.[36] Such regulation seeks to protect the site as both nature preserve and shared recreational space by preventing poaching, limiting and guiding foot traffic, and policing water usage, to name only a few examples. Such rules would seem to protect Garret Mountain from being ravaged by the feet that tread upon her. This muted arrival of Daphne, a tree-woman, again evokes the theme of rape as well as echoing the description of laurel around the mountaintop from early in book 1. Williams's manipulation of the Daphne myth suggests a longer tradition of equating women with nature, as the deixic function of the restroom sign pointing the way is replaced by an act of labeling in which the trees are identified as "Women." In this small gesture, Williams here links the particular women of Paterson with the mountain-wife. However, in maintaining the illusion of wilderness by limiting human interaction with the site (the picnickers cannot relieve themselves just anywhere), the regulations also limit the expression of human wildness. While the mountaintop conveniences maintain cleanliness and order, they lower any suggestion of reckless saturnalia to the level of banality. Williams foregrounds this act of regulation by adding an extra and insistent level of authority. Not only are there signs for the women's restroom, but a police officer is present to point to the sign that points away, beyond the visual scope of the stanza. The illusion of wilderness is thus preserved, as the ladies' room is tucked away out of sight, and punctured, as sign and signing finger remind the viewer of human bodily needs that must be anticipated by park conveniences.

Part 1 also concludes with a sign boldly stating: "NO DOGS ALLOWED AT LARGE IN THIS PARK" (61).[37] In the preface, the poet identifies himself as "just another dog / among a lot of dogs," one "Sniffing the trees" (3). The mandatory leashing of dogs in the park therefore also represents the tethering of vital impulses as well as placing poetry on a short leash.[38] That leash has implications for walking: like the dog restrained by rules, Paterson walks along the path at the leisurely pace of the flaneur, never breaking into an unrestrained run or joining Mary in her wild dance. The clearly legislated leash is matched by the soft law of park decorum: that Paterson seems uninterested in breaking into a dance or a gallop suggests that he has been successfully and unfortunately domesticated. And yet the rules are not always obeyed, as a few "guilty lovers and stray dogs" linger in the park as night comes on (80). Like the dancing figure of Mary, a handful of daring creatures can rise beyond the limitations of their rule-bound environment and achieve a moment of happiness and connection. That moment is achieved both in and against the park. The sylvan retreat invites these freedoms while the police-enforced regulations that help preserve the park as that architectural retreat act against the free movement of dog, city dweller, and poet.

While the limiting effect of park rules, and deadening social restrictions by extension, are to blame for some of the malaise on the mountaintop, Williams returns to Hamilton and SUM in the second section of book 2 for a more detailed critique of Paterson's ills. Garret Mountain morphs from a mythical to a biblical peak, as the immigrant preacher Klaus Ehrens delivers his sermon on the mount. Williams interlaces Klaus's personal testimony about the dangers of money with prose excerpts describing Hamilton's creation of the National Bank and the founding of Paterson, as Williams braids together the troubles of an individual laborer with a larger national history of finance and industry. Paterson walks to Klaus's open-air church to join the crowd for this Sunday sermon: "a cramped arena has been left clear at the base / of the observation tower near the urinals. This / is the Lord's line" (63). Klaus, mediator between heaven and earth, is wedged between observation tower and urinal. Fittingly, this location in the park serves as Williams's observation point as well, as he will cast a long glance back at Hamilton while connecting SUM's industrial program with the lives of Paterson's citizens in all their bodiliness, down to the waste that flows to the river. In this open-clearing-cum-bathroom, a semi-circular church is formed: "Several broken benches / drawn up in a curving row against the shrubbery" (63). While the ramshackle pews stand "against" the shrubbery, casting the underbrush as a limit to the human community in the clearing, Klaus preaches not only to the mostly apathetic park congregation ("Few listen. / Or, in fact, pay the least / attention" [65]) but also to the park, "calling to the birds and trees!" (64). Klaus's warnings about the dangers of profit and soulless labor address human, animal, and plant alike, which is appropriate, given that all are tangled in the same story of industrializing urbanization.

Klaus relates the tale of his immigration to America, his years of hard work, and the money he earned in the process: "I kept on making / money, more and more of it, but it didn't make / me good" (68). At this moment of discontent, Klaus received a message from God: "Klaus, get rid of your / money. You'll never be happy until you do that" (69). After this line, Williams interrupts the preacher with a prose segment summarizing several points from Hamilton's *Report on Manufactures* and then concludes with the beginnings of Paterson: "Even during the Revolution Hamilton had been impressed by the site of the Great Falls of the Passaic. His fertile imagina-

tion envisioned a great manufacturing center, a great Federal City, to supply
the needs of the country. Here was water-power to turn the mill wheels and
the navigable river to carry manufactured goods to the market centers: a
national manufactury" (70). Klaus's unhappiness contrasts with Hamilton's
utopian dreams of Paterson. The fertility of the valley is replaced by Hamil-
ton's fecund imagination that reduces the site to "water-power." The vision
of a natural manufactory results in subsequent generations of manufac-
turers and laborers, the glory of which crashes to the ground as the poem
flips back to the modern scene: a crowd of discontented working-class park
goers largely ignoring a preacher railing against filthy lucre. While SUM's
venture promised wealth, Klaus asks if wealth actually produces a goodness
beyond itself: "NO! he shouted" (68).

While Klaus's torments are the symptom of SUM's disease, the preacher's
act of giving away all his riches and committing his life to God is not pre-
sented as a sustainable option for either the people or the place. Although
Klaus is depicted sympathetically ("*le pauvre petit ministre* / did his best, they
cry"), he ultimately receives a negative reply: "Variously the dogs barked,
the trees / stuck their fingers to their noses" (79). As a parody of St. Francis,
Klaus is rejected by his nonhuman auditors, not only because his personal
renunciation fails to offer more substantive answers but also because his lan-
guage fails to lift the environment, the dogs and the trees, to expression, as
they cry, "No / poet has come, no poet has come" (79). Klaus's park sermon,
while partially addressed to the park, contains no mention of the physical
world around him, and so Paterson's attention drifts, seeking divine beauty
instead in "the view / and a fresh budding tree" (71). As Klaus leaves the
park, his departure is depicted as a death by water in the foliage of the
mountain: "swinging his arms, drowns / under the indifferent fragrance of
the bass-wood / trees" (82). The preacher's blithe ignorance of his failure,
captured in his swinging arms, is met by the consuming indifference of the
environment he overlooks.

Yet if Klaus fails, so too does Paterson as poet: "Be reconciled, poet, with
your world, it is / the only truth! / Ha! / —the language is worn out" (84).
The poet, too, has not yet successfully given voice to his scene with fresh
language and so, with the rest of the Sunday picnickers, flees the mountain-
top: "At nine o'clock the park closes. You / must be out of the lake, dressed,
in / your cars and going" (80). The final park regulation, closing time, re-
veals the fundamentally illusory nature of Garret Mountain. Just as it is no
place for ultimate answers, it is neither a viable dwelling place for civiliza-

tion and nature. The park offers the people of Paterson only a momentary respite from their work lives, and, like Arden, most often serves as a stage for reenacting the same mundane urban tragedies in pastoral costuming. The costly view enjoyed at the mountain's peak is also the poet's nadir, as book 2 concludes with Paterson descending into the dry stacks of the library below.

Williams's depiction of divorce and blockage within Garret Mountain Park echoes similar failures of the lofty ideals landscape architects like Olmsted hoped public parks could achieve. The combination of the two figures of nature walker and flaneur represents the admixture of urban and natural environments within this parkscape and, more broadly, Williams's desire for a healthy union of natural ecosystems and human habitats. Yet, in book 2, that admixture is ultimately unstable. The park cannot serve as a permanent home any more than simply entering it can undo the isolation suffered in the city. However, what the park can provide are fleeting moments of connection between man and woman, city and nature, person and place. The provisional nature of Garret Mountain's consolations raises the question: where is inhabitable ground? For Williams, the difficulty of discovering such ground is part of the challenge inherent in crafting a place-based poetics, let alone a shared American language rooted in the particulars of the local environment. In *Paterson,* Williams dramatizes his own often halting attempt to achieve those linguistic goals. While he succeeds in depicting the drama of this poetic venture and the ecological stage on which it is played, he fails in ultimately bringing about that imagined linguistic revitalization. As late as the third section in book 4, originally conceived of as the concluding segment of *Paterson,* the speaker frets over losing sight of his goal: "Haven't you forgot your virgin purpose, / the language? // What language?" (186). As critics have argued, book 4 is deeply ambiguous, and Williams seems uncertain about the overall success of his sprawling project: "perhaps / it is not too late? Too Late" (186). Is it too late in this long poem for the poet to attain his goal? The answer is unclear. However, just as the park can offer some moments of solace, Williams also finds beauty in even the waste and pollution of Paterson, abhorring and loving the clogged arteries of the Passaic River at once. The cost and the beauty can no more be disentangled from one another than can the human and natural elements of Paterson's environment.

to guide + restrict
tourism + preservationism
fantasy of wilderness

CHAPTER 4

Marianne Moore and the National Park Service

When Marianne Moore and her family motored their way to the foot of Mount Rainier on 25 July 1922, they did so armed with the National Park Service (NPS) guide to this unique combination of live volcano, glacier-topped mountain, and alpine meadow. Equally unique was the polyvocal NPS text, complete with maps, animal and plant identification guides, rules and regulations, hiking recommendations, and advertisements that sought to guide and restrict the experience of park visitors. This tension between tourism and preservationism marks the rhetoric of the entire guidebook, such as its description of the newly added Wonderland Trail. In 1915, this circular path around the peak of Mount Rainier was designed to accommodate the growing urban masses seeking an unspoiled wilderness experience: "Trails have been constructed with a view to making the wonders of nature within the park easily accessible as well as to provide patrol routes for the protection of the forests and game" (*Rules and Regulations Guide to Mount Rainier National Park* 13; hereafter cited as *Rainier Guide*). Much like Burnham and Olmsted's park paths, Wonderland Trail created the impression of wandering in an arctic wilderness while actually restricting human movement in a massive loop of pathways. In her long poem "An Octopus," Moore explicitly engages with the NPS's often conflicted landscape management philosophy as well as foregrounding the invisible architecture of the site. In acknowledging that visiting hikers are only "deceived into thinking that you have progressed" through the circular trail system, Moore positions the entire park as kind of wonderland in which the fantasy of wilderness can be indulged (71).

around base not peak

While Sandburg, Stevens, and Williams investigate how natures built into urban environments complicate distinctions between the organic and the artificial, Moore reveals how that division also dissolves in the national park by foregrounding just how human and strangely citified these last

citified?   emphatically urban animals
nature's circus
wilderness museums
120   BUILDING NATURES   curiosity shows

bastions of wilderness actually are. While national parks are often imag-
ined as the final remnants of unspoiled American wilds, they are in reality
sculpted and managed works of landscape architecture crafted to induce
a nature experience for urban consumers. Whereas the city park sought
to bring that experience within the confines of urban habitats, national
parks preserved it beyond city limits in response to the urban boom of the
early 1900s. These spatial wilderness museums, through their architectural
features, paradoxically simulated a nonhuman environment for human
consumption. "An Octopus" explores this mixture of human and natural
elements in the mountain's seemingly wild parkscape, only to ultimately
emphasize the place of the human in the landscape as visitor, guide, and ar-
chitect. The result is a poem that undermines NPS wilderness architecture
and rhetoric by revealing the way its inherent contradictions are played out
in the experience of the space, specifically in how visitors' guides attempt
to mediate that experience. Moore demonstrates how these wilderness ex-
cursions are informed by quintessentially urban fears and fantasies, thereby
framing the mountain as an object of consumption for the world-weary
city dweller. At the same time, Moore shifts the pleasures and virtues asso-
ciated with wilderness recreation to the rigorous pleasures of reading the
emphatically human text of the park, thereby turning nature appreciation
into art appreciation.

LANDSCAPE ARCHITECTURE AND THE NATIONAL
PARK SERVICE

The seeming unnaturalness of describing national parks as human, archi-
tectural spaces addressed to an urban public testifies to the NPS's success in
naturalizing their creations. However, the first American nature preserves
predate the NPS and responded to a fundamentally different set of public
concerns. The transition from those early efforts to the establishment of
the NPS and spaces like Moore's Mount Rainier demonstrates a shifting
national attitude toward wilderness in response to increasing urbanization.
In this regard, national parks are emphatically urban animals. Prior to the
national realization that the frontier was quickly disappearing, nature re-
serves functioned as curiosity shows and resource banks. The historian Rod-
erick Frazier Nash details these two functions of early reserves in Yellow-
stone National Park. When President Grant created Yellowstone in 1872,
the purpose was not to enshrine a wilderness experience. The landscape

was valuable inasmuch as it shaped city resource management and travel.[1] The forests of Yellowstone play a large part in regulating the flow of the Missouri and Snake Rivers, as they are located on the watershed for both. Protecting the forest meant protecting a source of potable water and maintaining the ease of travel on these river thoroughfares (Nash 113). As Nash and others have argued, early appreciation of Yellowstone and similar sites like Niagara Falls also evoked the idea of a kind of museum of natural oddities. The experience of a visitor to these sites was not that of the bushwhacking pioneer but of the spectator at nature's circus. In the statute that created Yellowstone, the location is first described as a "pleasuring ground for the benefit and enjoyment of the people" (qtd. in Nash 108). This "New Wonder Land" swiftly became a tourist attraction for visitors from home and abroad.[2] As Kathy S. Mason and Nash note, the American anxiety about competing with Europe was writ large on the landscape as sites like Yellowstone, Yosemite, and Niagara Falls were presented as majestic alternatives to the palaces of Europe. American natural curiosities upheld the glories of New World topography over and against European rivals.[3] In "An Octopus," Moore returns to this earlier idea of national park as resource bank and curiosity show or menagerie in her exploration of the parkscape's particularly American character. She also teases out latent concerns over the perceived uniqueness of that American landscape, as her descriptions of Rainier borrow freely from similar travel rhetoric about the Swiss Alps.

By the end of the nineteenth century, the national conversation moved from resources and curiosities to scenic wilderness preservation. As William Cronon has argued, it was at this moment that postfrontier anxieties combined with transcendental landscape ideals to create a new, conflicted national idea of wilderness. On the one hand, nature preserves were expected to enshrine a disappearing moment in American history by protecting landscapes associated with the era of the pioneer: "Those who have celebrated the frontier have almost always looked backward as they did so, mourning an older, simpler, truer world that is about to disappear, forever. That world and all of its attractions . . . depended on free land—on wilderness" (Cronon 71). Of course, it was the industriousness of the American pioneer that imperiled wilderness in the first place, and the success of that generation was manifest in the rise of American cities. As those cities grew larger and more numerous, the next generation sought spaces in which to relive the fantasy of the pioneer in seemingly untrammeled land. On the other hand, that desire intersected with a tepid version of sublime landscapes. As Cronon demonstrates, as these zones attracted an increasing number of tourists who were more invested in an impressive natural display than a mystical encounter with the sublime, wilderness expectations became domesticated. The sublime landscapes that produced awe and terror in writers like Wordsworth or Thoreau created a sweeter and softer impact in writers and park advocates like John Muir (73). However, the general features of what constituted a sublime landscape remained largely the same: mountaintops, waterfalls, and misty valleys. The idealization of these zones combined with the myth of the frontier, resulting in spaces that emphasized a sense of isolation, non- or prehumanness, and semi-sublime uplift.

Preserves were no longer primarily useful to urbanities as side shows or watersheds. Rather, their utility for disaffected city folk was precisely their semblance of uselessness.[4] Upon its creation, the National Park Service was placed in the awkward position of satisfying this impossible public desire for maintained, and yet nonhuman nature, while still negotiating many of the all-too-human commercial concerns attached to natural resource management and tourism. The push to preserve these spaces both for and from the American public troubled the NPS from its very beginnings. The founding of the NPS resulted from failed attempts to negotiate these tensions within the handful of preexisting preserves. Early managers had to compete for scarce funding that was split between the Department of the Interior and the Division of Forestry in the Department of Agriculture, the former of which tended to emphasize scenic preservation and the latter resource management.[5] In the absence of adequate funding, soldiers often served as park rangers, thus also entangling the War Department in land-management debates.[6] To resolve these difficulties, Congress passed the Park Service Bill in 1916 and charged Stephan Mather with heading the new National Park Service. Mason highlights the tensions inherent in Congress's commission of the NPS with both conserving "the scenery and the natural and historic objects and the wildlife" as well as providing for "public 'enjoyment' of the parks while leaving the natural attractions 'unimpaired for the enjoyment of future generations.'" To materialize this mission, Mather increased paved roads for automobile access to parks, coordinated with local businesses to improve park hotels, campsites, and restaurants, and developed educational programs for the public (73).

Landscape architects and park managers were then left with the challenge of designing spaces for both preservation and tourism. Tourists expected a nature experience that suggested the wildness of the pioneer and the sublime vistas of the transcendentalists, as well as recreational opportunities and convenient amenities. Designers created sites with meandering paths that kept visitors from crushing important flora underfoot and from glimpsing the all-too-human lines of tourists before and behind them. Equally crucial in park designs were the scenic lookout points that often served as a sublime culmination of the visitor's walk, in keeping with the narrative of the Romantic's mountain ascent. The value placed on isolated, wild peak views also dictated where conveniences might be placed, often at the foot of park mountainscapes in locations of low sublime potential and well out of view from the trail. The ideals behind these landscapes were much like those Olmsted articulated for city parks: increased health, an invigorated sense of civic virtue, and democratic access extended to all classes. And like city parks, national parks were often incapable of living up to the ideals undergirding their aesthetic. The working classes found the expenses attached to vacationing or recreating in national parks largely prohibitive, and, as Moore notes in "An Octopus," the long lists of illegal activities in park guides, like gambling and intoxication, demonstrates that mere exposure to the parkscape was not enough to foster virtue.

MOUNT RAINIER NATIONAL PARK

Much like the city of Paterson that was developed in fits and starts or the uneven realization of Burnham's *Plan,* Mount Rainier Park was shaped by many hands over the course of its management and public use. The ultimate result was a parkscape designed to conform to public expectations of an American wilderness experience. As early as 1870, local mountaineer James Longmire led tourist expeditions to the summit. The trip became popular enough to require the creation of several rudimentary roads and paths, as well as a hotel in 1884. By 1897, the Longmire family was running a successful tourism business as well as a small mining operation on twenty acres of land (Carr 209).[7] By the time John Muir climbed the mountain in 1888, scenic preservationists were already demanding that Rainier be protected from increased mining, grazing, and logging that were, ironically, facilitated by the roads created for tourists. Cyrus A. Mosier, inspector for the Department of the Interior, helped found the Pacific Forest Reserve in 1893, functionally protecting the forests at the foot of Rainier. Ethan Carr documents how Mosier appealed to a painterly landscaping tradition when he argued that logging would "tear the frame from this grand painting against the sky" (210). Whereas the Department of Forestry emphasized the utility of reserving future lumber stores, Mosier not only argued for scenic value but shifted that value from the forest proper to the "grand painting" of the mountain. The Pacific Forest Reserve serves as only the wooden frame around the sublime mountain. Mosier's image is a static one, as the still frame bounds the unmoving picture of Rainier. This sense of stillness also exposes a difficulty in preservationist pleas. Mosier's goal, and that of his fellow preservationists, was to actively manage the site in order to freeze the alpine peak in a lost historical moment, one imagined through the visual aesthetics of the transcendentalists.

While Mount Rainier was fully incorporated as a park by 1899, lack of necessary funding stalled substantial work on the site for several years. The first major improvements included the repair of existing trails and the extension of roads for automobile use. Under the direction of Hiram Chittenden, the engineer of the Yellowstone roadways, a gently rolling scenic road was installed (Carr 211).[8] By 1915, in response to increasing tourism and public interest, the park's budget expanded, and more than 150 miles of trail were developed.[9] By 1916, the year when the NPS was founded and officially took control of Mount Rainier Park, more than 200 miles of new trail had been laid, including the scenic Wonderland Trail loop. With the new boom in tourism came an even greater need for modernized accommodations. In 1917, the outmoded Longmire Lodge was demolished and replaced with Paradise Inn, a rustic-style hotel of two-and-a-half stories designed by the local firm of Heath and Grove Bell: "Furnished with handcrafted wooden furniture and wrought-iron details, the luxurious inn was everything Mather and the Rainier National Park Advisory Board could have wished" (Carr 217). Those furnishings were crafted of materials sourced from within the park. While new park regulations more effectively prohibited logging and mining, Paradise Inn was built from Alaskan cedar from the Silver Forest, an area that had experienced a severe fire in the 1880s and had turned into a grove of dead, silver-colored trees. Because the Silver Forest did not conform with the scenic standards of lush forest framing the mountain, this unique ecosystem was looked to as a source of lumber rather than an area worthy of protection. In the attempt to design a structure that provided luxury accommodations while presenting the front of the pioneer homestead, the architects harvested from the preserve and removed what scenic preservationists had considered a blot rather than an asset.

By the 1920s, when the Moores made their visit, debates about the proper management and development of the mountain park revealed increasing tensions between the demands for tourism and preservation. Mountaineering clubs, such as the popular Mazamas and the Mountaineers, wanted to maintain a sense of pristine wilderness during their climbs and so lobbied against increasing road access and hotels throughout the park. They did, however, desire improvements for their outdoor sports, such as the creation of the first permanent shelter, Camp Muir, in 1916 (Carr 219). Much of the debate centered on questions of automobile access, as Mount Rainier's proximity to Seattle attracted more automotive traffic than was usual at a national park. Motorists' clubs and the park managers regarded improved traffic flow as a benefit that would make the park accessible to a wider variety of visitors, as well as bringing revenue into the park concessions. In 1922, the Mountaineers went so far as to publish a pamphlet inveighing against the park administration, accusing them of running the park for profit rather than the public good.[10] Park managers were again placed in the difficult position of needing funds from tourists in order to maintain and preserve the park from human encroachment. Pressures from these various competing interests in preservationism, tourism, materials management, and different kinds of recreation continued to shape both the parkscape and the guidebooks that led visitors through this wilderness simulation. Mount Rainier was placed in the middle of these skirmishes as park managers and tour guides attempted to mask the human presence that shaped the site.

A GLACIAL OCTOPUS

When the Moores approached the entrance to Mount Rainier National Park on their scenic drive up to the grand, yet rustic Paradise Inn, they entered into both a wonderland and a battlefield of contested aesthetics, management practices, and community uses. In accepting the Rainier NPS guide, Moore had in hand an American landscape text that testified to these tensions, a text that she would significantly refashion when writing "An Octopus."[11] Unlike the more tacit park rules and light policing of park space in Paterson's Garret Park, NPS guidebooks not only trained tourists in proper park behavior but also fostered the hiker's sense of awe through long descriptive prose passages rhetorically shaped by the fusion of sublime and wilderness ideals. These guides teach the visitor to engage with the landscape architecture in a way that maximizes that sublime wilderness experience through both prohibition and encouragement. By following the guidebook's recommendation to appreciate particular vistas and lookout points, as well as keeping an eye out for certain flora and fauna, visitors are led to re-create a Romantically tinged pioneer experience. Understanding Moore's manipulation of guide rhetorics requires an approach to the document that reveals the polyvocality of the text in its strained attempt to embody NPS ideals while controlling visitors: its inconsistent treatment of authorship; abrupt changes in tone; veiled, often incestuous quotation practices; didactic concerns and poetic flourishes.

Beyond leading tourists to particular locations, NPS guides of the 1920s and 1930s fostered an appreciative attitude toward those locations through the use of remarkably purple prose. Muir's tendency to wax poetic over Paradise Valley, the alpine meadow of Mount Rainier, is typical of guide rhetoric: "It seems as if nature, glad to make an open space between woods so dense and ice so deep, were economizing the precious ground and trying to see how many of her darlings she can get together in one mountain wreath . . . among which we wade knee deep and waist deep, the bright corollas in myriads touching petal to petal" (*Rainier Guide* 9). Such language intersected with the text of the landscape in order to induce an experience of minor sublimity. The scene is infused with beauty, but all sense of terror is gone as the maternal mountain gathers together flowers and hikers in a single bright garland. Rather than describing a shocking experience of the mountain's alterity, Muir conveys a familial and tactile sense of intimacy, as the darling flowers touch the bodies of the wading walkers. The purpose of guidebook passages like these is not simply to mirror park architecture for the traveler. Rather, this kind of prose serves as a pedagogical tool used to train tourists in how to affectively participate with park aesthetics.

Nor were these documents relegated only to use within the parkscape. In 1920, so many motorists clubs, travel agents, and chambers of commerce had requested park brochures that the NPS was unable to keep up with the demand.[12] Guides doubled as travel literature for a variety of different readers, from armchair nature enthusiasts to motorists interested in scenic drives. The NPS published nearly 330,000 pamphlets in 1920, 25,000 of which were for Mount Rainier. In the official *Report of the Director of the National Park System to the Director of the Department of the Interior,* the director complains of lack of printing funds and estimates that "had our printing fund been sufficient, we could have profitably disposed of double the number printed" (31). This broader demand for park guides expressed the increasing public appetite for park literature that disseminated NPS ideals beyond park boundaries. These official NPS guides provided only one source of travel, adventure, and nature writing for an interested reading public. Unofficial travel and leisure books, like those from which Moore also quotes in "An Octopus," not only presented similar materials as their NPS counterparts but frequently lifted large portions of NPS guide text without any acknowledgment of the original source. For example, Joseph Hazard's *Snow Sentinels of the Pacific Northwest* (1923), one of Moore's source texts, paraphrases the *Rainier Guide,* which, in turn, quotes from Muir: "The flowers are so closely planted and so luxurious that it seems as if Nature were trying to see how many of her darlings she could get together in one mountain wreath" (Hazard 532). The result is a body of wilderness literature that obscures the specificity of the original observer while proliferating the same mass of controlling metaphors. When Moore began to write "An Octopus," she not only turned to her Rainier guide as a source but also composed passages in the margins.[13] In her use of unattributed quotation throughout "An Octopus," Moore mimics similar moves in her source archive. In doing so, she frustrates attempts to discover the original source or voice, much as attempts to discover an original, unmediated, prefrontier experience of the mountain are similarly thwarted.

Because contemporary park guides differ so significantly from their forebearers, in both social function and style, many critics have undervalued Moore's source archive in "An Octopus" and therefore have not fully acknowledged the ways she revises and parodies these texts. In investigating Moore's indebtedness to "business documents and school books" (Moore 267), critics often treat those documents, despite their differences, in a uniform manner: as unremarkable, nonliterary texts from which Moore mines quotes without much consideration for their larger context. As Elizabeth Gregory argues: "Moore borrows most often from pointedly unvaluable work," work including "such little-regarded sources as conversations overheard, park documents, and books of the sort we generally consider 'secondary material' . . . the pointedly unauthoritative" (129). Margaret Holley makes a similar observation: "As we have seen, Moore's quotations differ in a general way from Eliot's and Pound's in that hers offer us some unique or special phraseology, often from non-poetic sources, and are thus distinctly free of echo or literally allusion" (65). And yet, value, regard, authority, and literary character are always of a type. Park guidebooks, complete with rules and regulations, were literally and emphatically authoritative in the context of the park, as they employed the weight of law. And, as seen above, guides were also remarkably poetic in their style. These same texts were treated with high regard by an American public interested in travel and wilderness literature.

By downplaying the guides and travel literature quoted by Moore, critics also minimize the social function of those materials. As Bonnie Costello argues: "It is unlikely that the reader has been to this place [Mount Rainier], or cares to go" (87). On the contrary, it is likely that Moore's readers would have been quite interested in visiting a location like Mount Rainier. Attendance at national parks exploded through the 1920s and 1930s. In the first five years of its existence, only two thousand discrete visitors made the trek to Mount Rainier National Park. By 1925, that number had expanded to more than 173,000 visitors, 10,000 of whom came by car. These numbers are restricted to just Mount Rainier. The creation of the NPS was largely a response to the booming number of visitors, which, nationally, was well over 2 million by 1930 (Hazard 178). And Moore would have been aware of these attendance trends. In "An Octopus," she quotes from Hazard's popular mountaineering guide, from which these statistics are taken. Not only would Moore's audience likely have shared an interest in visiting national parks, but a large tourist industry was invested in stoking and accommodating that desire. The Northern Pacific and Union Pacific rail companies fiercely competed for right-of-way in Mount Rainier National Park. As the 1922 park guide notes: "During summer season, round-trip excursion tickets at reduced fares are sold from practically all stations in the United States to Tacoma and Seattle as destinations" (*Rainier Guide* 13). Moore's family joined throngs of tourists on that same train when they boarded together in Chicago in 1922.

One of the consequences of devaluing Moore's archive is a critical stance that valorizes the real, physical mountain in the poem over and against the source materials. One critic who has laudably acknowledged Moore's engagement with the NPS, Jennifer K. Ladino, places Moore in an antagonistic relationship with her materials. Ladino rightly acknowledges Moore's tripartite engagement with Mount Rainier: "Her encounters with the mountain were physical, textual, and intellectual" (286).[14] However, she reads these three forms of interaction as ultimately separable and so presents "An Octopus" as the drama of a natural location rising above and pushing against the rhetoric that surrounds it: "The poem distinctly contrasts nature, as represented by the glacial octopus, with the violence it locates in the time period" (288). Specifically, NPS rhetoric commits a kind of exploitative violence against the landscape it attempts to entrap as an object of consumption: "'An Octopus' . . . specifically implicates promotional travel literature (most obviously, that of the National Park Service) as participating in an 'enterprising,' capitalist venture to exploit nature's economic value" (288). In *Shifting Ground,* Costello comes close to articulating a similar reading: "The sense that we have turned Mount Rainier into a theme park for tourists enamored of the pseudo-rigors of outdoor life contends with proliferating details and jolts to our orientation that the contemplation of this place provokes" (100–101). While Ladino makes an important break from earlier critics who have undervalued Moore's NPS source texts, her reading villainizes these materials in a way that the poem does not as she repeats the gesture of downgrading their literary value: "Thus, these critics don't consider how the NPS is itself a powerful 'primary source,' not a poetic one, perhaps, but an institutional source that is influential" (288–89). More importantly, current readings like these detach the mountain, a prehuman environment equated with an idealized nature, from the NPS and wilderness tourism discourses that Moore presents as an intimate, integrated aspect of both the physical parkscape and the viewer's experience of it. The "proliferating details" that jolt the reader's orientation have their origins in the NPS guides that similarly seek to bring about contemplation in the viewer, just as the physical contours of the site are planned and managed toward the same end.

"An Octopus" is less about Mount Rainier as a raw material fact than it is about how the guidebook crafts the visitor's experience of an architectural space. By foregrounding guide rhetoric, Moore emphasizes the tensions between preservationism and tourism that shape both the guide and the park's design. She presents two interlocking texts, the space and the guide, to reveal how the contradictory pulls inherent in NPS management result in seams and fissures through which the human artificer can be seen. Rather than harshly critiquing this human presence, Moore alternately presents bumbling or awkward human interventions comically and impressive human interventions, both architectural and rhetorical, as moments of fine art to be enjoyed. She achieves this effect through three main techniques of source manipulation. First, she heavily quotes from the 1922 park guide, as well as from a variety of wilderness travel and mountaineering books, thereby studding the sublime face of the mountain with forty-five discrete and attributed quotes. Through this constant snow of quotation, Moore complicates the possibility of direct experience of the glacier by highlighting the several discourses that intervene to shape that experience. Second, beyond direct quotation, Moore also lifts large portions of text from her sources for use outside of discrete quotation marks. Experiences that typographically seem to fall outside of the wilderness script are very often from those same materials. It is then difficult, if not impossible, to distinguish between the voice of the speaker and the voices of the guides, resulting in a textual landscape that, like the mountain parkscape, is permeated by principles of aesthetics and land management that are ever-present and self-effacing. Third, Moore goes beyond acts of quotation by using the guide as a structuring principle for "An Octopus," as the poem follows the planned paths of the parkscape and the directions of the park brochure, while also revealing moments at which the sublime wilderness ideals of park aesthetics fall flat.

MOORE'S OCTOPI

Unlike much of Moore's verse, characterized by regular stanzas and measured syllabic lines, "An Octopus" is arranged irregularly, much like the sprawling arms of the glacier at the mountain's peak. As Patricia C. Willis has demonstrated, the twenty-eight sentences of the poem correspond to the twenty-eight glacial arms extending down Mount Rainier. Willis posits that the poem is also structured "by what might be called various elevations": "It first presents the whole mountain as seen from a great distance; then it draws the reader close to the base and moves upward to the mountain goat near the peak. Next it returns to the forest floor to examine its flora, only to ascend again. . . . At the end, the poem steps back to the long view of the mountain" (249). The structural principles that Willis attributes to elevation and telescoping perspective are actually the organizational principles of the Rainier guidebook. The recurring base-to-peak movement in the guide is meant to be read by the tourist who walks from base camp toward the peak, while noting flora, fauna, and scenic outlooks of interest along the way. "An Octopus" closely follows this textual tour of the park. Not only can Willis's topographical pattern be mapped onto similar sequences in the guide, but the guide in turn also explains lacunae. What Willis does not include is a later section in which Moore interlaces discussions of the ancient Greeks and Henry James with park rules and recommendations. When this section is taken into consideration, the thematic structure of the poem loosely follows the shape of the guide's table of contents: "General description, Mount Rainier's great proportions," "Notes on the wild flowers," "Twelve characteristic park birds," "Twelve characteristic mammals of the park," "Rules and Regulations" (5).[15] Beyond following this general schema, each individual portion of the poem hews closely to the corresponding material in the guide. For example, no animal is mentioned in the poem that is not mentioned in the characteristic fauna sections of the guidebook, with only two exceptions: the human tour guides and their pack ponies, of which more will be said later on. Moore's use of quotation also follows the guide, as early sections of the brochure tend to be found toward the beginning of the poem and later sections are quoted toward the end. The result is a poetic landscape that, like the landscape of the mountain, is crafted in accordance with NPS aesthetics.

The title of the poem and first major image of the mountain immediately engages with the guide's metaphorical language: "An Octopus / of ice. Deceptively reserved and flat, / it lies 'in grandeur and in mass'" (71). Moore's first note tells her reader that "Quoted lines of which the source is not given are from the Department of the Interior Rules and Regulations, *The National Parks Portfolio* (1922)" (273). As critics have noted, Moore lifts the top-down image of the sprawling glacier atop Mount Rainier as an octopus from *The National Parks Portfolio*. However, this glacial octopus recurs throughout several of the other texts from which Moore quotes in the poem, to the point that the image of the frozen octopus functions as a recognized rhetorical topos in the guides. Not only does the *Portfolio* include this quote, but the *Rainier Guide* for 1922 has an entire section entitled "A Glacial Octopus" (9). The *Portfolio* introduces the park with a massive heading, "THE FROZEN OCTOPUS" and explicitly references maps of Rainier: "Seen upon the map, as if from an aeroplane, one thinks of an enormous frozen octopus stretching icy tentacles down upon every side among the rich gardens of wild flowers and splendid forests of firs and cedars below" (85). In *Snow Sentinels of the Pacific Northwest*, Hazard also describes Columbia Crest, the chief peak of Mount Rainier, as "the eye of a glacial octopus" (177). Similarly, Clifton Johnson's scenic tour guide, *What to See in America* (1919), states: "From the snow-covered summit twenty-eight rivers of ice pour down the gashed slopes, reaching into gardens of wild flowers and splendid evergreen forests like the tentacles of a huge octopus" (534). Moore quotes from both of these travel texts later on in the poem.[16] Her emphasis on the "Deceptively reserved and flat" aspect of the glacier, as viewed from above, also evokes the several topographical maps of the mountain found within the guides that are designed to communicate elevation in a flat medium, a kind of deception of cartography. The question is then whether or not Moore, in the title and first lines of the poem, presents the reader with the mountain or with materials *about* that mountain. Critics like Bruce Ross read an impulse toward psychical specificity and sensory detail in the octopus metaphor: "The description of the metaphoric octopus and its environment illustrates the aesthetic conviction and metaphysical imperative to observe the world and to express one's response to it, always through attention to details" (334). But the fine details Moore presents here are those of park documents and tourist guides that attempt to communicate the details of the parkscape. "One's response" in this instance is to echo an already well-heeled metaphor. The result is that the distinction between guide and site begins to dissolve as the visitor's response to "the world" of the park is always mediated by the intervening text of the guide.

Rather than simply reusing the rhetorical commonplace of glacier-as-octopus, Moore fiercely literalizes the metaphor. She plays out the implications of the image in a way that the guides do not: "dots of cyclamen-red and maroon on its clearly defied pseudo-podia" (71). As Johnson's scenic tour guide notes: "Often there are seen on the snow mysterious patches of pink or light rose color, commonly spoke of as 'red snow.' Really each patch represents a colony of billions of microscopic plants" (535). Moore extends the spatial realm of the image into the botanical, another area of major interest in the guides, as the dots of red arctic algae become the suckers on the arms of the octopus. The word "pseudopodia" not only takes seriously this octopus through zoological language but also quietly hints at the very artifice of the metaphor. These tentacle-feet are only *pseudo*podia, and the tentacles of the octopus are no more properly feet than the glaciers are properly tentacles.[17] Moore then begins compounding the metaphors

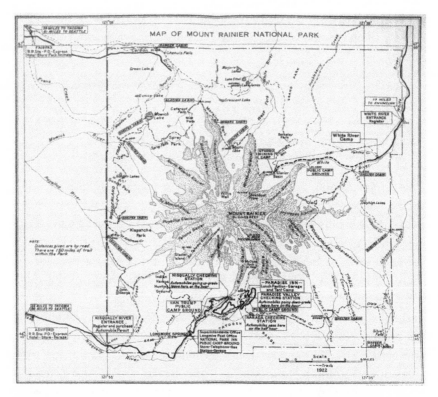

An aerial topographical map of Mt. Rainier from the 1922 NPS guidebook to Mount Rainier National Park. The gray areas represent the glacial fields.

with every line: the glacier system is like an octopus, each glacier is like a tentacle, each algae colony like a sucker, and the ice that forms the glacier is like "glass that will bend" (71). Moore may here be stealthily quoting from Hazard's mountaineering guide, as he describes the glacial "ice fields that are curved and bent" (28). Her note on the line, however, turns readers away from park materials and toward the work of Sir William Bell, who proposed several inventions that would revolutionize the modern world, including "a smooth road surface that will not be slippery in wet weather; a furnace that will conserve ninety-five percent of its heat" and bendable glass (*Complete Poems* 273). By likening the ice to bendable glass, "a much needed invention," the glacial octopus transforms into its own feat of modern engineering, as Moore equates the flexible ice with human ingenuity and construction.

The imaginary appendages then suddenly break free from their static expression on the map as the moving glacier becomes a deadly, compound animal:

> or killing prey with the concentric crushing rigor of the python,
> it hovers forward "spider fashion
> on its arms" misleadingly like lace;
> its "ghostly pallor changing
> to the green metallic tinge of an anemone-starred pool." (71)

This octopus / python / spider / anemone pool turns deadly as Moore renders the slow movement of the glaciers as a crushing attack. Like the pseudo-podia, the webbing between these glacial tentacles is "misleadingly" like a piece of lace, but here the deception is one of daintiness on the body of a predator. Delicate beauty gives way to danger, but a danger that, for the moment, is held at arm's length. Who or what is the "prey" of this monster? The mountain beneath it? The tourist beholding it? Or is there no analogous prey in this landscape for the metaphor to attack? By withholding the referent, Moore simulates the sense of domesticated terror and awe conveyed by the NPS guides as she creates a predator without real prey, a creature of strength but lacking a clear object upon which to expend its energy. Hikers wanted the thrill of perceived danger and hard going, while everyone fully anticipated returning home after their vacation in the park. Some were tragically mistaken in that assumption, a morbid reality Moore will return to at the poem's conclusion. However, here she forestalls real violence by creating an atmosphere of tense uncertainty about the actual dangers involved in visiting the park, as the attack of the glacial octopus remains a victimless affair.

Moore's sources for the quotes in this passage, provided in her notes, further diminish any sense of danger in this NPS version of the sublime. Both "spider fashion" and "ghostly pallor changing / to the green metallic tinge of an anemone-starred pool" originate from articles in the *Illustrated London News.* The first quote is taken from W. P. Pycraft's essay "Good News for the Gourmet" (1924), in which he describes a new dining craze: cala-mari.[18] The article provides close anatomical illustrations and descriptions of a variety of marine creatures often mistakenly taken for octopi (such as a variety of squid) in order to guide both diners and chefs in procuring a tasty and nontoxic morsel: "When 'sauntering' along it walks on these arms in a spider-like fashion, very 'creepy' to behold" (1224).[19] The second quote is actually an elaborated paraphrase from Francis Ward's "'Poison Gas' in Nature: The Lesser Octopus, a Summer Seaside Visitor to Be Avoided" (1923). Ward describes the physiology and habits of *Eledone cirrhosa,* a kind of octopus known to cause difficulties for fishermen and swimmers in some coastal regions of England. He provides two pages of illustrations and a full paragraph on *Eledonae* coloring: "If frightened, an intense ghostly pallor passes right over the animal. . . . Then rapidly the pallor passes off, and the cephalopod is again a deep terra-cotta red" (270). A layer of iridescent tissue below the upper membrane results in a "delicate green metallic tinge" (270). Both sources treat the octopi relative to human needs as either restaurant goers or beachside vacationers, as each links proper acts of zoological investigation with successful acts of human consumption and recreation. In even these emphatically scientific biological metaphors, Moore presents Rainier's glacial octopus as an object of recreational consumption through the use of these quotes. That her readers would be less aware of these articles than of the guides and travel literature quoted elsewhere in the poem induces the same disappearing act inherent in NPS aesthetics. Moore's glacial octopus is presented as a natural, wild creature when, in actual fact, these descriptions are rooted in the same kind of anthropocentrism that the NPS attempts to veil, with varying degrees of success.

The first nonfigurative description of Rainier follows these lines and is another unattributed quote from the guide: "comprising twenty-eight icefields from fifty to five hundred feet thick" (*Rainier Guide* 3).[20] In seemingly breaking from the rhetoric of the guide in favor of more direct language, Moore actually simply shifts among different guide styles and modes, from the figurative and literary to the terse and scientific. Moreover, the quote she does attribute to the guide, "in grandeur and in mass," does not refer primarily to Rainier in the original text but rather compares the mountain to a different peak: "Easily King of all is Mount Rainier," wrote F. E. Matthes, of the United States Geological Survey, reviewing that series of huge extinct volcanoes towering high above the sky line of the Cascade Range. "Almost 250 feet higher than Mount Shasta, its nearest rival in grandeur and in mass, it is overwhelmingly impressive both by the vastness of its glacial mantle and by the striking sculpture of its cliffs" (*Rainier Guide* 7). With this first attributed guide quote, Moore commits an act of double ventriloquism: she quotes the guide quoting Matthes. Like other guides of the day, Rainier's brochure functions as a kind of small nature-writing anthology. Besides numerous quotes from scientists like Matthes or preservationists like Muir throughout the text, both of whom are quoted on the first page of the guide, entire sections are written by a variety of noted contributors, such as park ranger J. B. Flett's "Notes on the Wildflowers" (22–23), and biologist and Department of Agriculture surveyor Walter P. Taylor's "Twelve Characteristic Park Birds" (23–27) and "Twelve Characteristic Mammals of the Park" (27–30). And yet the rest of the text speaks in an authoritative though unattributable voice. Although the name of Stephen T. Mather, director of the NPS, graces the cover of the guide, he has only approved the brochure, and the primary authors (or, more likely, authors) remain unidentifiable. Moore's playful shifts between attributed and unattributed quotation follow similar conventions in her source archive, resulting in a poem whose acts of bricolage are influenced by similar practices in the guides. This glacial echo chamber raises questions about both the authority and cohesiveness of the poetic voice describing the mountainscape. If the poem is about NPS descriptions of the park more than about the park itself, who is providing us with these descriptions? Who, exactly, is our guide through the space? Just as the site cannot be disentangled from the guide, the guide as a whole cannot be cleanly attributed to particular authors or observers, and so the poem fractures across the jagged edges of multiple voices the narrative of a single sensitive explorer achieving revelation on the mountaintop. Just as Williams uses Dr. Paterson to evoke and erase a real walking body, Moore's speaker plays on our desire to make contact with the glacier while never resolving into a coherent climber or well-defined body.

MOORE'S AMERICAN ARBORETUM AND MENAGERIE

In the next lines, Moore shifts from the glacier to the mountain's fir trees as they rise above the "maneuvers 'creepy to behold'" of the ice: "austere specimens of our American royal families, / 'each like the shadow of the one beside it. / The rock seems frail compared with their dark energy of life'" (71). The firs of Rainier are equated with a noble national pedigree, emphasizing the Americanness of the location, but they are also reduced to mere specimens. In this instance, Moore's scientific lexicon underlines the NPS's preservationist concerns. This arboreal sample is all that remains of the once sprawling American wilderness and is therefore in need of protection. However, "specimens" also contracts the acreage of protected forest, as boundless frontier morphs into a small sampling of woodland. For her description of this specimen, Moore combines quotes from both Ruskin and Muir. The first quote, "the magnitude of their root systems," is found in the guidebook and yet does not describe the fir trees: "The root system corresponds in magnitude with other dimensions of the tree, forming a flat far-reaching spongy network two hundred feet or more in width without any taproot" (13). Here, Muir details the root system of the famous sequoia he worked so hard to preserve, especially those found in the Grant and Sequoia National Parks. The original essay, "Our National Parks," was printed in the 1920 *Rules and Regulations for Crater Lake* and was subsequently reprinted in the *Rainier Guide*. Rainier is not home to the sequoia, but in describing the firs in terms of the sequoia, Moore again participates in the nebulous attribution issues found in her park materials. The royal firs seem interchangeable with their equally superlative American relatives, erasing the attentiveness of Muir's particular botanical description by transforming it into a moveable, generic description for any large trees in any park. The object of investigation within the poem is again placed at a farther and farther remove as more and more texts accrue between landscape and viewer.

The second fir tree quote, "each like the shadow of the one beside it. The rock seems frail compared with their dark energy of life," paraphrases from a long passage in Ruskin's *Frondes Agrestes: Readings in Modern Painters*, a 1875 collection of excerpts from Ruskin's earlier work, *Modern Painters*: "Each like the shadow of the one beside it—upright, fixed, spectral, as troops of ghosts standing on the walls of Hades, not knowing each other, dumb forever. . . . [T]he rock itself looks bent and shattered beside them,— fragile, weak, inconsistent, compared to their dark energy of delicate life, and monotony of enchanted pride—unnumbered, unconquerable" (118). In *Frondes Agrestes*, Ruskin combines descriptive passages about the Swiss Alps with a larger investigation of landscape painting and the artistic depiction of natural scenes. Not only does this quote originate from a non-American landscape in order to describe the nobility of an emphatically American forest, but the source text is more concerned with artifice and representation than with the physical landscape. As with the guides, Moore's use of the quote seems to present the forest in itself, when actually several artistic hands intervene: painters' depictions of landscapes, Ruskin's depiction of the paintings, the editor's selections of Ruskin. Like the trees, "each like the shadow of the one beside it," the alpine forests of Switzerland and Washington State become interchangeable environments. NPS guides similarly tout the unique American character of the landscape while constantly appealing to foreign equivalents to bolster a sense of importance and grandeur. An anxiety about the blueness of the fir forest's bloodline turns both the NPS and Moore back to the continent to establish credibility.

The reader's progression through Moore's guided tour of the mountain is interrupted by a direct address that foregrounds the presence of the trail: "Completing a circle, / you have been deceived into thinking that you have progressed, / under the polite needles of the larches" (71). The larches, polite both in a kind of architectural domestication and in their accommodation of the tourist, have helped to mask the trail's circuit. The spruce trees are also "conformed to an edge like clipped cypress," matching the politeness of the larch with the impression of grooming found in formal gardens. Even the needles of the larch are "hung to filter, not to intercept the sunlight," like decorative elements used to maximize a sense of brightness. Like the deceptive map, the shape and placement of the deceptive woodland trail gives the impression of wilderness wandering while keeping the tourist cordoned off in a tight loop. Moore manipulates the use of the second person in the guides, used to direct "you" toward a point of interest, to create a disconnect from the kind of experience the guide promotes. As the reader suddenly becomes aware of the trail, the inability to "progress" up the length of the mountain by this path becomes a type of conceptual failure whereby the viewer has not progressed in an awareness of the artificial character of the space.

The poem then pauses to describe the Goat's Mirror, a lake located near the mountaintop: "The Goat's Mirror— / that lady-fingerlike depression in the shape of the left human foot, / which prejudices you in favor of itself / before you have time to see the others" (71–72). In continuing an address to "you," the speaker stands at a remove from the parkscape. The voice that mapped the glacial ice from an aerial perspective in a totalizing tone when the poem began now slides to the odd absent-presence of guide voice that directs "you" along specific paths. This voice functions as an authority, commanding the reader-hiker through the landscape, while also standing at an increased remove, hovering in a directorial nowhere. However, unlike the guide, the speaker of "An Octopus" is familiar with the landscape while betraying the secret anthropocentrism that colors the tourist's experience of the space. For the visitor, the Goat's Mirror is rather a mirror of the human body, hand- and foot-like at once. As Costello notes:

"Unwittingly, the tourist is drawn to his own image, not to natural gran-
deur, in his experience of the glacier" (84). This similarity between lake and
body "prejudices you in favor of itself," and so the tourist finds pleasure in
scenic views that flatteringly remind her of herself, rather than transport
her out of her too-human experience.

After providing the general topography of the mountain and the place-
ment of the trail, the poem then follows the guide by detailing animals,
birds, and their particular habitats in the park. However, these observations
are not simply a matter of natural sensitivity or observational skill. Moore
takes her selection of fauna directly from the guide's descriptive lists of an-
imals and birds of interest. In these acts of selection, the poem embodies a
phenomenon naturalists refer to as target acquisition. In target acquisition,
when a certain animal is pointed out to a viewer, the viewer then sees that
target to the exclusion of others that have not been designated. Both the
speaker-guide and "you" see only those creatures already mentioned in the
park brochure as objects of interest, and so even an awareness of bears
and chipmunks is an eminently guide-crafted act of viewing. In the passage
following the Goat's Mirror, Moore spends time describing a variety of an-
imals the guide has preselected, including porcupines, rats, beavers, bears,
and a goat (72). The relationship of each animal to its habitat is depicted
in terms of property ownership and land management, as she transforms
the creatures into trenchant natives who refuse to be dispossessed and even
lightly comic park managers. The space they inhabit is the "property of the
exacting porcupine," left to them by "their ancestors," though they share
this inheritance with the rat "slipping along to its burrow." "Thoughtful
beavers" are seen "making drains which seem the work of careful men with
shovels," as Moore turns these animals into a small group of furry park
managers and construction workers. The home of the bears, however, is
obscured from view: "their den is somewhere else, concealed in the confu-
sion / of 'blue forests thrown together with marble and jasper and agate'"
(72). Black bears were protected in the park as early as 1899, and while the
guide states that they may be "found throughout the park in suitable situa-
tions," sighting one was a rare occurrence: "They do not seem to be abun-
dant, and they continue shy. The abundance of cover also militates against
their being seen, and there are undoubtedly many more bears in the park
than one might at first suppose" (*Rainier Guide* 27). The forest cover assists
in the park's continued preservation efforts, as it protects the bears from

the danger of illegal hunting. The "confusion" of "blue forests" represents not an untamed wilderness but an area intentionally underdeveloped according to the park's plan. Moore's bear ambles out of view, beyond the scenic scope crafted by the placement of the trail. This blind spot furthers the preservationist mission of the park, as it obscures the protected animal from view, while simultaneously frustrating the curious tourist.

Following the base-to-peak movement of the guide, the poem rises in elevation to consider "A special antelope":

> it stands its ground
> on cliffs the color of the clouds, of petrified white vapor—
> black feet, eyes, nose, and horns, engraved on dazzling ice-fields,
> the ermine body on the crystal peak;
> the sun kindling its shoulders to maximum heat like acetylene, dyeing
>   them white—
> upon this antique pedestal (72–73)

What Moore here calls an antelope is the mountain goat, listed as one of the twelve animals of interest in the park. While the guide describes the animal somewhat unflatteringly ("shaggy white hair, short unbranched horns, and awkward-appearing heavy body"), sighting one is listed as a special rarity for visitors, mostly for the grandeur of the animal's surroundings and its typical shyness: "Any mountaineer who is vouchsafed the sight of a mountain goat in the park may consider himself fortunate" (*Rainier Guide* 27).[21] Moore duplicates the pride of place given to this creature in the guide by setting off the goat in a frozen etching.

Critics, such as Alison Rieke, tend to read the goat as "[Moore's] astonishing emblem of the power of living magnificence": "The 'shoulders' of the white goat, a creature often associated with base instincts, are regally dressed in 'ermine' and glow as if they had been set on fire with an acetylene torch, intensifying their natural color of white" (165–66). And yet, the overinsistence and high artifice of this "magnificence" petrifies rather than enlivens, as there is remarkably nothing "living" about this depiction.[22] Whereas Moore animated the still, flat image of the glacial octopus, here she flash-freezes the goat that the guide characterizes by its bounding movement. The result is an overwrought, static presentation of what should be a leaping animal, much like the still chintz swan lodged in the candelabra of "No Swan So Fine."[23] The goat is "engraved" on the crystal background

A high-contrast image of
a mountain goat from *The
Rockies of Canada.*

of the mountain that itself is described as a "petrified" mass of vapor. The
"ermine" of its body suggests the black-dappled furs worn by royalty as
Moore first wraps the awkward hulk of the goat in a noble coat, and then
takes to it with a welder's torch: "kindling its shoulders to maximum heat
like acetylene, dyeing them white." Just as the guide emphasized the over-
all scenic effect of the goat's environment, here an atmospheric flash is
needed to dye the goat white (as if it was not white enough already), in
yet another artificial act of embellishment. Moore then places this glow-
ing totem animal on an "antique pedestal," as if it were a classical sculp-
ture. The description is overburdened in part due to its mixed media. The
stark black-and-white palette of the scene combines etching with hints of
the high contrast black-and-white photos found throughout the *Portfolio*
and *Rainier Guide,* as well as the unofficial companion guides. The goat
then uncomfortably becomes three-dimensional as Moore entangles fash-
ion (complete with furs and dye) with sculpture, resulting in a bizarre act
of mountaintop taxidermy. This pinnacle vision, rather than instantiating
a sublime vista, represents the zenith of park artificiality and the stasis of
preservationism by transforming this rare, bounding animal into a rare,
overly precious art object.

Moore follows this frozen tableau with yet another list of animals found in this park habitat, "home of a diversity of creatures":

those who "have lived in hotels
but who now live in camps—who prefer to";
the mountain guide evolving from the trapper,
"in two pairs of trousers, the outer one older,
wearing slowly away from the feet to the knees"; (73)

Moore comically describes this park species, the mountain guide animal, in language similar to that used in discussing the characteristic local fauna. In so doing, Moore punctures the wild landscape with a human presence while parodying the very grammar of wilderness writing. The evolutionary pressure of the parkscape morphs the trapper, once tasked with overtaking the wilderness and its inhabitants, into a later generation of guide possessed of similar mountaineering skills now used for preservation and tourism. To capture this animal's habitat and characteristic markings, Moore quotes from W. D. Wilcox's description of Bill Peyote, a very colorful trail guide, from the mountaineering book and travelogue *The Rockies of Canada:* "He usually wears two pairs of trousers, one over the other, the outer pair about six months older. This was shown by their dilapidated and faded state, hanging, after a week of rough work in burnt timber, in a tatter fringe knee-high" (119). What Moore excludes from her quoted caricature is the next sentence: "Part of this was affectation, to impress the tenderfoot, or the 'dude,' as he calls everyone who wears a collar" (119). Just as the park architecture performs the appearance of wilderness, so too does the guide play the role of seasoned pioneer and trailblazer, complete with appropriate costuming as displayed in Bill Peyote's formal portrait in the original text. In withholding the lines, Moore again returns to a quotation practice that mimics the acts of deception at play in the theater of the park: like Bill Peyote, the park guides perform the role of modernized pioneer for the citified public audience.

This tattered guide is accompanied by "the nine-striped chipmunk," "the water ouzel," "the white-tailed ptarmigan," and "the eleven eagles of the west" (73). While eagles do not appear in the list of characteristic birds, the bibliography of the guidebook includes Paul Fountain's *The Eleven Eagles of the West* (1906). The book is a collection of essays about Fountain's adventuresome travels in the region.[24] The eagles mentioned in the title are not actual animals but refer to the eleven westernmost states. Fountain's work is markedly elegiac for the vanishing frontier experience: "Already, in most

Bill Peyote in full regalia in *The Rockies of Canada*.

of these eleven States, nine-tenths of the game has been killed, nine-tenths of the trees destroyed, a sure sign of the immediate rise of a multitude of towns and cities, and human works of all description. The land can never again be known as I have known it: the past is a fleeting picture which I have endeavoured to fix ere it fades away forever" (x). Fountain here captures the sense of frontier loss in the face of urbanization and the desire to preserve a "picture" of that disappearing moment. The eagles that surround Moore's mountain guide in his worn slacks are actually floating representations of that frontier fantasy. The natural habitat for these flying phantoms is the national park that tries, like Fountain, to capture the wilderness "ere it fades away forever."

The eleven eagles of the West are followed by a quote with an unusual source: "'They make a nice appearance, don't they,' / happy seeing nothing?" (73). In her notes, Moore states that this line was "Overheard at the circus" (273). The spectacle of the national park is here brought back to its roots in the curiosity show by equating acts of park viewing with the spectatorship of the circus. The supposed awe inspired by natural vistas dotted with wild creatures is reduced to a "nice" affair, as that wildness is tamed by association with trained performing animals. Moore then further minimizes the scene into a pleasant emptiness: "happy seeing nothing." "They" casts a long shadow and refers to the entire list of preceding creatures, including the "mountain guide evolving from the trapper," whose descriptive evolutionary lineage equates him with the other animals that have evolved and adapted to their environment. The human is thus caught up in a pleasant delusion as a viewer, actually seeing nothing while pretending to see wilderness, and as a landscape element, one of the circus-like creatures who make a "nice appearance" in the park panorama.

These creatures all gather on ground that takes a dangerous turn: "Perched on treacherous lava and pumice— / those unadjusted chimney-pots and cleavers / which stipulate 'names and addresses of persons to notify in case of disaster'—" (73). The hazardous holes and hairline fractures on the glacier, referred to in mountaineering slang as types of human tools, require that the hiker provide an emergency contact list. Moore uses legalistic language like that found in the rules-and-regulation section to demand these "names and addresses." Here, she closely paraphrases a similar warning that the guide italicizes for emphasis: *"All persons starting on dangerous trips to the mountains or glaciers, unaccompanied by a registered guide, should register with the ranger in charge of the nearest station and give him details of proposed journey and name and address of the person to notify in case of serious accident"* (*Rainier Guide* 20). This warning concludes the section "How to Climb Mount Rainier," in which the hiker is both regaled with the splendors of visiting the mountaintop and seriously cautioned about the dangers of the ascent. These warnings were necessitated by the increasing popularity of the park. Novice hikers often attempted the strenuous ascent, thinking the task would be easier than it first appeared because of the accessibility of the trails.[25] Moore writes the official tone of this warning onto the mountainscape, as the topography, rather than the guide, stipulates the need for "persons to notify / in case of disaster." She here turns the glacier into a kind of park bureaucrat while obscuring the actual danger behind the legalese of the landscape.

The forewarning of serious harm is followed by a comically minor moment of danger as a marmot cries out in response to an unknown scare:

> where "when you hear the best wild music of the forest
> it is sure to be a marmot,"
> the victim on some slight observatory,
> of "a struggle between curiosity and caution,"
> inquiring what has scared it. (74)

The hoary marmot, also known as the whistler, is one of the twelve characteristic mammals of the park. This badger-like animal not only has a "shrill, penetrating whistle of clear quality and decided attractiveness" that is "among the best of the wild music of the mountains," but it also often sits "quietly on some convenient rock as one approaches, giv[ing] little evidence of the struggle between curiosity and caution taking place within" (*Rainier Guide* 28).[26] Marmot and tourist here blend together in anxious acts of viewing and listening. Like a tourist, the marmot is perched on an "observatory" as it attempts to identify some animal or landscape event. The struggle between "curiosity and caution" is also a defining characteristic of the guide's instructions for mountain climbers, as it vacillates between encouraging and warning against the ascent.[27] Instead of falling prey to some natural foe, the marmot is a "victim" of its struggle between these two extremes. The danger is not rooted in the landscape inasmuch as it is a by-product of the contradictory pulls of NPS rhetoric as it both fosters and forestalls engagement with the park.

Furthermore, this tableau of the inquiring marmot is ultimately a rhetorical creation: the park visitor has only heard the whistle, not beheld the scene. The image of the marmot is entirely a creation of the guide that provides visual details and a kind of character sketch occasioned by only the sound of the animal's distinctive whistle. Like the dens of the bears, both absent and imaginatively present to the visitor's view, the marmot's absent presence is an NPS textual creation that satisfies the visitor's desire for a fuller wilderness encounter with the animal when only the whistle immediately exists. As the lines progress, the poem follows the visitor following the imagined sources of the marmot's alarm: "a stone from the moraine descending in leaps, / another marmot, or the spotted ponies" (74). Not only does the progression of alternatives emphasize the tentativeness of each suggested cause of alarm, but it follows the gaze of a fantasy marmot, as the actual whistling animal is withheld from view. Marmot, tumbling stone, ponies, the flower fields the ponies graze in, and the flowers themselves are not physically immediate to the speaker. Rather, they are the imagined landscapes generated by the guide as possible scenes and wilderness adventures. The scenes that follow this imagined marmot's imagined gaze, while dense with vivid detail, all share in the provisional quality of their origin.[28] Even when describing the ground's "moss-beds" and "ferns" in this sequence, the poem has departed from terra firma to travel the fantasy textual parkscape of the guide.

As the speaker imagines the marmot's unknown source of alarm, new and peculiar animals are introduced: "the spotted ponies with glass eyes, / brought up on frosty grass and flowers / and rapid draughts of ice-water"

(74). The glass-eyed ponies mirror their cold environment and icy diet. "Glass" also verbally connects them with the glacial octopus, described at the beginning and end of the poem as a glassy animal. Moore notes Wilcox's *The Rockies of Canada* as the source of the pony reference, but the context of the quote seriously troubles the impression of arctic clarity and sheen suggested in the poem. Moore's spotted ponies are referred to by Wilcox as "Indian ponies." These animals were specially trained and bred as pack animals and were frequently used as trusty mounts for tourists:

> The Indian pony, or cayuse, probably owes its origin to a cross between the mustang and the horses introduced by the Spaniards in the conquest of Mexico. They are small horses with very great endurance and ability, combined with sufficient strength for all needful purposes. Some of them have "glass eyes," or a colourless condition of the retina, supposed to be the result of too much in-breeding. . . . The hardest time comes at the end of winter, when the snow melts and freezes alternately. Then the ponies must starve unless they are driven in and fed by their owners. (130)

Not only are these horses not entirely native to the American West, the children of local mustangs and Spanish horses, but they are ill-suited to arctic environments and rely on their owners to keep them alive in winter. While the pony in "An Octopus" appears at first introduction to be a native creature, in fact, it is a human import used for visitors' recreation that requires extensive care from the park rangers. Furthermore, the glassiness of eye that seems to link these animals to their glassy mountain environment is the result of serious inbreeding brought about by human husbandry invested in creating suitable beasts of burden. Their frosty eye is the product of human intervention, much as the bendable glass of the glacier was first imagined in terms of human inventiveness. Because of the pony's shared characteristics with the glacial octopus, a sense of inbreeding for the sake of human consumption diffuses through the shine and ice of the parkscape with which the ponies are identified. Again, by masking the anthropocentric context of this quote, Moore mimics the guide's attempts to hide the all-too-human pedigree of the park's incestuous noble lineage.

The presentation of the ponies then shifts to foreground that anthropocentrism and the tourist trade that necessitates the presence of these animals: "Instructed none knows how, to climb the mountain, / by business men who require for recreation / three hundred and sixty-five holidays in the year" (74). The source here is again *The Rockies of Canada:* "A crowd of the business men of Banff, who usually take about 365 holidays every year, stands around to offer advice and watch the sport" (116). The Banff businessmen watch a horseback procession out of town as a new group of guides and tourists pick up the trail.[29] Moore turns these lazy spectators of the wilderness adventurers, contrasted in Wilcox with the industry and heartiness of the tourists, into wilderness tourists themselves. Instead of contrasting leisure and rigorous recreation, as does Wilcox, Moore equates the leisure of the middle class with park recreation. The comedic excess of that recreation, a full year of holidays, underscores that these "business men" are people of some means. While the NPS emphatically argued that national parks were created for all citizens and struggled to keep park access somewhat affordable, the class divide seen in city parks grew into an even larger chasm in spaces like Mount Rainier National Park. Despite the democratic impulses of the NPS, working-class park goers were few in number, as a growing middle class was able to afford the travel fare, gear, admission, and time off needed for park visits. It is these middle-class businessmen who, "none knows how," instruct the ponies on how to climb the mountain. Horse trainer and park ranger are cut out of the picture as the glass-eyed ponies take a mysteriously communicated instruction in mountaineering from novices. Even the semblance of wild instinct is replaced by training at the hands of these urban businessmen for whose convenience the ponies have been reared.

These "conspicuously spotted little horses" manage almost to disappear in the mottled arctic flower field at the base of the glacier: "hard to discern among the birch-trees, ferns, and lily-pads, / avalanche lilies, Indian paint-brushes, / bear's ears and kittentails" (74). This mass of multicolored flora, taken from the wildflower guide found in the park brochure, is brought together as both a march of mounted riders and a cut of fabric: "the cavalcade of calico competing / with the original American menagerie of styles / among the white flowers" (74). As with the etched-photographed-dressed-sculpted goat, the meadow is described in artificial terms, both a military parade on horseback and a patch of flower-spotted calico fabric. David Ross Anderson argues that "An Octopus" articulates Moore's republican ideals for the nation as the mountain landscape "is conducive both to civic virtue and [to] diversity because the plants and animals must work together as a community if they are to survive" (39). Anderson reads this particular passage as emblematic of Moore's unifying national vision: "Indeed, the volcano's ecosystem embodies the motto *e pluribus unum:*

out of many, one. The entire habitat is praised as 'the original American menagerie of styles'" (39). However, the "menagerie of styles" refers not to the entire habitat, as it "competes" with the calico field. If anything, the habitat is marked by conflict as the spotted pony is engulfed in this floral stampede. The "original American menagerie of styles" may in fact refer to a collection much closer to the meaning of "menagerie": the different animals found in both landscape and guide as examples of American fauna of particular interest. As with the circus, the menagerie suggests an emphatically nonwild environment with selected creatures on display for human pleasure. The American zoo of the park competes with and is covered by the floral calico, much as the bear disappeared from view in the gem-like colors of the foliage. This competition is not truly ecological as much as it is visual: the tourist's view of the fauna is lost in the entirety of the flora, and thus competition here has less to do with Darwin than with scenic value.

Moore then breaks from this scenic description to contrast the delicacy of Greek culture and apparently robust American wilderness pastimes:

> "Like happy souls in Hell," enjoying mental difficulties, the Greeks
> amused themselves with delicate behavior
> because it was "so noble and so fair";
> not practiced in adapting their intelligence
> to eagle-traps and snow-shoes,
> to alpenstocks and other toys contrived by those
> "alive to the advantage of invigorating pleasures." (75)

The contrast here is not between contemplation and labor, but between different modes of enjoyment and habits of mind: the amusement of "delicate behavior" and the pleasure of the admittedly contrived "toys" of mountaineering. Instead of offering two mutually exclusive attitudes toward recreation and meditation, Moore rather presents two poles that define a spectrum that is negotiated by the parkscape, guides, and visitor. The phrase "Unimagined delicacy," here equated with the Greeks and classicism, originally refers to the glacier in the first sentence of the poem, whose movements and appearance vacillate between hard, rough surfaces with crushing power and smooth, delicate, mirrored surfaces possessed of stillness (71). Thus from the outset of the poem, the parkscape and the guide are already poised between these two extremes.

Critics have read the Greeks as trapped in the realms of Dante's limbo, the only "happy souls in Hell," and contrasted them with the speaker who travels up a kind of Mount Purgatory to the garden of Paradise, itself an echo of the Garden of Eden.[30] However, this reading makes much of the name of Paradise Valley, the official name of the alpine meadow, while disregarding patterns of movement and qualities of landscape that suggest other Dantean precedents. Mount Rainier is not topped by Paradise Park but by the glacier, and so the telos of this journey is much more like the icy center of hell than the lush crown of purgatory. Rather than meeting Beatrice at the mountaintop, the speaker is granted a mock sublime vision of a goat, associated with bodily desires and the devil. The visitor in the park also never makes any real advancement: the two modes of movement are either the deception of the circular trail that goes nowhere or a Sisyphean cycle of base to peak to base again. In making no true progression through this hellish paradise, the park visitor is more like those "happy souls in Hell" than it would at first appear. The limbo scene in the *Inferno* is also surprisingly parklike. When Dante visits the master Greek and Roman philosophers, they gather in an enclosed castle garden that is described as a meadow: "A meadow of fresh green within we found"; "Whence we the whole surrounding scene could view. / There on the smooth enamell'd green" (*Inferno* 30). This courtly garden, an enameled green characterized by the same smoothness Moore attributes to the Greeks, also shares the hard, slick finish of Paradise Valley as Moore presents it after a rain: "upon which moisture works it alchemy, / transmuting verdure into onyx" (74). Limbo, a pleasant though far-off alternative to heavenly paradise, serves a fit analogue for the park, a similarly pleasant though imperfect approximation of American wilderness in which the visitor is happily trapped.

The visitor to Moore's octopus also shares several characteristics with her presentation of the Greeks in this passage. Like the Greeks, the park goer has also "liked smoothness, distrusting what was back / of what could not be clearly seen" (75), including sights such as the "reserved and flat" glacier (71), the waters of the Goat's Mirror (72), the goat "engraved on dazzling ice-fields," and the glassy-eyed ponies (74). This smoothness is also a rhetorical slickness, as the poem mimics the guide's presentation of a shining wilderness veneer. However, the wilderness experience that Moore contrasts with the Greeks cannot be taken as a viable option to cool classicism, as Moore foregrounds the contradictions in the wilderness ideal while mocking NPS rhetoric:

> Bows, arrows, oars, and paddles, for which trees provide the wood,
> in new countries more eloquent than elsewhere—
> augmenting the assertion that, essentially humane,
> "the forest affords wood for dwellings and by its beauty
> stimulates the moral vigor of its citizens." (75)

Here, Moore links American eloquence with unsustainable attitudes toward the land. The list of "Bows, arrows, oars, and paddles" not only gestures backward, into a pioneering past, but also points to gear used for recreation in the park, while additionally suggesting the future of deforestation. While the noble firs of Mount Rainier Park enjoy special protection, the wilderness "toys" played with in the parkscape are constructed of less fortunate trees that "provide the wood." Moreover, the wild forest is made "essentially humane," both in terms of resource management and scenic value. The "moral vigor" of the pioneer is here tied to the acts of deforestation and settlement that eventually destroy his particular habitat and raison d'être, just as the use of "wood for dwellings" in turn will eventually destroy the "beauty" of the sylvan scene.

Moore then compares the remote "wisdom" of the Greeks to the rules and regulations of the guide, "odd oracles of cool official sarcasm" (75). She quotes at length from the prohibitions listed at the back of the guide:

> where "guns, nets, seines, traps and explosives,
> hired vehicles, gambling and intoxicants are prohibited;
> disobedient persons being summarily removed
> and not allowed to return without permission in writing." (75)[31]

Not only are the legislative tools required to preserve the morally invigorating landscape here laid bare, as the *Rainier Guide* excludes hunting tools from the toy box of wilderness games, but that moral power is undermined. Despite the claims of park designers and nature enthusiasts, simply beholding the uplifting parkscape is an insufficient guarantee of moral uplift, as the guide must explicitly prohibit gambling and drunkenness. The consequence of breaking these rules is expulsion from the garden. Moore scholars have linked this expulsion with Adam's exile from Eden. For example, Gregory reads the poem as a Genesis narrative in miniature: "These poems, which each involve the fall, the garden, and Adam and Eve, both take up where *Paradise Lost* leaves off: 'An Octopus' tells the story of life in exile from Eden" (175). And yet, Moore's inclusion of the exile's modification, "not allowed to return without permission in writing," contrasts the justice of God with the tedium of the park manager in the act of likening them. Just as hunting and drinking hardly amount to the gravitas of original sin, the attempt at gravitas in the guide is undermined by both its insistence and its bureaucratic loopholes (any sin against regulations is forgivable with the proper paperwork). In its analogy to heaven, the park falls short, just as the park goer makes a poor Adam: "such power as Adam had and we are still devoid of" (75). Park and visitor both fail to live up to the ultimate pastoral of our first garden.

The poem concludes with a last remote look at the mountain, prefaced by a reflection on the required habits needed to make the climb:

> It is self-evident
> that it is frightful to have everything afraid of one;
> that one must do as one is told
> and eat rice, prunes, dates, raisins, hardtack, and tomatoes
> if one would "conquer the main peak of Tacoma (75)

The "you" of early stanzas is replaced by the noncommittal and official "one." Just as the marmot fantasy placed immediate experience at a distance, here the poem eschews an actual mountain climb in favor of an abstract consideration of the requirements for such an endeavor. Again, Moore captures that consideration in terms of the guide, as she poaches from the climbing regulations without attributing her source. "How to Climb the Mountain" concludes with a long discussion about the appropriate diet for climbers: "Beef, tea, lean meat, all dry breakfast foods, cocoa, sweet chocolate, crackers, hardtack, dry bread, rice, raisins, prunes, dates, and tomatoes are all in order. The simpler the diet, on the whole, the more beneficial it is likely to be" (*Rainier Guide* 20). While nothing seems particularly frightful about this diet at first, the guide threatens catastrophe if the hiker fails to keep to these recommendations: "Moderation in diet and the avoidance of heavy food [of] any sort are precautions that can not be too urgently recommended. One should bear in mind that he is preparing for the most heroic kind of athletic work, and that such work is impossible on the conventional diet followed by most people" (*Rainier Guide* 20). The very heroism of the explorer is here bound up with this diet, and so the management of one's body through food becomes both an exercise in the virtue of temperance and the hook on which the success of the ascent hangs. So too is the overwhelming landscape replaced by an overwhelming textscape of compounding recommendations, mandates, rules, and procedures.

It is also unclear why, if eating prunes and dates is frightful, "one" is frightful as well: "it is frightful to have everything afraid of one" (75). The guide seems to suggest the exact opposite; the hiker has cause to be afraid of every slight feature of the glacier while hiking, not the other way around. However, this passage follows Moore's quotation of the guide's sundry prohibitions against hunting, fishing, and gambling. Her proffered sample of regulations is quite modest compared to the comprehensive five-page section given over to enumerating the dos-and-don'ts of the park (*Rainier Guide* 37–41). The presence of such regulations situates the visitor as an object of fear, an animal requiring careful management lest it harm itself or the parkscape. The fear over these "disobedient persons," an anxiety that possessed park managers as expressed in their detailed rules and regulations, is then written onto the land, as "everything," from marmots to red glacial algae, fears the equally terrified encroachment of the hiker. Situated between curiosity and caution, the visitor anxiously tries to enact park preservationism while indulging in his own act of recreation. Rather than resolving this impossible tension, Moore makes the human hiker as much a fantasy as the marmot, thereby leaving the poem frozen in indecision as the speaker can only ruminate about what "one would" have to do in order to reach the main peak, rather than actually attempting the task.

The glacial octopus, beyond fearing the hiker, also suffers from the stillness and distance required by this preservationist impulse:

> damned for its sacrosanct remoteness—
> like Henry James "damned by the public for decorum";
> not decorum, but restraint;
> it is the love of doing hard things
> that rebuffed and wore them out—a public out of sympathy with
>   neatness. (75–76)

The prohibitions of the guide take on religious proportions, as the mountain is both protected and damned to solitary confinement by holy laws against encroachment. Like the speaker, rebuffed by the difficulty of the ascent and the weightiness of these prohibitions, the American public fails to take up the hard task of reading the decorous, restrained work of James. Hiking and reading coalesce around difficult texts, both characterized by "Neatness of finish!" (76). Rather than a phenomenological text of unmediated confrontation with a mountain, the text Moore presents in the poem as an analogue to James is an object as monstrous and many-armed as the octopus, while possessed of a similar shine and smoothness. NPS rules, travel brochures, animal and plant identification guides, nature photography, landscape architecture, mountaineering regulations, preservationism, materials management, and tourism collide in the very contours of the space and the visitor's experience of it. The result is a mountain as text whose sticky tentacles cannot be cleanly removed from the several other texts that shape both it and our acts of viewing, traversing, and dreaming about it. The poem is American and Greek at once in its aesthetic, exploring the uneven, rocky, and contradictory principles of the NPS that are behind the smooth, glassy, even presentation of both glacier in particular and wilderness in general.

Moore is able to satirize the roughness lurking behind the NPS, and the times it uncomfortably comes to the fore, while enjoying the smooth facade for the thing it is: not nature *in ipsa,* but an art object beautiful for its neatness and difficulty. Such appreciation can be obtained by recognizing, rather than ignoring, the human presence that both crafts and moves through the crafted landscape: "Neatness of finish! Neatness of finish! / Relentless accuracy is the nature of this octopus / with its capacity for fact" (76). The glacier is described not as a natural phenomenon, but like a neatly finished painting or sculpture, imagined as a designed product in even elemental wear and tear: "planned by ice and polished by the wind." Nature, as in a particularly American vision of the vanishing frontier, is replaced by "relentless accuracy" and "capacity for fact." Again, the object possessed of these qualities hovers somewhere between embodied location and rhetorical node, as the image of the glacial octopus, that favorite metaphor of Rainier guides and tour books, returns for a final appearance. "Relentless accuracy" and "capacity for fact" are descriptions not only of the mountain but also of the encyclopedic NPS guides and travel literature at their best.

They are also qualities not to be taken lightly, as the octopus stretches out "its arms seeming to approach from all directions," and a final aerial view combines with a last threatening posture by the mountain-guide-creature:

> the glassy octopus symmetrically pointed,
> its claw cut by the avalanche
> "with a sound like the crack of a rifle,
> in a curtain of powdered snow launched like a waterfall." (76)

This final vision of the mountain combines glassy, still symmetry with the rough-cut claw shaped by the kinetic avalanche, both brought into balance *humanized the landscape*

by the overarching submarine imagery. The final, neat vision of that avalanche is achieved through humanizing language. The sound of the snow shifting is likened to the report of a hunter's gun, as the deadly avalanche resolves into both a decorative curtain of powder and a scenic waterfall for an arctic vista dangerous and fine at once. Moore sends us back to where we started, beholding the delicate and deadly glacial monster that we understand only through our own most human values. While the hiker has not progressed spatially through the wonderland of Mount Rainier National Park (indeed, with so many unrealized, imagined turns, it is unclear what ground the poem truly lands on), the octopus that is the poem has slowly progressed. It has done so by playfully picking apart NPS and travel rhetoric to expose the flaws and enjoy the occasional artful pleasures of this anxious wilderness fantasy built for a nation of city dwellers. The aesthetic awareness Moore brings to this crafted habitat serves as an invitation to progress in our understanding of national parks as complex, tentacled material texts, rather than succumbing to the deception of the seemingly natural.

Afterword

Like many modern art movements, landscape architecture has a fondness for declarations and manifestos. The bold claims made by the likes of Burnham and Olmsted pale in comparison to the 1966 Declaration of Concern penned by a cohort of environmentally minded landscape designers. By this time, the political, nationalistic, regional, and aesthetic values of the first generation of planners had expanded to a biospheric scale in response to an alarming ecological crisis. While early landscape architects linked the success of the American experiment with the success of their practice, the authors of the 1966 Declaration argued that "A key to solving the environmental crisis comes from the field of landscape architecture, a profession dealing with the interdependence of environmental processes" (Miller, "Declaration"). While their focus was still largely American and urban—the authors use American cities as evidence of ongoing pollution—the writers of the Declaration tasked landscape architects with nothing less than saving the planet. The initial response was the creation of the Landscape Architecture Foundation (LAF), now one of the leading professional organizations for landscape architects worldwide.

In June 2016, the LAF convened a summit to draft "The New Landscape Declaration." The need for this fresh declaration of purpose stems in part from an ongoing disciplinary anxiety, as old as the profession itself. As Richard Weller, a leading landscape architect and urban designer, bluntly asks in the title of his recent article: "Has Landscape Architecture Failed?" Arguably, the field has made little measurable impact in addressing the global environmental crisis, let alone generating a democratic American utopia, for reasons often far beyond the control of its practitioners. Like Burnham and Olmsted, contemporary landscape architects must watch as a grindingly slow political process dismantles their sweeping plans into smaller, cheaper bits of municipal work. And while landscape architects think of their work in terms of entire urban systems or bioregions, officials tend to utilize the skills of engineers or urban planners for big projects, leaving landscape architects the tiny terrain of individual parks and gardens. Nonetheless, Weller views the new declaration as an opportunity to reflect on the gap between the profession's altruistic goals and its ability to achieve them: "Consequently, we must ask if McHarg and his colleagues were justified in placing such a tremendous responsibility on the shoulders of landscape architects, why we have we failed so spectacularly to live up to their challenge?" ("Failed"). But the question behind the question is just as provocative. *Were* the authors of the 1966 Declaration justified in casting landscape architecture as an environmental cure-all?

Weller acknowledges that there are several good reasons to say no: the crisis is too large; it requires a massive global response; as a symptom of modern industrialism, environmental harm cannot be remediated by any single profession. Laudably, Weller and the LAF are not daunted by these obstacles and refuse to fall back on them as excuses. The 2016 "New Landscape Declaration" casts landscape architecture as an answer to the intertwined environmental and socioeconomic catastrophes facing the global community. The LAF reiterates landscape architecture's value in solving these problems because of its inherent multidisciplinarity that straddles the nature-culture divide: "As designers versed in both environmental and cultural systems, landscape architects are uniquely positioned to bring related professions together into new alliances to address complex social and ecological problems. Landscape architects bring different and often competing interests together so as to give artistic physical form and integrated function to the ideals of equity, sustainability, resiliency and democracy" (LAF, "New Landscape Declaration"). As with the earliest articulations of the profession, the "New Landscape Declaration" links an artistic practice with the realization of idealized democratic goals. But here, the scope stretches far beyond an American context as it considers both a planetary biosphere and a global economic and political community. However, while acknowledging the necessary diversity of that international human community, as well as the unique features of regional biomes, the Declaration also assumes a universal human desire for a connection with spaces coded as nature: "We vow to create places that nourish our deepest needs for communion with the natural world and with one another." But what counts as the "natural world," especially in a multicultural context?

As Weller demonstrates, the profession has had to adapt to developing, and often conflicting, understandings of nature, an ongoing theoretical debate that characterizes the current Declaration. He locates the 1980s as the moment when landscape architects began asking: "Design with which nature exactly and according to whose values?" ("Failed"). If the goal was no longer to preserve, let alone design, a stable, pastoral-inflected vision of nature embedded in a Western experience, what would the art objects and built environments of landscape architecture look like? Correspondingly, as the field of ecology developed, holistic models of ecosystem as either healthy organism or peak equilibrium gave way to resilience models and chaos theory. Weller advocates a form of landscape architecture where sustainability, a term that suggests a static, pinnacle state of nature, is replaced by resilience: "Rather than working deductively—as sustainable development principles might—to superimpose an image of 'good' upon a place and then work to reshape that place in a preferred image, resilience theory works from the local asset base outwards." The result is a design that never achieves a stable, finished form but that seeks to optimize the robustness of a constantly changing system. (Although Weller emphasizes the postmodernity of such an approach, it is an urban ecological vision the likes of which Carl Sandburg was performing a century ago.) Indeed, the LAF's "New Landscape Declaration" captures this contested moment in the profession by simply resolving these competing terms by placing them side by side in a call to "equity, sustainability, resiliency and democracy." And even the ecological theory of resilience dodges the issue: resilience, ultimately, for whom? And how would we recognize a state of resilience to begin with? The danger is that this term becomes the new nature without our even realizing it.

What's provocative in the context of this exploration is the amount of common, albeit ever-shifting ground shared by landscape architecture and ecocritics or scholars in the environmental humanities. Many of the questions raised above are familiar to those who have tracked nearly parallel debates in ecocritical circles. My goal here is not to solve these quandaries (a task that requires its own book, if not the work of one's lifetime). Hence an afterword rather than a conclusion. In the words of the architect Ignasi de Solà-Morales, this rhetorical space is a *terraine vague:* the indeterminate, wasted urban space that escapes the controlling efforts of design and regulation while receiving its very identity in opposition to the planned landscape that bounds it.[1] Most city dwellers are familiar with these abandoned, irregular plots and their admixtures of cyclone fencing, broken bottles, dandelions, and feral cats. Like an afterword, it is internal and external to the city at the same time, located within and yet falling outside of the controlling logic of its surroundings. It is the kind of space that tempts the architect in its potential, while its lack of formal shaping invites anxieties about the similar civil disorder that might play out in this unstructured nowhere. The architecture of the preceding literary analysis feels like it should incorporate the ecological and political virtues of these poems and places, with critiques of ways their vision fails in our contemporary environmental discourse. But what I have offered here is a descriptive analysis of a moment in American verse and public space. My goal has not been to uphold that moment, or the poetic texts arising from and commenting upon it, as morally correct or environmentally desirable. I would not, for example, critique Daniel Burnham's view of nature by saying that it should be more like Carl Sandburg's or the Sierra Club's or deep ecology's view of nature.

My hesitation to do so comes from disciplinary concerns about how we do what we do in the environmental humanities. The temptation for ecocritics has always been to import our particular shade of environmentalism into our readings, so that what counts as "green" literature is that which conforms to our ideas of good ecology. Likewise, environmentally "bad" or harmful literature deviates from that ideal. In *The Future of Environmental Criticism,* Lawrence Buell captures the danger of this importing/exporting act: "Although there is something potentially noble about human attempts to speak ecocentrically against human dominationism, unless one proceeds very cautiously there soon becomes something quixotic and presumptuous about it too. All too often, arguments about curbing species self-interest boil down to setting limits you mostly want to see other people observe" (8). And excellent work has been done to avoid just such a quixotic tumble. In his preface and introduction to *The Ecology of Modernism,* Joshua Schuster emphasizes that judging modern poetry against our contemporary ecological ideals is both anachronistic and unhelpful. As his lucid history of the origins of ecology illustrates, ecosystems, and the quadrat method on which ecology is based, are human boundaries designed to facilitate the *descriptive* study of material interactions (or we may follow Karen Barad and say *intra*-actions) as observed within that bounded space-time. And, as Dana Phillips would also remind us, our popular notions of ecology, with a lexicon grounded in health and disease, are based on an older, now quite outdated model in which the ecosystem was metaphorically likened to an organism, one that could be sick or well. But ecosystems are not animals and have no ideal state in and of themselves. Hence the italics above. Ecology is *descriptive, not prescriptive*. It can observe what happens in the ecosystem it defines, but whether or not any given happening is labeled as desirable is an inevitably human intervention. I regard my approach to these texts as therefore deeply ecological not just in its focus on spaces and material systems but in its primarily observatory stance. The readings of these landscape texts, whether literary or spatial, unearths what kinds of natures they construct, critique, or eschew, without valorizing any given one as the right state of material affairs.

This is not to say, however, that this investigation of built natures is without consequence in current environmental conversations but rather that those consequences belong in this *terraine vague* rather than in the official boulevards of the preceding analysis. Indeed, the poetry boasts a unique relevance as the locations explored by the poets persist today and continue to present communities with civic and environmental quandaries. Burnham's lakefront parks and Olmsted's greenswards continue to suggest wholesome, nonhuman environments in the densely populated zones many of us call home. The promise of scenic vistas extended by the NPS still masks the busy acts of human intervention needed to create these panoramas for visitors fleeing from urban centers. And the difficulties of these spaces, as presented by the poets, also persist. Urban habitats are still largely unhealthy environments for a variety of life, including humans. City parks continue to testify to class tensions rather than ameliorating them. National parks remain prohibitively distant and costly for large portions of the population.

One of the major environmental consequences of these readings is an invitation to abandon a land ethic invested in the preservation or reclamation of a pristine nature that is more the child of our nostalgia than its own reality. The poetic awareness of artifice found throughout the works of these poets summons the specter of the artificer responsible for shaping our cities, parks, and nature preserves. That awareness has potential consequences for the way American communities continue to shape and use those habitats. If nature persists in the American imagination as a zone apart from and diametrically opposed to the city, American environmentalism is reduced to preserving animals and landscapes "out there" while it fails to address adequately that densest of human environments, the city. We increasingly need an environmentalism that embraces the possibility of sustainable urban living as a vibrant solution to ecological disaster. A modern ecology, whose root comes from the Greek οἶκος, meaning "household," must be grounded in the very sediment, grout, and brick of our homes. For the bulk of us in the United States, and for the community with the greatest environmental impact, that home is to be found within the limits of a city or suburb.

Emphasizing the city as a node of interactions intimately existing within wider ecosystems can better enable environmentalists to mobilize urban dwellers, a population that comprises the majority of world consumers and nearly 80 percent of the American population. For example, in the world of urban sustainability movements where these conversations are taking place, one marks continuing divisions between what Alex Steffen has called dark green and bright green environmentalism. Dark green environmentalism generally takes a wary stance toward human technology and industrialism while valorizing direct contact with the land. The bright green movement, as the name implies, argues for increasing technological innovation to create sustainable futures for industry and urbanism. If the deep green utopian city looks more like a colonial farming community, the bright green vision is something closer to a zero-impact, ultradense metropolis the likes of which dot science-fiction landscapes. There are many shades of green on this spectrum, but the poles of the debate are cast as a tension between nature and technology, the organic and the mechanic.

What our poets would remind us is that such distinctions are ultimately unreal in a modern American context. No landscape unsullied by the touch of the human exists; no unshaped plot is possible. The question actually revolves around tool usage, design, and outcomes. Whether we live in a log cabin or a smart LEED apartment, use a hoe or a self-monitoring hydroponic system matters less than how we define desirable outcomes and how our tools and designs help us achieve those goals. A modern environmentalism is inevitably Promethean and human; the question is only one of degree. Reframing the conversation along these lines could help designers, community organizers, and environmentalists work from more shared common ground.

The representation of built natures in the poetry reminds us that we must be held accountable for the consequences of the natures we build. Such accountability becomes even more urgent when we undertake new acts of management, planning, and preservation, even when that means shoring up earlier ones. Consider, for example, the afterlives of the spaces presented by these poets. On 7 November 2011, the National Park Service officially dedicated Passaic Falls Park in Paterson, New Jersey, in an attempt to save the location from continued pollution. The Park Service was also tasked with preserving the remnants of the early mills, themselves once the source of that pollution, from either development or total decay. NPS materials describing the park demonstrate this juggling act between natural and cultural preservation. The official park website describes the landscape in a way that erases any tension between the site's industrial past and ongoing environmental harm: "Waterfalls and ancient geology, engineering landmarks and the economic birth of a new nation—these are just a few of the things you will discover on your visit to the City of Paterson and the Paterson Great Falls National Historical Park" ("Plan Your Visit").

The same month in 2011 that Paterson's old mills came under the purview of the NPS, the Environmental Protection Agency accepted the City of Chicago's new water safety plan. The city government would have faced massive fines unless it took steps to decrease the hazardous bacterial load in the Chicago River. Once considered an engineering marvel, the submerged concrete bed at the river's bottom prevents the safe decomposition of sediment. Currently, the Arrgone National Laboratory is in the third year of a seven-year mapping project that tracks the river's bacterial cycles. While declared safe enough now for boating, Chicagoans are still cautioned against swimming in or eating fish from the river. At the same time, the city is developing and extending the Chicago Riverwalk, a green pedestrian trail that connects the river with the lakefront park system first proposed by Burnham. The design consists of several "rooms," or platforms, overlooking the river, connected via a series of pedestrian arcades. The Riverwalk, also known as Chicago's "Second Lakefront," offers a seamless pedestrian path from the river downtown all along Lake Michigan (Koziarz, "Riverwalk Expansion").

While the Audubon Society offers birding excursions in the shadow of skyscrapers on riverside trail in Chicago, on the West Coast, webcams keep live watch on Mount Rainier's snowcapped peak, as well as the parking lot below. Compared to surveys first taken in 1913, the glacier has lost over a quarter of its volume due to the rising temperatures of global warming. The original survey by Matthes and the same glacial map found in Moore's Rainier guide are used as comparison points for contemporary aerial images of the glacier to help geologists determine the rate of melt. In 2011, that melt rate was so high that rivers connected to the glacier flooded onto the roads and bridges in the park as the newly freed glacial sediment rolled downhill. Concrete piers were placed around Longmire lodge to keep the rising levels of the Nisqually River from destroying the historic cabin. As summer comes to Mount Rainier, rangers brace themselves for peak tourism season as the alpine flowers begin to bloom. Nearly every interested hiker will arrive to see this colorful alpine garland by car. The park's website, the modern guidebook equivalent, warns travelers: "Parking is limited in many areas of the park. Wait times at the Nisqually and White River Entrances can be up to an hour on the very busiest summer weekends and holidays" ("Operating Hours & Seasons").

In 2016, while motorists jammed the gates of Rainier and the LAF summit met in Philadelphia, the residents of Hartford celebrated the annual Rose Festival in Elizabeth Park. Members of the Friends and Enemies of Wallace Stevens recited his poetry feet from the rustic arbor. Dedicated staff and volunteers worked to make the weekend another success, even as the park conservancy faces another year of difficult decisions. Many of Wirth's original wooden rose arches need to be repaired or replaced, and there is also a pressing need for a permanent stage structure at the end of the lawn adjacent to the rose garden to accommodate the many cultural events held in the park. The roses also took a hit during harsh winters in 2014 and 2015, particularly the climbers that usually smother Wirth's arches, so funds must be diverted to save or replace the blighted stock. The conservancy is looking to collaborate with a new landscape architecture firm to help them create a master plan that will guide decisions such as these in the future.

Should traffic be restricted in Mount Rainier National Park for preservation concerns, or should roads be increased and modernized to accommodate even more visitors? Should Chicago spend money developing a trail along a toxic river? Or will that trail raise public investment in cleaning up the watershed? And should the city feel tied to Burnham's *Plan* at all as it builds up its waterfront? Is the Passaic Falls Park primarily a nature or a culture preserve? If the former, should the last remnants of the mills be torn down and the landscape restored? If the latter, should the old mills be reconstructed for historical purposes? Should work in Elizabeth Park focus on restoring the original Wirth design or anticipate the needs of its contemporary park goers? And how will new amenities, like a permanent stage, change patterns of park usage or affect the environmental impact of the location?

The spatial texts that so intrigued Sandburg, Stevens, Williams, and Moore persist. They shape us, we shape them. Our communities alter these architectures as needs arise, and our community uses change as spaces flood, freeze, infect, bloom, fall into neglect, and rise into new forms. For all of the contemporary aesthetics, tools, and concerns we bring with us into these built natures, the root issues that troubled early planners and the poets who explored these spaces remain. What form should nature take in this place? How will the design of that nature shape the human and more-than-human communities that use it? What state of affairs do we hope this architectural green world will bring about, and why is that state of affairs a desirable one? Can the architecture even realize those goals? The way we answer these questions will have real, measurable consequences in the physical world, down to the placement of a pond or the paving of a trail. And thus the amalgam of nature and city, organic and crafted presented in the poetry of Sandburg, Stevens, Williams, and Moore is more than a historical curiosity that shapes their verse. Rather, these poets offer us the imaginative tools needed in our present moment as we build and rebuild our green worlds.

Notes

1. CARL SANDBURG AND THE LIVING AMERICAN CITY

1. That figure does not include population increases throughout the wider Chicagoland area. Cook County's population reached 1,192,000 by 1890. The population count for the city also jumped in 1889 due to the annexation of 134 miles of land into the city limits. For specifics on these figures, see Burnham Jr. and Kingery's *Planning the Region of Chicago*.

2. While I am here more concerned with the general principles of early American city planning than with their correctness, the significant gap between theory and practice has been explored elsewhere. In *Dreaming the Rational City: The Myth of American City Planning*, Christine Boyer explores the tension between this idealistic theory of the rational city and the difficulties of actual plan implementation.

3. The theory that citizens would absorb virtue from orderly surroundings was shared by the wider City Beautiful movement. The City Beautiful movement drew from both Beaux-Arts and classical architectural precedents, emphasizing uniformity and harmony of design. The McMillan Plan for Washington, D.C., and the Columbian World's Exhibition in Chicago are both regarded as prime examples of City Beautiful planning. For more on this movement, see William Henry Wilson's *The City Beautiful Movement*.

4. The first run of a thousand leather-bound volumes sold for twenty-five dollars apiece to a select group of subscribers. The *Plan*, coauthored by Burnham and Edward Bennett, also included an afterword by Walter L. Fisher: "Legal Aspects of the Plan of Chicago." Although the question of the *Plan*'s authorship is a vexed one, I will follow convention and refer to Burnham as the principal author. For more on the collaborative nature of the document, see Kristen Schaffer, "Fabric of City Life: The Social Agenda in Burnham's Draft of the *Plan of Chicago*."

5. "Fifty years ago, before population had become dense in certain portions of the city, people could live without parks; but we of to-day cannot. We now regard the promotion of robust health of body and mind as necessary public duties, in order that the individual may be benefited, and that the community at large may possess a higher average degree of good citizenship. And after all has been said, good citizenship is the prime object of good city planning" (*Plan* 123).

6. "The need for breathing spaces and recreation grounds is being forced upon the attention of practical men" (47).

7. With the help of Charles Wacker and Eugene Taylor, Moody gave more than five hundred talks to more than 150,000 auditors in the course of seven years, as well as papering the city with tens of thousands of related pamphlets. In May 1911, Moody printed an abbreviated version of Burnham's design entitled *Chicago's Greatest Issue: An Official Plan,* which he distributed for free to property holders. In 1916, he also published the sensational pamphlet *Chicago Can Get Fifty Million Dollars for Nothing!* in support of Burnham's plan to use the lakefront as a dumping site to be covered eventually by a public park. Wacker's *Manual of the Plan of Chicago* was also published to provide a wider number of Chicagoans with an affordable and accessible version of the *Plan.* By 1920, more than seventy thousand copies of the manual had been sold. Moody supplemented his print propaganda with the film *A Tale of One City,* which provided Chicagoans with a flickering representation of the *Plan* in more than sixty movie theaters throughout the city. In 1919, Moody even engineered a massive *Plan* push through Chicago's Christian communities by instituting Nehemiah Day, during which pastors took a quote from the Book of Nehemiah, "Therefore we, his servants, will arise and build," as a text for sermons supporting the *Plan.*

8. Some of those material alterations include the widening of several key thoroughfares, the rerouting of miles of track, the erection of a new Union Station, the linking of the north and south sides of the Chicago River via a dual bridge along Wacker Street as well as a bridge along Michigan Avenue, the straightening of the south branch of the river, the construction of Navy Pier, and the creation and landscaping of the lakefront park as well as of the forest preserves.

9. For example, the widening of Twelfth Street (now Roosevelt Road) received approval in 1912, but the project did not get under way until four years later, following complicated public legal battles regarding the city's seizure of property. In 1917, when the project was completed, the city threw "a celebration that drew close to 100,000 spectators" (Smith 134).

10. For more on the Great Migration in the context of Chicago, see James R. Grossman's "The White Man's Union: The Great Migration and the Resonance of Race and Class in Chicago, 1916–1922."

11. This is especially true of the upper-north side of the city. Burnham intended Lake Shore Drive to serve as a highway to Milwaukee following the contour of the lake, but the project was never fully completed. Lake Shore Drive abruptly ends at Hollywood and Sheridan, north of which several city blocks simply end and open up directly onto the beach.

12. Similarly, *Plan* critics often charged Burnham with ignoring the specifics of living conditions for the working classes in his designs. Complaints about the *Plan*'s neglect of working-class dwellings began before the advertising push had even started: "Well before Moody was hired, numerous individuals, including some wealthy Chicagoans, raised one of the most persistent criticisms of the *Plan:* for all its environmentalist slant, it pays scant attention to housing or the day-to-day lives of working people" (Smith 126).

13. While many American cities boast that they were home to the first sky-scraper, Chicago's Home Life Insurance Building is widely considered to be the first of its kind. Chicago also has the honor of receiving the first "skyscraper" designation in print. There are two ways of classifying skyscrapers. The first is based on physical construction components. In that category, Chicago is a front-runner for the city with the first skyscraper: "Most experts agree that the first real skyscraper was the Home Life Insurance Building in Chicago, designed by William Le Baron Jenney in 1883 and built in 1884–85. . . . Jenney went one step further and introduced a theoretical concept that would make the construction of really tall buildings possible. He took the dead load off the building's walls and placed it on the skeletal framework or iron that was concealed inside the masonry" (Douglas 21). For more on the history of skyscrapers, see George H. Douglas's *Skyscrapers: A Social History of the Very Tall Building in America*. The second method is relational. Since a skyscraper only scrapes the sky in relation to the surrounding cityscape, any building called a skyscraper is one by comparison to its surroundings, irrespective of construction components. In this category, Chicago is the clear winner, as it is the first place mentioned in print as possessing a skyscraper: "The 'sky-scrapers' of Chicago outrival anything of their kind in the world" ("Skyscraper").

14. Much has been said of Sandburg's socialism and depictions of the working class, such as in Mark Van Wienen's "Taming the Socialist: Carl Sandburg's *Chicago Poems* and Its Critics" and Philip R. Yannella's *The Other Carl Sandburg*. While critics emphasize Yannella's recovery of Sandburg as a political radical, he also argues that Sandburg's success as Lincoln's biographer depended on a market saturated with prairie nostalgia. That same prairie nostalgia colors Sandburg's depiction of the sky-scraper, as well as his depiction of Chicago in "Windy City."

15. The diversion of the river's flow from the lake back to the Mississippi was largely a response to the cholera epidemic of 1885. While the river remained little more than an open sewage drain for decades, mandates from the Clean Water Act of 1972 brought about a serious improvement in water quality. The reversal of the river's flow was considered one of the major public engineering feats of the 1900s.

16. Originally founded as Holabird and Simonds in 1880, the firm of Holabird and Roche was also well known for opulent design, as seen in their work on the Palmer House hotel in Chicago. By 1890, the firm was one of the largest in the United States.

2. WALLACE STEVENS AND THE AMERICAN PARK

1. Barbara Church was wife of Henry Church, editor, patron of the arts, and friend to whom Stevens dedicated *Notes Toward a Supreme Fiction*. As noted by George Lensing, even after Henry's death, Stevens maintained a friendly correspondence with "Mrs. Church," as he refers to her in his correspondences (362).

2. Olmsted presented "Public Parks and the Enlargement of Towns" to the American Social Science Association in Boston on 25 February 1870. This presen-tation was designed to generate enthusiasm for the Emerald Necklace project in Boston, another of Olmsted's celebrated park systems.

3. As the urban historian John S. Berman shows, the prominent use of public greens by European immigrants was, in small part, an improvement over the upper-class domination of the space during its first years of use. Laws prohibiting large gatherings on the greens functionally excluded Irish and German immigrant populations, who enjoyed the kind of large picnics Stevens here describes on their Sunday afternoons. Once management of the park shifted from the state to the city, changes in park regulation turned the park into the working-class playground first envisioned by Olmsted and Vaux, even though the laws still did little to foster cross-class contact. The sheer numbers of working-class visitors, suggested also by Stevens's description, also threatened to overwhelm the park, and Olmsted often expressed dismay at the illicit use of fenced-off greensward for such picnicking and play. For more on class conflict in the early years of Central Park, see Berman, *Central Park*.

4. The "We" refers to Stevens and his walking companion that afternoon, Walter Butler.

5. These displays offended his concept of tastefulness: "Olmsted objected to much of the specimen planting and flower-bedding by gardeners of his time because it went against the 'spirit of place' and thus against his conception of good taste. His main criterion for tastefulness was that a design should be 'fitting' and proper in its setting, not clashing and incongruous" (Beveridge and Rocheleau 32). Fitness, while congruous with an emphasis on native plants, did not always exclusively mean local flora. Olmsted would, on occasion, import plants similar to native varieties for his compositions. The principle of fitness therefore hovers between the ecological and the aesthetic, with aesthetic fitness ultimately serving as the ground for such choices.

6. In this presentation to the Missouri Botanical Society, Mill also provides a useful history of botanical gardens, from ancient Greece and Rome, through the Middle Ages, and up to the modern era. He notes that Kew was something of an oddity in its lack of university affiliation: "Kew, having no connection with any university of educational establishment, differs markedly in this respect. . . . Her sphere of usefulness is largely concerned with the economic aspect of botany, and it is her aim and object to encourage and assist, as far as possible, the scientific botanists, travelers, merchants and manufacturers, in their varied botanical investigations" (209).

7. "Tea" was first published in the March 15 edition of *Rogue* and was later included in *Harmonium*.

8. According to Kristine Paulus, the current plants records manager for the Botanical Garden, the caladium varietals around 1902 included *argenteum, grandiflorum, albansese, argyvictus,* "New Century," and "*Emile Verdier,*" along with caladium accessions lacking legible varietal designations (personal communication, 1 Aug. 2016).

9. Caladium has several common names, including angel's wings and heart of Jesus. The leaves are often two-toned, with a red interior and green ring on the edge of the leaf, but white and lavender variations can also be found (Coombes 30). Native to South America, caladium cannot survive winter temperatures below 55 degrees and prefer warm, moist conditions in the summer. Leaves can grow in excess of two feet long and wide (Kellum 51). For more on caladium, see Kellum, *Southern Shade: A Plant Selection Guide.*

10. Stevens uses tea drinking and ceremonies as refined, artistic, meditative practices in other pieces, such as in *Three Travelers Watch a Sunrise*. He was an avid tea enthusiast and often sought out exotic blends that were hard to come by in the States. For more on tea in Stevens's works and life, see Nico Israel's "Wallace Stevens and the World of Tea."

11. Alan Filreis also comments that Stevens's "feelings for natural landscape was for the most part confined to frequent walks in Elizabeth Park," particularly during "his daily and especially Sunday strolls" (*Modernism* 236, 237), as does Gyorgyi Voros, who states that Stevens "regularly walked to work through Elizabeth Park" (31). Peter Brazeau also suggests the Stevens purchased their home in Hartford because of its proximity to the park (231).

12. In the Annual Reports of the Board of Park Commissioners for the City of Hartford, the Olmsted Brothers are listed as consulting landscape architects from 1896 through 1901. While some historians classify Elizabeth Park as an Olmsted creation, the firm only provided broad recommendations for the entire park system and occasionally contributed small pieces of design as needed. Wirth is named as designer on official park schematics for Elizabeth Park, and the overall vision for the space is his own creation.

13. The management of later superintendents who more clearly segregated the garden areas from the open greens emphasized the seams between the pastoral and botanical styles. George A. Parker served as superintendent after Wirth moved on to design the Minneapolis Park system in 1906. Parker's main alterations included removing vegetation around the park's border, installing streetlights, and constructing specific recreational areas such as a baseball diamond and playground (Cornelio 20). Parker's alterations tried to "protect" the gardens from the "vagrants and drunks" who "misused these public places" by taking advantage of the dense shade and cover afforded on the margins of the lawn (Cornelio 20).

14. Peter Sharpe stops short of identifying Elizabeth Park as the site of this catalepsy but does note that "the tenuous equilibrium gained by this opposing of forces provides the quiet moment of contemplation on a real bench in Hartford" (262).

15. *Owl's Clover* was first published in a limited edition by Alcestis Press in 1936. After cutting more than one hundred lines, Stevens then included it in *The Man with the Blue Guitar* (New York: Knopf, 1945), 39–72. The longer, original version also appears in *Opus Posthumous* (New York: Knopf, 1966), 43–71. Both the 1936 and the 1945 versions are reprinted in *Collected Poetry and Prose*. I have chosen to use the 1936 version largely so as to treat the same text as do the scholars I cite in the following analysis. For more on the textual history of *Owl's Clover,* see Filreis's "Stevens in the 1930s."

16. For more on the history of Prospect Park, see Colley and Colley's *Prospect Park: Olmsted and Vaux's Brooklyn Masterpiece*.

17. Louis Harman Peet's immaculately detailed *Trees and Shrubs of Prospect Park* list both Japanese and English yew in the park setting: "If you happen to pass it in early autumn you may chance to see its beautiful red-pink seed cups hanging brightly all through its dark green, like little bells" (168).

18. In *The Final Sculpture*, Michael North expertly details Stevens's engagement with public statuary, paying special attention to his focus on equestrian works in *Owl's Clover* and "The American Sublime." He argues that "the equestrian statue continues to find a place in Stevens's work as the symbol of a difficult, nearly impossible, compromise" made among poet, readership, and politics (189). While North explores the artistic and social context of Clark Mill's statue of Andrew Jackson on horseback in relation to "The American Sublime," his treatment of the statue in *Owl's Clover* necessarily lacks similar specificity as the location of the park had yet to be determined. His exploration of equestrian statuary as a whole, however, remains highly applicable, especially given MacMonnies's participation in similar kinds of statuary styles explicated by North.

19. Similarly, MacMonnies's work on the Soldiers and Sailors Memorial Arch explicitly references the Arc de Triomphe. MacMonnies also supplemented his income by frequently selling smaller copies of his most popular pieces, and so Stevens's concerns here about how reproduction degrades aesthetic experience may apply to MacMonnies's career as a whole. For more on MacMonnies and Prospect Park, see Michele H. Bogart, *Public Sculpture and the Civic Ideal in New York City, 1890–1930*. For more on MacMonnies's career, see E. A. Gordon's *The Sculpture of Frederick MacMonnies: A Critical Dialogue*; and Mary Smart's *A Flight with Fame: The Life & Art of Frederick MacMonnies, 1863–1937*.

20. Robert Moses served as the first parks manager for a unified New York park system and was a major, albeit controversial, force in New York City planning from the 1930s through the 1960s. For more on Moses, see Hilary Ballon's *Robert Moses and the Modern City: The Transformation of New York*.

3. WILLIAM CARLOS WILLIAMS AND THE FAILURES OF PLANNING

1. Williams relied heavily on William Nelson and Charles A. Shriner's comprehensive history of Paterson from its founding to 1914. In relating the founding of Paterson and SUM, they provide several excerpts from the original charter and minutes from early board meetings: "On July 4, 1792, a meeting of the Society for Useful Manufactures met at the house of Abraham Godwin to hear a full report of the recent topographical survey completed by General Schuyler: 'The committee appointed for the purpose of fixing upon a proper place on the waters of the Passaick [*sic*] for the seat of the factory, for fixing the town of Paterson and making the necessary purchases of land'" (325). Nelson and Shriner's text is a massive compendium of a wide variety of primary sources, including local myth, newspaper accounts, letters, business minutes, geographical surveys, and photography.

2. Hamilton's enthusiasm for industrialization was not shared by all. Both Benjamin Franklin and John Adams, for example, retained the Edenic ideal of a nation of farmers (Miller 284). The *Report* argued that an agricultural nation would be poorly prepared for war because of its dependence on foreign nations for goods like weapons and cloth. An industrial nation would also further Hamilton's federalist program by uniting the states through broader shared commerce, as well as fostering

a mutually beneficial relationship between American corporations and the national government, as these new businesses would enjoy tax cuts and funding provided by the Bank of the United States, and they, in turn, would increase the overall wealth of the nation. For more on the specifics of the *Report on Manufactures*, see Miller's *Alexander Hamilton and the Growth of a New Nation*, 278–96.

3. It is difficult to determine the extent to which Hamilton should be depicted as the main character in SUM's narrative. Officially, Hamilton kept a low profile: "Hamilton seems not to have been a formal promoter, if only because that would have been in conflict with his function in the Treasury. He may have drawn the act of incorporation, which had certain features resembling those he included in the charters of the Bank of New York and the Bank of the United States" (Mitchell 181). However, behind closed doors, Hamilton was responsible for most of SUM's large-scale decisions. The board frequently communicated with him for advice, and Hamilton even attended several meetings in person. He was also responsible for selecting the planner, engineer, and governor, as well as the majority of the board members. The new governor, William Durer, was also a close business acquaintance of Hamilton's before joining SUM. Hamilton's involvement with SUM was most prominent when the Society met with financial difficulties, as it did very soon after its creation, since his own reputation was already entangled with the success or failure of their projects. For more on Hamilton's involvement with SUM, see Mitchell's *Alexander Hamilton: The National Adventure, 1788–1804*.

4. But, as Garner notes, the term was first coined in late nineteenth-century America as a kind of insult to describe mining camps in the Monongahela Valley: "It is always used pejoratively and has carried a stigma that has not gone away" (3). My use of "company town" here follows that of Garner, in that I am referring to a particular economic and architectural arrangement and am not necessarily evoking that negative connotation.

5. Company towns are controlled by a single company that oversees the construction of both the works and laborers' quarters. While Paterson bears all the architectural markers of the standard company mill town, it is more properly a corporation town since SUM did not directly run the manufactures. Rather, they invested in the site and sold shares to businessmen who then took over the day-to-day operations of the mills. The difference, however, is organizational rather than architectural.

6. For a brief moment in the early stages of planning, SUM's ideal city went beyond the boxy, uniform brick structures of the standard mill town and toward a more elegant, classical plan. SUM originally hired Charles Pierre L'Enfant, whom Hamilton knew well and recommended for the job. In selecting L'Enfant, Hamilton chose a planning visionary but also a designer who constantly went over budget and often had difficulties implementing his plans, and so was not the most prudent choice of an engineer. In L'Enfant's plan, Paterson was to be organized in a grand sunburst pattern of open boulevards radiating out from what would come to be called Colt Hill. L'Enfant also proposed long, classical stone aqueducts for the raceways that were required for the mills. However, this design proved to be prohibitively expen-

sive, "a scheme that would have absorbed more money than was invested in all the manufacturing establishments in America at the time" (Nelson and Shriner 330).

7. Every alderman wanted to ensure that the park would be situated in his district, and so debates about the final location were long and involved. Eventually, the alderman split the baby, opting for two parks, one on each side of town, in order to appease all parties: "On Feb 28, 1889, the aldermen passed an ordinance creating a commission whose duty it should be to take charge of the two parks (Washington and Lincoln on the East and West side respectively)" (Nelson and Shriner 402).

8. The Passaic Falls featured in a variety of travel guides and collections of American landscape sketches. For example, *Appleton's Railroad and Steamboat Companion* (1847) recommends taking the fifty-cent train ride from Bergen to Paterson: "Here are the *Passaic Falls,* which are celebrated for their picturesque beauty, and are much visited by strangers" (Williams 194). N. P. Willis's *American Scenery, or Land, Lake, and River Illustrations of Transatlantic Nature* also includes a sketch of the Passaic Falls and a short entry about its history.

9. Though primarily a literary journal, the *Casket* goes on to provide directions for tourists at the Falls: "By mounting upon an embankment of stones in front of the Falls, to the Canal reservoir, and thence ascending a flight of steps to a gate and house of refreshments, the upper level of the Passaic is reached" (68). The presence of a "house of refreshments" further suggests the Falls' success as a tourist attraction. Irving's poem "The Falls of the Passaic" also praises "the cliff's dizzy borders . . . / Where the torrent leaps headlong embosom'd in foam."

10. Edgar Williams, an architect, ultimately designed the location several years later: "Ironically, the ground that was to be the so-called 'Isle of Safety,' is now the Borough's World War I Memorial Monument, designed in 1920 by Edgar Williams" (Leith).

11. "Another day I watched Uncle Irving shooting with an air gun of unusual power. . . . At last the squirrel fell, all bloody at our feet" (*Autobiography* 7).

12. Paul Mariani, Williams's biographer, begins his narrative with a December 1950 visit Williams made to the park with his grandson. Only two months earlier, Williams had concluded book 4 of *Paterson,* and now his grandson asks how deep the falls are. Mariani imagines the exchange: "To see it all as it must have been before they'd fouled it, dumping garbage and even excrement into it. To see it, at least in the mind's eye, once more as it must have been: a new world naked. How deep had it gone?" (2).

13. While Williams's first plans for *Paterson* included only four books, he added a fifth and had started working on a sixth shortly before he died. The five-book version of *Paterson* was first published in its entirety in 1963. There are several textual variations among the original separate volumes, their reprints, and subsequent collections. For this study, I am relying on the edition revised by Christopher MacGowan in 1992. For more on the textual history of Paterson, see MacGowan's preface to *Paterson.*

14. This dynamic is also not restricted to *Paterson.* Ann W. Fischer-Wirth provides

a compelling analysis of marriage throughout Williams's oeuvre in "'A Rose to the End of Time': William Carlos Williams and Marriage."

15. It is unclear if either plant is native, was ever included in the landscape plantings for the park, or if they are to be found there at present. As early as 1866, the amateur botanist Anne G. Hale recommended cacti for domestic planting, stating some are "hardy enough to venture as far north as New England" (195). According to the naturalist Geoffrey A. Hammerson, prickly pear, notable for its showy yellow flower, can be found in sandy soils in Connecticut, though such a discovery is rare as the prickly pear does not grow abundantly there due to harsh winters (165). Laurel may here refer to the mountain laurel, or spoonwood, a poisonous ornamental evergreen with pink blossoms brought to North America in the 1700s. Mountain laurel is not actually a member of the laurel family but is found throughout the East Coast and as far inland as Indiana (Wells 147–49).

16. Grooming functions as a metaphor for poetic composition later in book 2, as a man in tweed, a T. S. Eliot stand-in, combs out the hair of his collie, brushing the strands into waves and combing out pieces of "The Love Song of J. Alfred Prufrock" in the process.

17. Nelson and Shriner note that, as with many early SUM ventures, the Passaic Water Company was severely underfunded: "quite without money, with an utter lack of experience; with a very inadequate conception of what a water supply to a city meant; with everything to learn and at a period when only the larger cities had introduced water" (408). In organizing a water utility company this early in its history, Paterson declared an intent to be as prominent as "the larger cities" of New York and Boston. However, as in Chicago, using the river as both a source for potable water and a sewage canal resulted in public health issues that plagued the Passaic Water Company. By 1911, the courts reversed the initial decision of the legislature, stating: "The Legislature had no right to pollute a river flowing through a thickly settled territory" (383). A new canal was constructed that dumped Paterson's waste directly into the salt water of New York Bay.

18. Williams plays with "SUM" and mathematics throughout *Paterson*. For example, the sum of SUM's efforts comes to nothing in part 3 of book 2: "Look for the nul / defeats it all // the N of all / equations" (77).

19. This is not to say that the grid layout is unique to American cityscapes. As early as 450 BC, the Greek planner Hippodamus utilized this pattern in his plan for the city of Piraeus. However, between the fall of Greece and the sixteenth century, European street patterns tended to look more vascular than rectilinear, often growing to accommodate community usage rather than a predetermined plan. As a frontier nation, America was often in the position to plan cities before, rather than after, the fact, and so the grid became ubiquitous in a fashion that it could not in the older cityscapes of England. The 1787 Northwest Ordinance Act and the 1862 Homestead Act officially set the grid pattern as a national urban standard, as well as making the buying and selling of frontier property easier on the federal government.

20. While some architects, like L'Enfant, praised the logic of the grid, others like

Olmsted and H. W. S. Cleveland criticized its homogeneity and inability to accommodate local topography. Burnham employed the grid in Chicago but argued that this layout is particularly well-suited to a flat prairie location and was absurd in a site like San Francisco.

21. This is also a central concern throughout Williams's oeuvre. He locates the potential for new poetry in the newness of the American vernacular: "From speech, from American speech as distinct from English speech . . . from what we hear in America. . . . A language full of those hints toward newness of which I have been speaking" (*Selected Essays* 289–90).

22. For example, Temple Street on the north side of the river becomes Main Street on the opposite bank. Similarly, Wayne becomes Spruce, Arch becomes Bridge (not to be confused with another street named Bridge farther north that is not in any way connected to Bridge on the south side of the city), and Halendon splits on the southeast bank to become Lafayette and Straight Street (which is not at all straight and veers south in several loops following the bank of the river). These name changes reveal the difficulty of imposing a grid system over a city bisected by a curving river.

23. Critics like Joel Conarroe have suggested a wide variety of other literary sources for *Paterson* that are similarly invested in the activity of walking or journeying, as well as with landscape: "The pilgrimage or quest motif, for example, relates it to *The Canterbury Tales*, to *Endymion* (Williams' first long poem was imitation Keats), and to Shelley's *Alastor*. In its handling of the awakening sensibility of the poet and treatment of landscape as 'a kind of emotional topography' it claims kinship with Wordsworth's *The Prelude*" (15). The present analysis is not an argument against any of these sources but is rather a contribution to the complex constellation of influences that shape Williams's presentation of Paterson as walker.

24. For more on the long tradition of the flaneur, see Keith Tester's introduction to *The Flâneur*.

25. I am here emphasizing acts of seeing, but this is not to say that the flaneur is limited to only one of his senses (nor is the nature walker). While sight and spectacle play a prominent role in *flânerie*, critics have investigated the function of touching, tasting, and hearing as well (see David Frisby's "The *Flâneur* in Social Theory"; Barry Smart's "Digesting the Modern Diet: Gastro-porn, Fast Food and Panic Eating"; and Bruce Mazlish's "The *Flâneur*: From Spectator to Representation" respectively). The role of hearing in *flânerie* may provide even more points of contact with *Paterson*, as the command to "Listen!" emerges later on in book 2.

26. The following account of the nature walker draws on Scott Slovic's "Nature Writing and Environmental Psychology." Slovic argues that the fundamental narrative of the nature walker emphasizes human acts of epiphany and cognition more than it foregrounds the physical environment. Nature is the occasion that initiates an essentially artistic process of understanding and realization.

27. The nature walker is admittedly a broader conceit than the flaneur. I am here reappropriating Slovic's usage of the term "nature writer." His analysis argues that the act of writing or verbal articulation is part of the nature walker's act of cognition and synthesis: "Putting things into language helps people see better; and this

can happen either at the moment of confrontation or in retrospect while sitting at a desk hours later" (355). At the end of book 2, Mr. Paterson retreats to the library to conduct research and begin writing. However, in the pieces Slovic investigates, the narrator is most often identifiable with the writer in a manner that cannot be easily mapped onto *Paterson*, and so I have altered the designation.

28. "Most nature walkers, from Thoreau to the present, walk a fine line (or, more accurately, *vacillate*) between rhapsody and detachment" (Slovic 353). Slovic refers to this mode of vacillation as a "dialectical tension between correspondence and otherness" and cites examples from Henry David Thoreau, Annie Dillard, and Edward Abbey. As Slovic notes, the degree of vacillation can vary from writer to writer.

29. My thanks to Edward Smyk, official historian of Passaic County, for this information about Garret Mountain Reserve.

30. Critical analyses of book 2 at times have difficulty negotiating this relationship. For example, Roger Gilbert rightly notes that "the park is not a true wilderness but an urbanized parcel of 'nature,'" but he goes on to say that it is "contaminated" by that urban modern culture (128). In this construction, the park is contaminated just by being the thing that it is. In contrast, Walter Scott Peterson emphasizes the importance of human activity over and against an interest in the environment: "More important, Paterson also sees the human beings who surround him" (47). In one critical formulation, human presence infects landscape; in another, landscape is simply a backdrop for human activity. Neither reading is wrong in its content, but both overemphasize one aspect of the human-nature relationship. It is the quality and dynamism of that relationship that is Williams's focus in book 2.

31. Williams returns to and revises the pastoral throughout his poetic career, in landscapes as varied as back alleys and junk-ridden backyards. For more on Williams and the pastoral tradition, see Mickelson's "'The Truth about Us': Pastoral, Pragmatism, and *Paterson*."

32. Priapic statues came in a variety of forms but often served as a kind of scarecrow made of local materials: "Country people would cut any branch from a tree that resembled a phallus, carve a rough face in it, and set it up in their garden, sometime decorating it with wreaths of flowers and sometimes a splash of red paint" (Redfield 1169). Priapus also stands on the boundary between classes, as poorer farmers outside of the cities regarded him as a powerful deity, whereas city dwellers treated Priapus as a bawdy comedic figure associated with awkward sexual gestures.

33. Ornithologists refer to this group-protective behavior in birds as mobbing: "Mobbing birds rarely attack the predator; they merely harass it. However, the harassment is often sufficient to cause the hawk or owl to fly. When it flies, the mobbing birds follow it with enhanced vocal efforts. . . . Mobbing isolates and identifies a predator at relatively little risk to the individual mobbing birds" (Kricher 308). For more on mobbing techniques, see "Mobbing" in Kricher's *A Field Guide to Northern Forests*.

34. "Their pitiful thoughts do meet / in the flesh—surrounded / by churring loves! Gay wings / to bear them (in sleep)" (52).

35. Peterson compellingly demonstrates that the reappearance of the grasshoppers in later scenes also extends the hope of genuine love throughout book 2: "The

Cupids that surround the lovers ('Churring loves'—cf. grasshopper lyric) suggest that love, at least in some form, remains" (64).

36. "Law—and lawlessness—are . . . the twin axes around which the history of conservation revolves" (Jacoby 2). Jacoby analyzes the implementation of conservation law in several different national parks in order to argue that these laws often made the land practices of working-class immigrant or country communities suddenly illegal, such as bans against using park water for laundry or daily cooking. The same tactics were often employed in the creation of smaller public parks. For example, the plot selected for Central Park was home to both a landed African American community and a diverse population of squatters. The site was effectively cleared by legislating the inhabitants away as police were given authority to arrest and evict anyone lighting a fire or poaching on the property. For more on the history of park legislation and class dynamics, see Jacoby's *Crimes against Nature: Squatters, Poachers, Thieves and the Hidden History of American Conservation*.

37. It is worth noting that, as of 2011, the New Jersey Audubon Society sited "disturbance from visitors and unleashed dogs" as two continuing and significant threats to the preservation of Garret Mountain as a nesting habitat for local birds ("Garret Mountain").

38. Thomas LeClair's article, "The Poet as Dog in *Paterson*," provides a thorough and lengthy study of dogs throughout the poem, such as the sexually adventuresome Musty and ChiChi. LeClair argues that the image of the dog allows Williams to explore his role as poet, as well as the mongrel possibilities of an American poetics. LeClair cites this prohibition against unleashed dogs as an example of blockage that frustrates the poet's craft.

4. MARIANNE MOORE AND THE NATIONAL PARK SERVICE

1. In the case of the Adirondacks, the preserve was founded largely thanks to the heavy petitioning of New York businessmen, led by the chair of the Chamber of Commerce, Morris K. Jesup: "Jesup petitioned the legislature that it was necessary to save the forests because 'their destruction will seriously injure the internal commerce of the State.' Moreover, the merchants believed that if drought eliminated the Erie-Hudson route as a means of shipping goods, railroads would have a monopoly and be able to raise rates at will" (Nash 119). As Nash's example shows, the first American preservationists were largely city industrialists and businessmen.

2. "More typical of the general reaction [to the park's creation] was the . . . description of the 'New Wonder Land' as a place whose attractions were limited to unusual natural phenomena such as geysers" (Nash 111). These natural wonderlands were of huge importance to American rail companies, such as Union Pacific, that sought to make a profit transporting tourists to and from these attractions. For more on Union Pacific and American parks, see Nash.

3. "In 1872, with the creation of Yellowstone National Park, Congress set a precedent for the preservation of the monumental, the extraordinary, and even the

bizarre in nature. Early visitors to the parks expected to see grand natural phenomena that would rival Old World architectural attractions" (Mason 2).

4. The debate surrounding Adirondack Park serves as an excellent example of this shift. Whereas the preserve was first designed to protect urban interests in potable water and transportation, by 1894 the language had moved toward wilderness preservation. David McClure, an attorney who advocated permanent preservation of the site in the New York constitution, combined earlier arguments about the utility of the location with pleas to consider "the higher uses of the great wilderness": "In fact McClure declared that the 'first' reason for preserving it was 'as a great resort for the people of this State. When tired of the trials, tribulations and annoyances of business and every-day life in the man-made towns, [the Adirondacks] offer to man a place of retirement. There . . . he may find some consolation in communing with that great Father of all'" (Nash 121).

5. Gifford Pinchot, who founded the Division of Forestry in 1898, focused on regulating lumber resources rather than scenic preservation and often battled with the Department of the Interior and the Sierra Club, founded by the naturalist John Muir, over the ultimate value of scenic preservation (Mason 72–73).

6. In 1915, four of the twelve existing parks were still under the control of the army, resulting in serious management difficulties. Their ownership also testified to the difficult transition from taming to preserving wilderness: "In the nineteenth century, the army's intervention in the parks was a natural extension of the military's mission to pacify and 'civilize' western frontier lands. As the army's role in the West decreased in the early twentieth century, however, so too did the War Department's interest in the national parks" (Mason 69).

7. The following history of landscape design in Mount Rainier Park draws from Ethan Carr's *Wilderness by Design: Landscape Architecture and the National Park Service.* Carr traces the history of landscape design in the early era of the NPS, using Mount Rainier as one of his chief examples.

8. The Government Road, now known as Nisqually Road, was an engineering feat of some note. Eugene V. Ricksecker served as the assistant engineer and is credited with maintaining a 4 percent maximum grade over the complex terrain while also guaranteeing that "the road passed all points of interest" (Carr 212).

9. "Under Superintendent Hall and his successor, Ethan Allen, budgets increased from three thousand dollars in 1911 to an average of almost fifteen thousand dollars annually for 1913 through 1915" (Carr 214).

10. The Rainier National Park Company was a concession monopoly meant to solve the problem of poor service provided years earlier by a variety of privately owned companies. By the early 1920s, shareholders who had funded projects like the new Paradise Inn were expecting returns. Park managers therefore felt considerable pressure to keep increasing the amount of annual visitors. As Carr notes, this tension was hardly unique to Mount Rainier Park, as similar clashes plagued the Yosemite National Park Board (221).

11. "An Octopus" went through several revisions during its publication history.

Moore's notes in 1923 indicate that she originally imagined "An Octopus" and "Marriage" as a single long piece that was subsequently broken into two. The version that was first published in the *Dial* in 1924 is several lines longer than that which would later appear in *Complete Poems*. The majority of excised material deals explicitly with Moore's Greek materials, such as the *Aeneid*. The current analysis refers to the final copy in *Complete Poems*.

12. That year, the director of the NPS reported to the Department of the Interior: "Such heavy demands for the rules and regulations booklets have been made on the Washington office by different organizations that we now have a mailing list of automobile clubs, highway associations, chambers of commerce, travel bureaus, etc., all over the United States, to which we send supplies of the pamphlets as they are issued. These are used in furnishing tourists information regarding tours of the national parks. This feature is so popular that we are unable to adequately meet requests for the booklets" (*Report* 31).

13. Margaret Holley provides the following description of Moore's early draft: "What Moore's own underlined copy of the pamphlet shows us is that not only did she copy into her poem numerous phrases from the pamphlet's text, tables, notes, and even its bibliography, but also that she actually composed some portions of her poem in the margins of the pamphlet" (Holley 67).

14. "[Moore] experienced the direct and strenuous contact of the climber, the linguistically mediated and physically distanced perspective of the tourist, and the more cerebral positions of poet and naturalist, all of which enhance her narrative approach" (Ladino 286).

15. Loosely, because Moore also excises a great deal of material, mostly having to do with transportation and lodging, such as "Administration," "How to reach the park," "Free public camp grounds," "Information, utilities, etc." (5).

16. An interesting variation on this submarine image occurs early in the Rainier guide. The guide quotes F. E. Matthes, head researcher for the United States Geological Survey: "Cascading from the summit in all directions, they (the glaciers) radiate like the arms of a great starfish" (7).

17. "Pseudopodium" is a zoological and a botanical term. It refers both to tentacle appendages in animals and to elongated tendrils extending from moss (*OED*, def. 1 and 2).

18. "The merit of the octopus as food for man—as well as whales—has lately been very freely discussed, and the verdict, on the whole, is greatly in its favour" (Pycraft 1224).

19. Pycraft is not optimistic about the ability of the layman to make the correct identification. The article concludes: "I must end as I began. How are we to know which is the 'octopus' which we are to eat 'fried to a golden brown'? We have a bewildering variety to choose from and as like as not we shall choose the wrong one" (1224).

20. The Rainier guide opens with a table entitled "The National Parks at a Glance." The name, location, area in square miles, and "distinctive characteristics" are listed for each park. Rainier's description is as follows: "Largest accessible single

peak glacier system—28 glaciers, some of large size—48 square miles of glacier, 50 to 500 feet thick—Wonderful subalpine wild flower fields" (3).

21. The guide continues: "Living amid glaciers, rocky crags, precipitous cliffs, and pumice fields, the mountain goat has a habitat on Mount Rainier the superior of which in scenic grandeur would be very hard to find. Though present in some numbers about the mountain, one must hunt with exceeding care to see him at all. Remarkably light on his feet for so heavy-bodied and clumsy-appearing an animal, he is able to negotiate ice and rock slopes of unbelievable steepness. His size, sure-footedness, conspicuousness, herding habit, and unapproachability make the mountain goat unquestionably the most interesting animal in the park" (27).

22. For example, Costello treats the goat as a touchstone in the chaotic environment of the park: "The goat and antelope 'engraved' become surrogate figures that allow us to see ourselves in the painting and to organize the flux of sensations, against the turbulence in which the poem began" (85).

23. In "No Swan So Fine," Moore contrasts the vitality of a live swan with "gondoliering" legs to a chintz china swan embedded in a Louis XV candelabrum.

24. Moore replicates an error in the bibliography. The correct title of Fountain's work is *The Eleven Eaglets of the West*.

25. "Altogether too many people have attempted the ascent immediately upon arrival from the city, without having permitted their hearts and lungs to become accustomed to the rarefied air of the higher altitudes and without having toughened their muscles for the great task. As a consequence they have either came [*sic*] back exhausted to the verge of collapse or else they have altogether failed in the undertaking. And there is unfortunately more than one case on record of persons who have permanently injured their health by such ill-considered proceeding" (*Rainier Guide* 19–20).

26. The hoary marmot entry provides yet another example of the guide's emphasis on scenic vistas, even when providing details for animal identification: "The picture furnished by the glorious amphitheaterlike cirques of the park, with their precipitous walls, glaciers, snow fields, and rock slides, and their forests and flowers, would scarcely be complete without the whistler" (28).

27. The hoary marmot is itself a careful mountain climber: "The facility with which the animal traverses rock slides and steep slopes would scarcely be anticipated in an animal so heavy-bodied and awkward an appearance" (*Rainier Guide* 28).

28. "All" here encompasses the list starting at line 111 and concluding at 128 with the description of Paradise Valley's alpine meadow. After 128, also the end of a sentence, the poem shifts to a discussion of aesthetics.

29. "The picturesque train of horses with their wild-looking drivers files out through the village streets under a fusillade of snap-shot cameras and the wondering gaze of new arrivals from the east. But these evidences of civilization are soon left behind and after a few miles the primitive wilderness is entered" (Wilcox 116).

30. For example, Patricia Willis argues that Moore moves the Greeks to the happy garden of Paradise atop Mount Purgatory: "Marianne Moore in effect moves the Greeks from the Inferno to the Purgatorio by applying to them the phrase 'like

happy souls in hell'" (264). Gregory also likens Moore's topography and description of the alpine meadow to Milton's description of Paradise (175).

31. As with many of her quotations, this is a loose paraphrase of different sections of the rules and regulations, including: "Visitors entering or traveling through the park to places beyond must, at entrance, report and surrender all firearms, traps, nets, seines, or explosives in their possession to the first park officer and, in proper cases, may obtain his written leave to carry them through the park sealed" (38); "Gambling in any form, or the operation of gambling devices, whether for merchandise or otherwise, is prohibited" (39); "Persons who render themselves obnoxious by disorderly conduct or bad behavior shall be subjected to the punishment hereinafter prescribed for violation of the foregoing regulations, or they may be summarily removed from the park by the superintendent and not allowed to return without permission in writing from the Director of the National Park Service or the superintendent of the park" (40).

AFTERWORD

1. De Solà-Morales begins his study of *terraine vague* with a discussion of urban photography, though the concept applies to the primary site as well, one he describes as "unincorporated margins, interior islands void of activity, oversights." The *terraine vague* is "foreign to the urban system, mentally exterior in the physical interior of the city" (26). For more on the *terraine vague*, see *Terraine Vague: Interstices at the Edge of the Pale.*

Bibliography

Anderson, David Ross. "The Woman in the Tricorn Hat: Political Theory and Biological Portraiture in Marianne Moore's Poetry." *Journal of Modern Literature* 22.1 (1998): 31–45.

Ballon, Hilary. *Robert Moses and the Modern City: The Transformation of New York.* New York: Norton, 2007.

Barad, Karen. *Meeting the Universe Halfway: Quantum Physics and the Entanglement of Matter and Meaning.* Durham: Duke University Press, 2007.

Berman, John S. *The Museum of the City of New York: Central Park.* New York: Barnes and Noble Press, 2003.

Beveridge, Charles E., and Paul Rocheleau. *Frederick Law Olmsted: Designing the American Landscape.* Ed. David Larkin. New York: Universe, 1998.

Board of Park Commissioners. *The 40th Annual Report of the Board of Park Commissioners of the City of Hartford for the Year Ending 1900.* Hartford, CT: Case, Lockwood, and Brainard, 1900.

Bogart, Michele H. *Public Sculpture and the Civic Ideal in New York City, 1890–1930.* Washington, DC: Smithsonian Institution Press, 1997.

Boyer, Christine M. *Dreaming the Rational City: The Myth of American City Planning.* Cambridge: MIT Press, 1994.

Brazeau, Peter. *Parts of a World: Wallace Stevens Remembered.* New York: Random House, 1983.

Buell, Lawrence. *The Environmental Imagination: Thoreau, Nature Writing, and the Formation of American Culture.* Cambridge: Harvard University Press, 1995.

Burnham, Daniel H., and Edward H. Bennett. *Plan of Chicago.* Chicago: Chicago Commercial Club, 1908. Facsimile ed. New York: Princeton Architectural Press, 1993.

Burnham, Daniel H., Jr., and Robert Kingery. *Planning the Region of Chicago.* Ed. John Barstow Morrill and Paul O. Fischer. Chicago: Chicago Regional Planning Association, 1956.

Buttel, Robert. *Wallace Stevens: The Making of Harmonium.* Princeton: Princeton University Press, 1967.

Buttel, Robert, and Frank Doggett, eds. *Wallace Stevens: A Celebration.* Princeton: Princeton University Press, 1980.

Callahan, North. *Carl Sandburg: His Life and Works.* University Park: Pennsylvania University Press, 1987.

Cambon, Glauco. *The Inclusive Flame: Studies in American Poetry.* Bloomington: Indiana University Press, 1963.

Carr, Ethan. *Wilderness by Design: Landscape Architecture and the National Park Service.* Lincoln: University of Nebraska Press, 1998.

City of Hartford Parks Department. *Elizabeth Park General Plan Designed by Theodore Worth, Corrected Jan. 1904.* Hartford, CT: Parks Department, 1904.

Cleveland, Horace William Shaler. Preface. *Landscape Architecture, as Applied to the Wants of the West: With an Essay on Forest Planting on the Great Plains.* Chicago: Jansen, McClurg, 1873.

Colley, David P., and Elizabeth Keegin Colley. *Prospect Park: Olmsted and Vaux's Brooklyn Masterpiece.* New York: Princeton Architectural Press, 2013.

Conarroe, Joel. *William Carlos Williams' Paterson: Language and Landscape.* Philadelphia: University of Pennsylvania Press, 1970.

Cook, Eleanor. *A Reader's Guide to Wallace Stevens.* Princeton: Princeton University Press, 2007.

Cook, Geo H. *Final Report of the State Geologist: Topography, Magnetism, Climate.* Vol. 1. Trenton, NJ: John L. Murphy Publishing, 1888. Googlebooks. Accessed 8 Aug. 2016.

Coombes, Allan J. *Dictionary of Plant Names.* Portland: Timber, 1994.

Cornelio, Alicia. *Elizabeth Park: A Century of Beauty.* Virginia Beach: Donning, 2003.

"A Correct View of the Passaic Falls near Paterson, New Jersey." *Casket, or, Flowers of Literature, Wit, and Sentiment* 2 (Feb. 1827): 68. ProQuest. Accessed 8 Aug. 2016.

Costello, Bonnie. *Marianne Moore: Imaginary Possessions.* Cambridge: Harvard University Press, 1981.

———. *Shifting Ground: Reinventing Landscape in Modern American Poetry.* Cambridge: Harvard University Press, 2003.

Cranz, Galen. *The Politics of Park Design: A History of Urban Parks in America.* Cambridge: MIT Press, 1989.

Cronon, William. "The Trouble with Wilderness, or, Getting Back to the Wrong Nature." *Uncommon Ground: Rethinking the Human Place in Nature.* Ed. Cronon. New York: Norton, 1996. 69–90.

Crutzen, Paul J. "Geology of Mankind." *Paul J. Crutzen: A Pioneer on Atmospheric Chemistry and Climate Change in the Anthropocene.* Ed. Crutzen and Hans Gunter Brauch. Cham, Switzerland: Springer, 2015. 211–16.

Cummings, E. E. *Selected Poems.* Ed. Richard S. Kennedy. New York: Liveright, 1994.

Dante Aligheri. *Inferno.* Trans. Anthony Esolen. New York: Random House, 2005.

Davison, Gideon Miner. *The Traveller's Guide through the Middle and Northern States and the Provinces of Canada.* Saratoga Springs, NY: Davison and G. & C. & H. Carvill, 1834.

DeMause, Neil. *The Complete Illustrated Guidebook to Prospect Park and the Brooklyn Botanic Garden.* New York: Silver Lining, 2001.

Douglas, George H. *Skyscrapers: A Social History of the Very Tall Building in America.* Jefferson, NC: McFarland, 1996.

Dudley, Dorothy. "November in the Park." *Poetry: A Magazine of Verse* 7 (Oct.–Mar. 1915–16): 67.

Durnell, Hazel. *The America of Carl Sandburg: An Analytical Study of His Works and of the National Mind.* Geneva: Journal de Geneve, 1963.

Elder, John. "The Poetry of Experience." *Beyond Nature Writing: Expanding the Boundaries of Ecocriticism.* Ed. Karla Armbruster and Kathleen R. Wallace. Charlottesville: University of Virginia Press, 2001. 312–24.

Eliot, T. S. *The Complete Poems and Plays: 1909–1950.* New York: Harcourt, Brace and World, 1971.

Fein, Albert. *Frederick Law Olmsted and the American Environmental Tradition.* New York: Braziller, 1972.

Filreis, Alan. *Modernism from Right to Left: Wallace Stevens, the Thirties, and Literary Radicalism.* Cambridge: Cambridge University Press, 1994.

———. "Stevens in the 1930s." *The Cambridge Companion to Wallace Stevens.* Ed. John N. Serio. Cambridge: Cambridge University Press, 2007. 37–47.

Fischer-Wirth, Ann W. "'A Rose to the End of Time': William Carlos Williams and Marriage." *Twentieth Century Literature* 36.2 (Summer 1990): 155–72. JSTOR. doi: 10.2307/441819.

Frisby, David. "The *Flâneur* in Social Theory." *The Flâneur.* Ed. Keith Tester. London: Routledge, 1998. 81–110.

Fountain, Paul. *Eleven Eaglets of the West.* New York: Dutton, 1906. Googlebooks. Accessed 8 Aug. 2016.

Garner, John S. *The Company Town: Architecture and Society in the Early Industrial Age.* Oxford: Oxford University Press, 1992.

"Garret Mountain." New Jersey Audubon Society. www.njaudubon.org/sectionibba /ibbasiteguide.aspx?sk=3156. Accessed 8 August 2016.

Gilbert, Roger. *Walks in the World: Representation and Experience in Modern American Poetry.* Princeton, NJ: Princeton University Press, 1991.

Gordon, E. A. "The Sculpture of Frederick MacMonnies: A Critical Dialogue." Diss. New York University, 1998. Digital.

Gregory, Elizabeth. *Quotation and Modern American Poetry: "Imaginary Gardens with Real Toads."* Houston: Rice University Press, 1996.

Grossman, James R. "The White Man's Union: The Great Migration and the Resonance of Race and Class in Chicago, 1916–1922." *The Great Migration in Historical Perspective: New Dimensions of Race, Class, and Gender.* Ed. Joe William Trotter Jr. Bloomington: Indiana University Press, 1991. 83–105.

Hale, Anne G. "Domestic Economy, or, How to Make the Home Pleasant." *New England Farmer* (Apr. 1867): 195–200. Googlebooks. Accessed 8 Aug. 2016.

Hammerson, Geoffrey A. *Connecticut Wildlife: Biodiversity, Natural History, and Conservation.* Lebanon, NH: University Press of New England, 2004.

Harvey, David. *Justice, Nature and the Geography of Difference.* Malden, MA: Blackwell, 1996.

Hass, Joseph, and Gene Lovitz. *Carl Sandburg: A Pictorial Biography.* New York: Putnam's Sons, 1967.

Harman Peet, Louis. *Trees and Shrubs of Prospect Park*. New York: American Printing House, 1902.

Hazard, Joseph T. *Snow Sentinels of the Pacific Northwest*. Seattle: Lowman and Handford, 1932.

Holley, Margaret. *The Poetry of Marianne Moore: A Study in Voice and Value*. Cambridge: Cambridge University Press, 1987.

Hughes, Langston. *The Collected Poems of Langston Hughes*. Ed. Arnold Rampersad. New York: Vintage Classics, 1995.

Israel, Nico. "Wallace Stevens and the World of Tea." *Wallace Stevens Journal* 28.1 (Spring 2004): 3–22.

Jackson, Kenneth T. *Crabgrass Frontier: The Suburbanization of the United States*. Oxford: Oxford University Press, 1985.

Jacoby, Karl. *Crimes against Nature: Squatters, Poachers, Thieves, and the Hidden History of American Conservation*. Berkeley: University of California Press, 2001.

Johnson, Clifton. *What to See in America*. New York: Macmillan, 1919.

Kellum, Jo. *Southern Shade: A Plant Selection Guide*. Jackson: University Press of Mississippi, 2008.

Kimmelman, Michael. "The Climax in a Tale of Green and Gritty: The High Line Opens Its Third and Final Phase." *New York Times*, 14 Sept. 2014, C1.

Knickerbocker, Scott. *Ecopoetics: The Language of Nature, The Nature of Language*. Amherst: University of Massachusetts Press, 2012.

Koehler, Stanley G. *Countries of the Mind: The Poetry of William Carlos Williams*. Lewisburg, PA: Bucknell University Press, 1998.

Kolodny, Annette. *The Land before Her: Fantasy and Experience of the American Frontiers, 1630–1860*. Chapel Hill: University of North Carolina Press, 1984.

———. *The Lay of the Land: Metaphor as Experience and History in American Life and Letters*. Chapel Hill: University of North Carolina Press, 1975.

Koziarz, Jay. "Construction Crews Continue Work on Chicago Riverwalk Expansion." *Curbed Chicago*. 1 Apr. 2016. chicago.curbed.com/2016/4/1/11346488/chicago-river-walk-construction-update. Accessed 6 Aug. 2016.

Kricher, John C. *A Field Guide to Eastern Forests: North America*. Ed. Roger Tory Peterson. New York: Houghton Mifflin, 1998.

Ladino, Jennifer K. "Rewriting Nature Tourism in an 'Age of Violence': Tactical Collage in Marianne Moore's 'An Octopus.'" *Twentieth-Century Literature* 51.3 (Autumn 2005): 285–315. JSTOR. www.jstor.org/stable/20058770.

LeClair, Thomas. "The Poet as Dog in *Paterson*." *Twentieth-Century Literature* 16.2 (Apr. 1970): 97–108. JSTOR. doi: 10.2307/440864.

Leith, Rod. "W. C. Williams, Recreation and Parks." E-mail message to the author. 13 Oct. 2011.

Lensing, George. *Wallace Stevens and the Seasons*. Baton Rouge: Louisiana State University Press, 2003.

Lentricchia, Frank. *Modernist Quartet*. Cambridge: Cambridge University Press, 1994.

Limerick, Patricia Nelson. *The Unbroken Past of the American West*. New York: Norton, 1987.

MacGowan, Christopher. Preface. *Paterson.* New York: New Directions, 1992. ix–xv.

———. "Paterson and Local History." *William Carlos Williams Review* 24.4 (Sept. 2004): 49–60.

Mariani, Paul. *William Carlos Williams: A New World Naked.* New York: Norton, 1981.

Marsh, John. *Hog Butchers, Beggars, and Busboys: Poverty, Labor, and the Making of Modern American Poetry.* Ann Arbor: University of Michigan Press, 2011.

Mason, Kathy S. *Natural Museums: U.S. National Parks, 1872–1916.* East Lansing: Michigan State University Press, 2004.

Mazlish, Bruce. "The *Flâneur:* From Spectator to Representation." *The Flâneur.* Ed. Keith Tester. London: Routledge, 1998. 43–60.

McCarthy, Jeffrey Mathes. *Green Modernism: Nature and the English Novel, 1900 to 1930.* New York: Palgrave Macmillan, 2016.

McLaughlin, Charles Capen. "The Environment: Olmsted's Odyssey." *Wilson Quarterly* 6.13 (Summer 1982): 78–87. JSTOR. 23 Jan. 2012.

Michelson, Max. "In the Park." *Poetry: A Magazine of Verse* 8.2 (May 1916): 66.

Mickelson, Ann. "'The Truth about Us': Pastoral, Pragmatism, and *Paterson.*" *American Literature* 75.3 (Sept. 2003): 601–27. Project Muse. muse.jhu.edu/article /46634.

Mill, Arthur W. "The History and Functions of Botanic Gardens." *Annals of the Missouri Botanical Garden.* 2.1/2 (Feb.–Apr. 1915): 185–240. JSTOR. doi: 0.2307/ 2990033.

Miller, Campbell et al. "Declaration of Concern." *Landscape Architecture Foundation.* lafoundation.org/about/declaration-of-concern. Accessed 6 Aug. 2016.

Miller, J. Hillis. *Poets of Reality: Six Twentieth-Century Writers.* Cambridge: Harvard University Press, 1966.

Miller, John C. *Alexander Hamilton and the Growth of the New Nation.* New York: Harper and Row, 1959.

Mitchell, Broadus. *Alexander Hamilton: The National Adventure, 1788–1804.* New York: Macmillan, 1962.

"Mobbing." Def. 1. *Oxford English Dictionary Online.* Accessed 8 Aug. 2016.

Monroe, Harriet. *John Wellborn Root: A Study of His Life and Work.* Boston: Houghton Mifflin, 1896.

———. *You and I.* New York: Macmillan, 1914.

Moore, Marianne. *Complete Poems.* New York: Macmillan, 1994.

Morton, Timothy. *Ecology without Nature: Rethinking Environmental Aesthetics.* Cambridge: Harvard University Press, 2007.

Nash, Roderick Frazier. *Wilderness and the American Mind.* New Haven: Yale University Press, 2001.

National Parks Portfolio. Ed. Robert Sterling Yard. Washington, DC: National Park Service, U.S. Government Printing Office, 1921.

Nelson, William, and Charles A. Shriner. *The History of Paterson and Its Environs: The Silk City.* New York: Lewis Historical Publishing, 1920.

"The New Landscape Declaration." Landscape Architecture Foundation. lafoundation .org/news-events/2016-summit/new-landscape-declaration.

Nicholson, Carol J. "Elegance and Grass Roots: The Neglected Philosophy of Fredrick Law Olmsted." *Transactions of the Charles S. Peirce Society* 60.2 (Spring 2004): 335–48. JSTOR. www.jstor.org/stable/40320995.

North, Michael. *The Final Sculpture: Public Monuments and Modern Poets*. Ithaca, NY: Cornell University Press, 1985.

Oliver, Elisabeth. "Aestheticism's Afterlife: Wallace Stevens as Interior Decorator and Disruptor." *Modernism/Modernity* 15.3 (2008): 527–45.

Olmsted, Frederick Law. *Landscape into Cityscape: Frederick Law Olmsted's Plans for a Greater New York City*. Ed. Albert Fein. Ithaca, NY: Cornell University Press, 1967.

———. "Public Parks and the Enlargement of Towns." *Civilizing American Cities: A Selection of Frederick Law Olmsted's Writings on City Landscapes*. Ed. S. B. Sutton. Cambridge: MIT University Press, 1971. 52–100.

———. *Walks and Talks of an American Farmer*. New York: Putnam, 1852.

———. "The Yosemite Valley and the Mariposa Big Tree Grove." *America's National Park System: Critical Documents*. Ed. Cary N. Dilsaver. Lanham, MD: Rowman and Littlefield, 2016. 5–20.

Olmsted, John Charles. "Report to the Annual Meeting of Park Superintendents." *Hartford Courant*, 10 July 1901, 37.

"Operating Hours & Seasons." National Park Service. www.nps.gov/mora/planyourvisit/hours.htm. Accessed 6 Aug. 2016.

Patterson, Anabel M. Introduction. *Pastoral and Ideology: Virgil to Valéry*. Berkeley: University of California Press, 1987. 1–18.

Paulus, Kristine (plant records manager, New York Botanical Garden). E-mail message to the author. 1 Aug. 2016.

Perlis, Alan. *Wallace Stevens: A World of Transforming Shapes*. Lewisburg: Bucknell University Press, 1976.

Peterson, Walter Scott. *An Approach to Paterson*. New Haven: Yale University Press, 1967.

Phillips, Dana. *The Truth of Ecology: Nature, Culture, and Literature in America*. Oxford: Oxford University Press, 2003.

Pinkerton, Jan. "Political Realities and Poetic Release: Prose Statements by Wallace Stevens." *New England Quarterly* 44.4 (Dec. 1971): 575–601. JSTOR. doi: 10.2307/364475.

"Plan Your Visit." *National Park Service*. www.nps.gov/pagr/planyourvisit/index.htm. Accessed 6 Aug. 2016.

Pound, Ezra. *Selected Poems of Ezra Pound*. New York: New Directions, 1956.

"Pseudopodium, n." *Oxford English Dictionary Online*. Accessed 8 Aug. 2016.

Pycraft, W. P. "Good News for the Gourmet." *Illustrated London News*, 28 June 1924, 1224.

Redfield, James M. "Priapus." *Gods, Goddesses, and Mythology*. Ed. C. Scott Littleton. Tarrytown, NY: Marshall Cavendish, 2005. 1168–69.

Report of the Director of the National Park Service to the Director of the Secretary of the Interior. Washington, DC: National Park Service, U. S. Government Printing Office, 1920.

Riddel, Joseph N. "'Poets' Politics': Wallace Stevens' *Owl's Clover.*" *Modern Philology* 56.2 (Nov. 1958): 18–132. JSTOR. www.jstor.org/stable/435520.

Rieke, Alison. "'Plunder' or 'Accessibility to Experience': Consumer Culture and Marianne Moore's Modernist Self-Fashioning." *Journal of Modern Literature* 27.1/2 (Autumn 2003): 149–70. JSTOR. www.jstor.org/stable/3831843.

"Rose Garden." *Elizabeth Park Conservancy.* elizabethparkct.org/rose-garden.html. Accessed 7 Aug. 2016.

Ross, Bruce. "Fables of the Golden Age: The Poetry of Marianne Moore." *Twentieth Century Literature* 30.2–3 (1984): 327–50.

Rules and Regulations Guide to Mount Rainier National Park, Washington. Washington, DC: U.S. Government Printing Office, 1922.

Ruskin, John. *Frondes Agrestes, Readings in "Modern Painters."* Ed. The Younger Lady of the Thwaite, Coniston. New York: Wiley and Son, 1875. Googlebooks. Accessed 9 Aug. 2016.

Sandburg, Carl. *Always the Young Strangers.* New York: Harcourt, Brace, 1952.

———. *Chicago Poems.* New York: Henry Holt, 1916.

———. *Slabs of the Sunburnt West.* New York: Harcourt, Brace, 1922.

———. *Smoke and Steel.* New York: Harcourt, Brace, 1921.

Sankey, Benjamin. *A Companion to William Carlos Williams'* Paterson. Berkeley: University of California Press, 1971.

Schaffer, Kristen. "Fabric of City Life: The Social Agenda in Burnham's Draft of the *Plan of Chicago.*" *Plan of Chicago.* Chicago: Chicago Commercial Club, 1908. Facsimile ed., New York: Princeton Architectural Press, 1993. v–xvi.

Schuster, Joshua. *The Ecology of Modernism: American Environments and Avant-Garde Poetics.* Tuscaloosa: University of Alabama Press, 2015.

Sharpe, Peter. *The Ground of Our Beseeching: Metaphor and the Poetics of Meditation.* Selingsgrove, PA: Susquehanna University Press, 2004.

"Skyscraper." Def. 4. *Oxford English Dictionary Online.* Accessed 8 Aug. 2016.

Slovic, Scott. "Nature Writing and Environmental Psychology: The Interiority of Outdoor Experience." *The Ecocriticism Reader: Landmarks in Literary Ecology.* Ed. Cheryl Glotfelty and Harold Fromm. Athens: University of Georgia Press, 1996. 351–70.

Smart, Barry. "Digesting the Modern Diet: Gastro-Porn, Fast Food and Panic Eating." *The Flâneur.* Ed. Keith Tester. London: Routledge, 1998. 158–80.

Smart, Mary, and Adina E. Gordon. *A Flight with Fame: The Life & Art of Frederick MacMonnies, 1863–1937.* Madison, CT: Sound View, 1996.

Smith, Carl. *The Plan of Chicago: Daniel Burnham and the Remaking of the American City.* Chicago: University of Chicago Press, 2006.

Solà-Morales, Ignasi de. "Terraine Vague." *Terraine Vague: Interstices on the Edge of the Pale.* Ed. Manuela Mariani and Patrick Barron. New York: Routledge, 2013.

Spurr, David Anton. *Architecture and Modern Literature.* Ann Arbor: University of Michigan Press, 2012.

Steffen, Alex, and Arnie Cooper. "The Bright Green City: Alex Steffen's Optimistic Environmentalism." *Sun.* Apr. 2010. thesunmagazine.org/issues/412/the_bright_green_city. Accessed 6 Aug 2016.

Stevens, Holly. *Souvenirs and Prophecies: The Young Wallace Stevens.* New York: Knopf, 1977.

Stevens, Wallace. *Collected Poetry and Prose.* Ed. Frank Kermode and Joan Richardson. New York: Library Classics of the United States, 1997. Cited parenthetically as *CCP.*

———. *Letters of Wallace Stevens.* Ed. Holly Stevens. New York: Knopf, 1966.

———. *The Necessary Angel: Essays on Reality and the Imagination.* New York: Random House, 1965.

Sweeting, Adam. "Writers and Dilettantes: Central Park and the Literary Origins of Antebellum Urban Nature." *The Nature of Cities: Ecocriticism and Urban Environments.* Ed. Michael Bennett and David W. Teague. Tucson: University of Arizona Press, 1999.

Tester, Keith. Introduction. *The Flâneur.* Ed. Tester. London: Routledge, 1998. 1–21.

"To Turn South Water into Fine Boulevard." *Chicago Daily News,* 21 Nov. 1917.

Turner, Fredrick Jackson. *The Frontier in American History.* New York: Henry Holt, 1920.

Van Wienen, Mark. "Taming the Socialist: Carl Sandburg's Chicago Poems and Its Critics." *American Literature* 63.1 (1991): 89–103. JSTOR. doi: 10.2307/2926563.

Vendler, Helen Hennessy. *Wallace Stevens: Words Chosen out of Desire.* Cambridge: Harvard University Press, 1984.

Voros, Gyorgyi. *Notations of the Wild: Ecology in the Poetry of Wallace Stevens.* Iowa City: Iowa University Press, 1997.

Ward, Francis. "'Poison Gas' in Nature: The Lesser Octopus, A Summer Seaside Visitor to Be Avoided." *Illustrated London Monthly,* 11 Aug. 1923, 270.

Weller, Richard. "Has Landscape Architecture Failed?" *Dirt.* American Society of Landscape Architects. 23 Mar. 2016. dirt.asla.org/2016/03/23/has-landscape-architecture-failed. Accessed 6 Aug. 2016.

Wells, Diana. "Mountain Laurel." *100 Flowers and How They Got Their Names.* New York: Algonquin, 1997. 147–49.

Wilcox, W. D. *The Rockies of Canada.* New York: Putman's Sons, 1900.

Williams, W. *Appleton's Railroad and Steamboat Companion: Being a Traveller's Guide through New England and the Middle States, with Routes in the Southern and Western States and Also in Canada.* New York: D. Appleton, 1847. Googlebooks. Accessed 8 Aug. 2016.

Williams, William Carlos. *The Autobiography of Williams Carlos Williams.* New York: Random House, 1948.

———. *Paterson.* New York: New Directions, 1992.

———. *Selected Essays of William Carlos Williams.* New York: Random House, 1954.

———. *Selected Letters of William Carlos Williams.* Ed. John C. Thirwall. New York: New Directions. 1957.

Willis, N. P. *American Scenery, or Land, Lake, and River Illustrations of Transatlantic Nature.* London: George Virtue, 1811. Googlebooks. Accessed 8 Aug. 2016.

Willis, Patricia C. "The Road to Paradise: First Notes on Marianne Moore's 'An

Octopus.'" *Twentieth Century Literature.* 20.2/3 (1984): 242–66. JSTOR. doi: 10.2307/441116.

Wilson, William H. *The City Beautiful Movement: Creating the North American Landscape.* Baltimore: Johns Hopkins University Press, 1989.

Wirth, Theodore. *Elizabeth Park General Plan.* Hartford, CT: City of Hartford Department of Public Parks, 1900.

Yannella, Phillip R. *The Other Carl Sandburg.* Jackson: University Press of Mississippi, 1996.

Index

Page numbers in italics indicate illustrations.

material in, 11, 62; neoclassical styles in, 52, 75–77; notion of sublime and, 121–22; politics and, 155–56; rise of profession, 50, 55. *See also* Olmsted, Frederick Law; Vaux, Calvert; Wirth, Theodore

Landscape Architecture Foundation (LAF), 155–57, 162; Declaration of Concern (1966), 155, 156

land use legislation, 8

laurel plant, 96–97, 115, 173n15

LeClair, Thomas, "The Poet as Dog in *Paterson*," 176n38

Leith, Rod, "W. C. Williams, Recreation and Parks," 92, 172n10

L'Enfant, Charles Pierre, 171–72n6, 173–74n20

Lensing, George, *Wallace Stevens and the Seasons*, 68, 69, 167n1

Lentricchia, Frank, *Modernist Quartet*, 53

Limerick, Patricia Nelson, *The Unbroken Past of the American West*, 9

Longmire, James, 123

Lycurgus, 23

MacGowan, Christopher, *Paterson*, 92–93, 94

MacMonnies, Frederick: *The Horse Tamers* sculpture, 75, *75*, 76, 77, *78*, 79–80, 83, 170n18; Soldiers and Sailors Memorial Arch, 76, 81, *82*, 170n19

Mariani, Paul, *William Carlos Williams*, 172n12

Marsh, John, *Hog Butchers, Beggars, and Busboys*, 17

Mason, Kathy S., *Natural Museums*, 121, 122, 176–77n3, 177nn5–6

Mather, Stephen T., 122, 136

Matthes, F. E., 135–36, 161, 178n16

McCarthy, Jeffrey Mathes, *Green Modernism*, 4

McClure, David, 177n4

McKim, Mead & White, 75, 76. *See also* White, Stanford

Michelson, Max, "In the Park," 6

Mill, Arthur W., "The History and Functions of Botanic Gardens," 59, 168n6

Mill, Clark, 170n18

Miller, Campbell, "Declaration of Concern," 155

Miller, J. Hillis, *Poets of Reality*, 53, 54

Miller, John C., *Alexander Hamilton and the Growth of a New Nation*, 89, 170–71n2

Milton, John, *Paradise Lost*, 180n30

Minneapolis, park system of, 50, 169n13

Mitchell, Broadus, *Alexander Hamilton*, 89, 90, 171n3

modernity: built natures and, 9; new approaches to, 16–17; Stevens and pressures of, 13

Monadnock Building (Chicago), 36, 46

Monroe, Harriet: as editor of *Poetry*, 6; *John Wellborn Root*, 47–48; "A Play Festival in Ogden Park," 6

Montauk Block (Chicago), 36

Moody, Walter L., 28, 166n7

Moore, Marianne, 3, 7; "Marriage," 178n11; "New York," 14; "No Swan So Fine," 140, 179n22; visit to Mount Rainier National Park, 119, 125. *See also* "Octopus, An" (Moore)

moral panic, parks and, 11–12

Morton, Timothy, *Ecology without Nature*, 8

Moses, Robert, 84, 170n20

Mosier, Cyrus A., 123–24

Mount Rainier National Park, 7, 119–53; attendance trends, 128, 147, 162; bears in, 139–40; climbing regulations, 151–52; creation of, 123–25, 177nn8–10; dangers of, 134, 144–45, 153–54; fauna in, 139–47; fir trees, 136–38, 150; glaciers, 130, 161–62; global warming in, 161–62; Goat's Mirror lake, 138–39, 149; guidebook for, 119, 126–27, 128, 130–31, *133*, 135–37, 139–41, 144–45, 150–53, 161, 178n18, 178–79nn20–21, 179nn25–27; hoary marmots in, 144–45, 151, 179nn26–27; Moore's por-

RECENT BOOKS IN THE SERIES
UNDER THE SIGN OF NATURE: EXPLORATIONS IN ECOCRITICISM

Kate Rigby • *Topographies of the Sacred: The Poetics of Place in European Romanticism*

Alan Williamson • *Westernness: A Meditation*

John Elder • *Pilgrimage to Vallombrosa: From Vermont to Italy in the Footsteps of George Perkins Marsh*

Mary Ellen Bellanca • *Daybooks of Discovery: Nature Diaries in Britain, 1770–1870*

Rinda West • *Out of the Shadow: Ecopsychology, Story, and Encounters with the Land*

Bonnie Roos and Alex Hunt, editors • *Postcolonial Green: Environmental Politics and World Narratives*

Paula Willoquet-Maricondi, editor • *Framing the World: Explorations in Ecocriticism and Film*

Deborah Bird Rose • *Wild Dog Dreaming: Love and Extinction*

Axel Goodbody and Kate Rigby, editors • *Ecocritical Theory: New European Approaches*

Scott Hess • *William Wordsworth and the Ecology of Authorship: The Roots of Environmentalism in Nineteenth-Century Culture*

Dan Brayton • *Shakespeare's Ocean: An Ecocritical Exploration*

Jennifer K. Ladino • *Reclaiming Nostalgia: Longing for Nature in American Literature*

Byron Caminero-Santangelo • *Different Shades of Green: African Literature, Environmental Justice, and Political Ecology*

Kate Rigby • *Dancing with Disaster: Environmental Histories, Narratives, and Ethics for Perilous Times*

Adam Trexler • *Anthropocene Fictions: The Novel in a Time of Climate Change*

Eric Gidal • *Ossianic Unconformities: Bardic Poetry in the Industrial Age*

Jesse Oak Taylor • *The Sky of Our Manufacture: The London Fog in British Fiction from Dickens to Woolf*

combo of nat'l human
pastoral + wilderness
commingling of classes (doesn't work)
locus of despoilation (PATERSON)

CPSIA information can be obtained
at www.ICGtesting.com
Printed in the USA
LVHW090531080519
616961LV00003BA/410/P

9 780813 940847

In *Building Natures*, Julia Daniel establishes the influence of landscape architecture, city planning, and parks management on American poetry, showing how modernists engaged with the green worlds and social playgrounds created by these new professions in the early twentieth century. Using the combined approaches of ecocriticism, urban studies, and historical geography, *Building Natures* unveils the urban context for seemingly natural landscapes in several modernist poems, such as Marianne Moore's "An Octopus" and Wallace Stevens's *Notes Toward a Supreme Fiction*, contributing to the dismantling of the organic-mechanic divide in modernist studies and ecocriticism.

"Daniel's book moves into original territory, building upon the turn in modernist studies toward a reconsideration of 'nature,' inclusive of urban settings. Its dialogue between American poets and those who were designing and planning the settings that inspired them offers a worthy model for future study." BONNIE KIME SCOTT, San Diego State University, author of *In the Hollow of the Wave: Virginia Woolf and Modernist Uses of Nature*

"Daniel's deftly written and astutely researched book brings together American modernist poetics and landscaped parks as two kinds of 'built natures.' She shows how poems and parks interweave the pastoral and the urban, the organic and the artificial, into an ecological form and content. Daniel's book goes on a jaunty and studious walk through 'park poems.' In these poems she examines the fantasies and anxieties around the democratic ideals attached to green spaces that sprang up in the modernist period and still resonate today." JOSHUA SCHUSTER, Western University, author of *The Ecology of Modernism: American Environments and Avant-Garde Poetics*

JULIA E. DANIEL is Assistant Professor of English at Baylor University.

*Under the Sign of Nature:
Studies in Ecocriticism*

UNIVERSITY OF
VIRGINIA PRESS
Charlottesville and London
www.upress.virginia.edu

COVER ART: Detail from a map showing Calvert Vaux and Frederick Law Olmsted's design for Prospect Park. (From William Bishop, *Manual of the Common Council of the City of Brooklyn*, 1871/ Wikimedia Commons)
COVER DESIGN: Jill Shimabukuro

ISBN 978-0-8139-4084-7

90000

9 780813 940847